FROM
CABIN 'BOYS'
TO CAPTAINS

FROM
CABIN 'BOYS'
TO CAPTAINS

250 YEARS OF
WOMEN AT SEA

JO STANLEY

The
History
Press

This book is dedicated, with respect, to all women seafarers, and in particular to Akhona Geveza, Victoria Drummond, Edith Sowerbutts, my great aunt May Quinn and Lucy Wallace.

Cover illustrations. Front, left: Cabin 'boy' Anne Jane Thornton waving in 1835 (redrawn by Val Mitchell); *right:* Captain Barbara Campbell mirroring Thornton, aloft on the *Tenacious*, 2015. (Barbara Campbell) *Back:* Conductress Edith Sowerbutts stands on deck in the uniform she concocted for herself. (Janet Buttifont)

First published 2016

The History Press
The Mill, Brimscombe Port
Stroud, Gloucestershire, GL5 2QG
www.thehistorypress.co.uk

© Jo Stanley, 2016

The right of Jo Stanley to be identified as the Author of this work has been asserted in accordance with the Copyright, Designs and Patents Act 1988.

British Library Cataloguing in Publication Data.
A catalogue record for this book is available from the British Library.

ISBN 978 0 7524 8878 3

Typesetting and origination by The History Press
Printed in Turkey

CONTENTS

ACKNOWLEDGEMENTS

Many women seafarers shared their stories, at length and with generosity, and enabled me to better understand their successors. There is no bank of stories ready made and accessible for any internet browser, no archive full of paper life stories, no countrywide network of offices full of hordes of video tapes awaiting the researcher of seafarers' lives. The real live seafarers themselves have to speak. They did, generously, and thereby provided the bricks for this book. As the mortar-supplier and the architect I'd be unable to act without them. Thank you. They include Judie Abbott, Ellie Ablett, Mary Anne Adams, Julia Ashton, Kathy Atkinson, Nina Baker, Jackie Banyard, Leslie Barnes, Hilary Beedham, Sally Bell, Joy Bennington, Denise Bonner, Freddy Bosworth, Una Brown, Arleen Cameron, Barbara Campbell, Carol Cole, Lesley Cox, Sara Coxon, Jill Coulthard, Sarah Craig, Sara Coxon, Carole Critchley, Clare Cupples, Sue Diamond, Rachel Dunn, Caroline Eglin, Becky Elliott, Marjorie Ellison, Linda Forbes, 'Nancy Foxley', Sadie Grist, Susan Godding, Anita Hellewell, Robina Herrington, Muriel Hocking, Gloria Hudson, Lisa Jenkins, Fazilette Khan, Rose King, Inge Klein Thorhauge, Val Lawson, Lynn Littler, Christine McLean, Victoria McMaster, Margaret Mace, Ann Madsen, Tina Maude, Frances Milroy, Sabine Machado-Rettau, Maud McKibbin, Louise Merrill, Frances Milroy, Tina Mobius, Susie Newborn, Margaret Newcombe, Jane Nilsen, Caroline Norman, 'Belle Norris', Irene Organ, 'Alice Pickles', 'Caroline Pritchard', Margaret Rennison, Pat Rickard, Joan Roberts, Maureen Ryan, Fiona Rush, Denise St Aubyn Hubbard, Lesley Schoonderbeek, Rosemary Selman, 'Madeline Shurrocks', Linda Simkins, Sue Spence, Freda Taylor, Sally Theakston, Sue Thomson, 'Sally Townsend', Carol Peacock, Jessica Tyson, Ros Vallings, Debbie Wilson, Katy Womersley and her colleagues at Clyde Marine, Jane Yelland, Jean Washington, Barbara Wells, Sue Wood, Eve Wright and Sha Wylie (quotation marks indicate a pseudonym). The brevity of their stories in these pages in no way reflects the extent of their helpfulness; they infuse the book in all sorts of subtle and huge ways.

I also thank the seawomen I've been interviewing since the mid-1980s. Many enriched this book. Those directly quoted include Margaret Arthur, 'Merry Black', Dianne Drummond, Edwina Parcell, Norah Rivers and Marie Smith.

Some of the modern seawomen who helped me with this specific book are now reluctant to be named, or even anonymously quoted. I appreciate them very much, including for what their reticence taught me.

Some seawomen have left written or spoken records that have been invaluable. I hope others will be inspired to follow suit, and put their accounts in archives. My thanks go to writers and story-givers such as Edith Sowerbutts, Joan Phelps and Ida Digweed for their efforts and for allowing public access to their stories. Relatedly, I thank the interviewers (especially those at Southampton's former Oral Heritage Unit) for their good interviewing, and the Southampton City Archive for making the records available.

Many family historians have posted stories about women relatives on websites. These have enriched maritime historiography. So too have the websites where seafarers chat to each other relatively unguardedly about sea life (I'm sorry, but yes, I *am* listening). Thank you for posting.

I offer immeasurable thanks to all those women and men who linked me up with seawomen they knew, or who gave me background information. They include Colin Atkinson, Colleen Arulappu, Dave Baker, Colin Banyard, Mark Barton, John Butt, Tim Carter, Don Cockrill, Peter Collinge, Zak Coombs, Vera Corner Halligan, John Crosbie, Peter Cutmore, Godfrey Dykes, Pam Farmer, John Goddard, Henrietta Heald, Graham Hellewell, Martyn Hird, Bob Hone, Derek Ings, Terry Kavanagh, Alston Kennerley, Jan Larcombe, Natalie Lashley, Peter Lay, Stuart Le Fevre, Louise Miller, Tony Morris, John Mottram, Brian and Lisa Murray, Maurice Onslow, Bob Redmond, Denise and Martin Reed, Michael Robarts, Martin Robson, Albert Schoonderbeek, Tony Selman, Colman J. Shaughnessy, Sitling Tull, Debbie Snaishall, Bernard and Sally Stonehouse, David Sweet, Gary Hindmarch and Danielle Ronaldson at South Tyneside College, Southampton's Retired Stewardesses' group, Fred M. Walker, Derek Warmington, Brian White, Martin Wilcox, D.G.A. Williams, Willie Williamson, Tony Winder, Robert Wine, Kevin Winter, Mark and Keith Winterbottom, Stuart Wood. Of course, any mistakes are my responsibility, not theirs.

Relatives and friends of deceased seawomen have been invaluable in sharing pictures, documents and stories. Those who've kindly done a lot of searching in attics and grappling with scanners include Ros Balfour, Jan Buttifont, Jeremy Chandler-Browne and Susan Browne, Sue Freeman, Mrs Hobbes, Ian Hugh McAllister, Bob Proudlock, Edith and David Ross, Peter Smith-Keary, Cathy Spratlin, Frank and Heather Taylor, Lindsay and Bruce Urquhart and Susan Young.

Some hub people invited me to reunions or connected me to their retired seafarers' newsletters and websites. They include Sue B. (who was almost my agent), John Butt, Pam Farmer, Robina Herrington, Janice Jefferies, Jill Jones, Peter Mayner, Brian Smith, John Squires, Graham Wallace, and several anonymous hosts.

Other writers on relevant subjects shared knowledge with astounding generosity. They include Ros Barker, David Davies, Joan Druett, Henrietta Heald, Terry Kavanagh, Sari Mäenpää, Rebecca Mancuso and Louise Miller. M.A. Fish kindly shared invaluable statistical work on the Women's Royal Naval Service (WRNS).

I would like to thank my family, who were Liverpool seafarers in both the Merchant and Royal Navies. Their legacy, partly interpreted by Vera Stanley's lively curiosity about seafaring's subjective meanings, was a cornerstone in envisaging this book.

For decades and all over the world my network of generous maritime historians made this encyclopedic foray possible. I especially thank Skip Fisher, Marcus Rediker and Greg Dening. I've been supported by being part of several intellectual communities. In the UK they include the institutions where I am Honorary Research Fellow: Lancaster University's Centre for Mobilities Research and Hull University's Maritime Historical Studies Centre. Belonging to the Women's History Network and the oral history community has been crucial. I especially thank Joanna Bornat, Mary Chamberlain, Anna Davin and Sheila Jemima for helping shape my thoughts and for discussing methodological issues.

Professional archivists, librarians, press officers and statisticians who have helped me include Celia Saywell at the Association of Wrens, Ben Davis at the British Medical Association, Alice Marshall at the Department for Transport (DfT), Maureen Whatry and Sian Wilks at Liverpool University's Special Collections Library; Mark Jackson at the Marine Society, Lloyds Register public relations staff including Anne Cowne; *Lloyds List* staff, including Nicola Good; Robert Merrylees at the Chamber of Shipping; Merseyside Maritime Archives and Records; Mike Demetriou, Kate Patfield and Richard Lavender at the Ministry of Defence (media offices); the Modern Record Centre at the University of Warwick, especially Carole Jones; Jane Owens and Vanessa O'Sullivan at the Maritime and Coastguard Agency; Glenys Jackson at the Merchant Navy Training Board; The National Archive; staff at the National Museum of the Royal Navy especially Victoria Ingles; Caird Library staff at the National Maritime Museum; headquarters staff at Rail, Maritime and Transport Workers' Union, including Jessica Webb and Dan Crimes; Jo Smith at Southampton City Archive; Morag Bremner and Margaret Urquhart at Tain and District Museum; and Lesley Hall and colleagues at the Wellcome Institute. Special thanks go to Nautilus International staff, including Andrew Linington, Sarah Robinson, Debbie Cavaldoro, June Cattini, the Women's Forum team headed by Maryanne Adams, Lisa Carr, the equalities officer, as well as Carole Jamieson and Steve. They've been supportive, efficient and hospitable.

It's always a pleasure to write a book that includes many pictures, because it means I can create a mini exhibition to delight readers. For their part in this I thank Val Mitchell, John Blakeborough and Ron and Joan Druett. Hazel Sedel kindly sponsored an expensive photograph. Over the years many have kindly loaned or given me pictures for my Eve Tar Archive. Others have kindly waived or reduced the permissions charges. Thank you. You have enriched this book.

Grants from the Society of Authors and the Society for Nautical Research enabled me to meet some interviewees, not just phone them.

I also thank my successive volunteer helpers: Emma Watson, Harjot Hayer, Teresa Stenson and Ailish Woollett. Hazel Seidel and Janet Perham helped the cutting-back process and provided some wise arguments. I appreciate the help of everyone at the publishers including my commissioning editor Amy Rigg, copy-editor Jessica Cuthbert-Smith, Glad Stockdale on the design team and Helen Bradbury, who did the marketing.

Regrettably this book will probably have minor errors; because it breaks new ground there are few predecessors to check against. Books covering long periods – 250 years in this case – are also more prone to errors. Everything that can be checked has been. Every effort has been made to trace copyright holders and to obtain their permission for the use of copyright material. The publisher apologises for any errors or omissions and should be notified of any corrections. They can then be incorporated in future editions of this book. The interpretations in this book are my own, although based soundly on many seafarers' versions of what happened and what they recall. People's inclusion in the book does not mean that they agree with me or my interpretation.

Even if some people's help isn't visible in *this* book, it will enrich later articles and conference papers. Nothing is wasted. Some people rightly belong to more than one category in these acknowledgements, but to save space I have only included them once. They know they are valued for multiple kindnesses. Thank you all for helping me build this book.

INTRODUCTION

Anne Jane Thornton and Barbara Campbell, pictured on the cover, illustrate this book's theme: real and inspiring seafaring women from 1750 who wanted to find adventure at sea and explored themselves and the world. Anne Jane Thornton (1817–77) was one of those pioneers who had to don breeches and pretend to be a boy in order to sail; others chose to be married to a helpful man with a handy ship attached. Today a modern captain, Barbara Campbell, is one of scores who worked their way up and command ships in their own right.

In the next pages of this chapter you will find an explanation of some basics, including the historical roles of women at sea as 'boys', 'wives', 'maids' and finally as equal human beings; the different types of ship and services in which they worked; and the difficulties they faced and still face as women in a traditionally male world. Chapter 2 gives a period-by-period summary of what seawomen faced, over all.

Each of the next chapters then shows what happens in a cluster of jobs. I start with the traditionally male jobs of making the vessel work. Chapter 3 describes the breakthrough of women in deck (sometimes called 'navigation') work. Chapter 4 details the impressive story of their boilersuited counterparts who toiled in the ship's 'magical mystery garden', the engine room, and in other technical jobs at sea.

Subsequent chapters deal with the women who worked with passengers in the hotel side of ships. Chapter 5 explores housekeeping work. Chapter 6 reveals women's roles in health care. Chapter 7 explains how the role of emigrant matron became transformed into the authoritative conductress and eventually segued into entertainment director. Chapter 8 describes the progress of women from stenographers to hotel managers. Chapter 9 introduces the story of hairdressers, beauty therapists and shop staff. Chapter 10 tackles the many other jobs that women have done at sea – some new, some now extinct. My conclusion attempts to draw together this story of puzzlingly patchy progress and examine how seafaring changed women's sense of their potential to traverse the world, metaphorically as well as literally. Finally, the Appendices offer more detailed information for those interested in going further.

Technical work: Junior Radio Officer
Fazilette Khan adjusting the radio
dials on her first ship in 1984.
(Fazilette Khan)

Linda Grant De Pauw, an early historian of women seafarers, argues, 'The history of seafaring women is just beginning; the golden age of seafaring, in which gender is irrelevant, is still in the future.'[1] (By gender she means imposed social and cultural differences rather than biological ones. Babies are born one *sex*, usually. But *gender* is thrust upon them, starting with girls wearing pink clothes and boys being given toy trains, not dolls.) These pages show the mixed progress of British women on the waves as they – maybe – move forward towards that golden time, venturing into the most challenging of all the elements: not air with its high spaces, clouds and winds; not land with its hills and bogs and modern brigands; but the beautiful, vast, challenging sea.

I write about these women because I can't stop wanting to understand them and I want to share my wonder at these pioneers of masculine spaces. For me it was important to grasp that the foreign parts women seafarers visited were not only physical countries but the very vessels on which they sailed. My own fascination with these floating worlds is that they're places that are both like and unlike land. Shipboard life holds up a mirror to life on shore and helps us wonder at what we human beings do when we are away, unsecured, out there. Physical mobility is a wonderful gift: it helps us shift our thinking, our sense of all the possibilities life can offer. Working in long-haul sea and air transport is the main way that people without fortunes travel and manage to be repeatedly moving to places where they learn how very much 'normality' varies. I hope you will share my interest in this seafaring life that can inspire women to see they can do far more with their lives than they imagined. It can be a quest. Seafaring can mean far more than simply being the seaborne counterpart of a truck driver or flight attendant.

When my research for this book began, three women had recently been made captains of major cruise ships. Initially I celebrated that that such extensive progress had been made. After four decades of struggle, these intrepid seawomen were being allowed to do the job they wanted, regardless of their gender. This seemed to be justice. For once, it appeared that progress was linear; good initiatives cumulatively produced desirable outcomes. I wonder if the UK Navy will have women admirals before these pages finally become foxed. But recent years of researching into post-1970s developments have shown me that women's progress in all sorts of non-traditional work at sea is more complex. It's often a process of one step forwards, one step back. That's not to mention several steps around and a couple of daring seven-league-boot-style leaps over an extra range of obstacles.

What starts a woman on a seafaring path? One single novel, read by chance in girlhood, inspired many such girls to seek seafaring careers, despite difficult odds. For some it was *Treasure Island* or *Swallows and Amazons*: they imagined themselves as a young Jim Hawkins or Nancy Blackett. Sometimes it was a book about male sailors; sometimes it was about a woman breaking through in a job on land, like Body Shop founder Anita Roddick. The TV series *The Love Boat* shaped many people's ideas about what women did on ships. I myself probably developed the interest that led to my writing *Bold in her Breeches: Woman Pirates Across the Ages* in part because years earlier, I'd seen a TV repeat of Jean Peters swashbuckling in the 1951 movie *Anne of the Indies*.

But the dearth of practical how-to information meant girls and women often didn't know they could go to sea. Or they went to sea without helpful knowledge of its gendered realities and history. Unnecessary difficulties added to their struggle. Far too many didn't know they could be anything other than a stewardess, a housemaid afloat. I hope that reading this book about pioneers will inspire many young women to take to the sea, survive the problems and discover that they can be in life, literally as well as metaphorically, commanders of their chosen vessels.

This book is dedicated to someone who was defeated by the odds, and whose pivotal story reveals how hard seafaring life can be, especially if race as well as gender and age aren't in your favour. Cadet Akhona Geveza disappeared from her ship, British-registered *Safmarine Kariba*, in 2010. Her body was found drifting in the sea off the Croatian coast three days later.[2] It's still not clear whether she committed suicide or was murdered, but her loss exposed a seminal situation. It opened up international concern about the extent of shipboard sexual bullying, including rape. Sex and power struggles are at the heart of too many of the traumatised sea lives I've heard about. If a book is to be truthful this must be said. And my biggest struggle was to know how much this was true of the past too, or if it became far worse after the 1970s. Unfortunately, as US Navy captain Edward L. Beach acknowledged, although a large part of the battle for seawomen to be treated respectfully has now been won, 'sex and sexual customs as well as the primordial sexual urge are at the bedrock of what still must be done.'[3]

We don't know how rare Akhona's situation was, because recent and current seafaring women tell such differing stories about how painfully riven by gendered ideas (and consequent abusive behaviour) a modern ship can be. Today many keep silent for safety and their careers. Several stipulated they would only speak to me off the record. While women of the 1950s, 1960s and 1970s referred with odd lightness to flirtation and gallantry and the occasional man's 'silliness', their modern peers dare to use the words 'systemic sexism' and are clear that harassment is an institutional matter to be tackled.

Other women have chosen not to speak to me at all, because they think gender is not a germane issue. They want to be seen as seafarers, not *women* seafarers. This book, to them, is discriminatory. A few modern seawomen imagine that it doesn't matter whether you're a woman or a man these days. However, most gender-aware people think it's necessary to be discerning about the continuing destructive power of categories such as 'women' and 'men' in the UK's still-stratified society.

Elizabeth Louise Williams, who blogs about railways, is definite that the idea of women working *in* and *on* transport is, remarkably, still a challenge for trolls who derogate her: 'There is an astonishing[ly] brusque, domineering, arrogant, dismissive and sexist culture which seems to revel in bullying women.'[4]

Just as women, especially in technical jobs, are rare in transport, so are published accounts of their experience. This sparseness is paralleled by the scarcity of histories of women as bus, coach and lorry drivers, and of women airline pilots. So it's a pleasure to be augmenting published knowledge of all the hyper-mobile women who dared, and who deserve so much respect for their efforts.

FINDING NEEDLE SHARDS IN ODD HAYSTACKS

Women's work at sea is a story that's hard to piece together because so many women were unnoticed, written out of the record, or not counted. For example, when I emailed Bob Proudlock, the widower of Wynne O'Mara, one of the first female ship's surgeons sailing in the 1950s, he said she had no idea she'd been preceded four decades earlier by Dr Elizabeth MacBean Ross. Similarly, although it was in the 1920s that Victoria Drummond became the very first marine engineer, it took another sixty years for her biography to emerge. Then the National Union of the Marine, Aviation and Shipping Transport Officers (NUMAST), the Merchant Navy officers' union, started bringing to notice all the other women who'd made major steps in the maritime world. They set up the Victoria Drummond Award to mark their achievements.

When I tell people I write about gender and the sea they ask if I'm one of the admirable group of pioneers. A Wren? A stewardess? A would-be pirate? 'Are you that first New Zealand woman captain, Joanne Stanley?'[5] No, I'm the great-niece of May Quinn, a stewardess on ships sailing to West Africa. One of my great-grandfathers, Reg Stanley, was a captain. Another, Peter Quinn, was a ship's barber sailing to Japan and Canada. But from the 1980s I became one of the pioneers in studying these seafaring women who took the helm, wielded the duster or slashed with their cutlasses.

I've made two trips as a guest lecturer on cruises (yes, you *can* call that work). And, dedicated to finding out the realities for women like Anne Jane Thornton, last year I climbed the mainmast as guest crew of a sail training brig, the *Stavros S. Niarchos*. But, the more I look at this subject, the more it's clear that sailing is not my cup of happy tea, nor my heady cocktail. Ships are enclosed and restrictive institutions, even though seafarers are some of the most freewheeling human beings who ever did a job. I can't easily fit into that life.

Instead I look for and listen to those who try it, with my voice recorder and curiosity switched on. Oral history is often the best way of securing knowledge of women's pasts. Finding documentary evidence of what it was like for women at sea has been as challenging (and therefore satisfying) as finding needles in haystacks. Seasoned private eyes like V.I. Warshawski would have demanded extra fees, bourbon and a lie-down to compensate for the difficulty.

Looking through these rich pages now, you will see so many female presences that you might forget how rare women are in the formal records of maritime history. It's a barren land with an almost total absence of women, except for one-line clues in crew agreements (mass contracts for a ship's voyage) at the Maritime History Archive in Newfoundland and in a few company archives at the National Maritime Museum. Logicians have a maxim: 'absence of evidence is not evidence of absence.' They cite the classic story that the finding of a single black swan disproved the previous idea that all swans must be white. Similarly, I have found much absence of evidence of women ever doing this or that job at sea. But that is not evidence that women were not there, sailing.

The evidence is scarce mainly because records of seafarers' lives, whatever their gender, at the lower end of the scale don't exist. Anyone below captain was seen as negligible. The problem has been compounded by space-poor shipping companies now junking their old ledgers and filing cabinets. Also women in general have tended to assume their lives are not of interest, therefore not worth writing.

Publishers have previously perpetuated this erroneous idea (hence the low ratio of women's to men's autobiographies). Additionally Rosalin Barker, who has studied life under sail in the Whitby area, believes that the lack of extant memoirs by the many waterborne wives and daughters of masters is the result of the poorer ones being so overworked as ship's cooks that they had no time to write, or were not literate. If women did record their story, perhaps only in letters, their descendants didn't necessarily think to deposit the documents in public archives, which were imagined to be repositories only for grand folks' records. Wartime bombing also destroyed several city archives.

Still, I found fragments of 'needles', sometimes several whole needles, in many places. And I also realised it was useful to see what they lay next to, the direction they faced and how buried they were in the haystack. For example, campaigner Charlotte O'Brien's 1881 claims that women emigrants were not looked after on ship was initially denigrated. She really had got her facts awry, yet the government inquiry which ensued after the hullabaloo brought forward a by-product: good evidence about women crew.[6]

We can't know if the thousands of tiny and diverse fragments, 'the needles', are representative or atypical. And so no one alive today can really be certain that this account of women's history is anything like what the women themselves experienced and saw with such different eyes to those of today's women. That's why well-imagined novels about the subject, such as Linda Collison's *Surgeon's Mate*, are so fascinating.

I am proud to be part of a 'community' of writers such as Joan Druett, Suzanne Stark, Linda Grant de Pauw and Minghua Zhao,[7] who have written about women at sea, often focusing on one of the navies, on particular roles and on particular periods. The study of gender in seafaring is sometimes implicit in such books. Other scholars, such as Valerie Burton, Lisa Norling and Margaret S. Creighton, explore gender in relation to seafarers.[8] I try to write about women *and* gender.

In these pages you will find a largely 'British' story, meaning that the book refers to women and ships of the British archipelago, including Ireland. The definition is tricky today because so many ships are seen as of the UK, yet formally registered (it's called 'flagged') in places such as Panama. This book is certainly the first women's maritime history that tries to combine the past and the present, Merchant Navy and Royal Navy. Many of the women you will read about were in commercial shipping, that is, the Merchant Navy, because women rarely went to sea with the Royal Navy before 1991. Although a few books about women sailing in specific periods exist, this book is the first to attempt to give an overview of 250 years in both navies, and from a UK perspective. I have created what seems to be the best-fitting narrative of how women broke through into non-traditional jobs on ships. Many experts on the very different haystacks have discussed the puzzling needles with me. They, and

I, have done our utmost to deduce carefully and hypothesise soundly, and we look forward to future writers disagreeing.

I welcome any insights that you, as a reader and perhaps a seafarer, may give. Do feel free to contact me via the publisher, so that the next broad history book about women at sea is an even richer and better-informed one.

I have deliberately written this book in popular, not academic, style in order to make the story of women maritime pioneers as widely available as possible. But every chapter was researched and initially written in a very scholarly way. The pile of discarded data on my cutting-room floor is high. Each chapter was actually at least eighty pages long, and many will become, instead, academic papers and blog entries. I have also created 'documents' for posterity by recording interviews with women. When I could I collected their photographs. These documents will be deposited in appropriate maritime museum archives.

If, after reading this book, you want to learn more, please use the bibliography at the back. Information about my articles and next books as they are published will be on my blog at genderedseas.blogspot.com and on my website, www.jostanley.biz. Please feel free to send me your story of seafaring.

As you read on, I hope the stories you find here will delight and inspire you. They are about a workforce that deserves huge respect. I feel honoured to bring these women's lives to the attention they have long deserved.

Jo Stanley PhD
Fellow of the Royal Historical Society,
West Yorkshire, 2016

1

BRITAIN'S FORGOTTEN WOMEN SEAFARERS

Challenging huge Japanese whalers, Susi Newborn's brief time life at sea was sometimes as exciting as that of women pirates 250 years earlier. For mobile women, wanting to explore their own selves as well as the world, seafaring can be the ultimate in adventuring and acting with agency. In the 1970s this Greenpeace activist described herself as leaping accurately – glad of her T'ai Chi training – into one of the *Rainbow Warrior*'s tiny fast Zodiacs (rigid inflatable boats) 'as it thrashes and jerks like a rodeo yearling'. Barefoot and braced for bullets, she sailed at her targets in the name of peace and protecting the environment.

Green Campaigner Afloat

Susi Newborn (b. 1950s) became a founding director of Greenpeace and crewed on Greenpeace's iconic campaigning vessel *Rainbow Warrior* in the 1970s and early 1980s. She is from an Argentinean diplomatic family but was born in London. Like most people on board Greenpeace ships, she had many roles, from Zodiac crew to deckhand to cook. Today she is a filmmaker and the campaigns co-ordinator for Oxfam New Zealand. She is still on the water every day, taking the Fullers' ferry *Quick Cat* (many of whose crew are women) from Waiheke Island, where she now lives.[1]

Susi Newborn on the *Rainbow Warrior* in 1978 during the campaign against Icelandic whaling. (David McTaggart, courtesy of Greenpeace, GP026C6)

Susi loved the challenge, and her daring was rather akin to that of the world's most famous women pirates, Anne Bonney and Mary Read, who swashbuckled in the Spanish Main in the eighteenth century. Their sailing era ended in 1720, thirty years before the period covered by this book, but such female *boucaniers* whetted the appetite of potential seafaring women and influenced common ideas today of 'lady tars' on all the world's seas. ('Tar' is short for tarpaulin, the bitumen-covered cloth garments that seafarers – so-called 'knights of the tarpaulin' – used to wear to repel water.)

Archetypal Pirates of the Past

Cork-born Anne Bonney (1698–1782) is probably the most famous woman pirate, and always linked to her cross-dressed counterpart, Londoner Mary Read (1691–1721). Now archetypal 'piratesses', these two adventure-seeking footloose women sailed on the pirate sloop *Revenge* in the 1710s. Anne was Captain Jack Rackham's lover, later his wife. By contrast, Mary (whom she heterosexually fancied) was passing as a male crewmember. Both were able to succeed in this seafaring lifestyle because in their childhood relatives had disguised them as boys, as a way to make enough money to live on. This meant that they grew up bold and relatively unconstrained by ideas of normality. Anne gained her chance to sail because she was enterprising (ready for a new life, free of a feckless husband), in the right place at the right time (Nassau waterfront bars where buccaneers recruited) and attractive to a captain who had the power to keep a partner on board. Mary gained her opportunities because she was already skilled at passing as a soldier.[2] Their stories reached the public through popular potted, excitingly written biographies, especially Captain Johnson's *General History of the Pyrates*. It's hard to disentangle myth and fact; they may have sailed for several years. Their careers ended when they were arrested and brought to trial. They escaped hanging by swearing they were pregnant (an unborn child could not be punished for the sins of its mother).[3]

Susi Newborn of Greenpeace, too, was outside the law. And she learned firsthand about opportunistic sea tactics, violent enemy ships, storms, long-haired, hoop-earringed shipmates – and tedium. The reason she, a woman without seafaring skills and without that crucial seafarer's passport, the British Seaman's Discharge Book, could even be on board was that she was effectively one of the owners. As a volunteer on a small ship, she could freewheel between tasks. She even did the dirty work of cleaning bilges; as the smallest person aboard, she could fit into the narrowest spaces.

Susi was unusual, like Anne and Mary. Almost all the thousands of British women working at sea since 1750 were essentially domestic employees. Like my Great-Aunty May going to and fro, to and fro, between Liverpool and West Africa, these

'Yes, I'm a woman.' 1720s Pirate Mary
Read reveals herself to a vanquished enemy.
(Image from P. Christian, *Historie des Pirates et
Corsaires*', 1852, engraving by A. Catel from
a sketch by Alexandre Debelle)

stewardesses travelled regular routes, making passengers' beds as routinely as any chambermaid might. Their floating hotels initially seemed more exciting, and were certainly more challenging socially and geographically, than below-stairs life in a hotel or grand house. They had few choices and no stashes of Spanish doubloons.

But many elements of Susi's experience were typical of those early women's sea lives too. They saw the world. They seized opportunities. They defied restrictive views of a woman's place. And they survived months on the Atlantic, Pacific, South China Seas and beyond, with male crewmembers who thought a ship no place for a lady. Unlike Anne or Mary, these women were 'out' as women, meaning they were visibly female (which brought them into contact with the ship's gendered hierarchy). Ironically, they gained their freedom to rove because of the limited and confining contemporary idea that lady passengers must be waited upon by females, oceangoing maids.

Two other categories of women sailed too. There were those who got opportunities because they were relatives of the master (as captains are called). An accommodating husband who wanted a travelling wife, and had the authority to take her with him, was a ticket to ride. US wives in the nineteenth century seemed to travel far more readily their British counterparts.

A further category includes women like Anne Jane Thornton, who disguised themselves as men and did men's jobs. They belonged to the world of the vessel, the technical machine, rather than the neat bedroom. It was only in the second half of the twentieth century that it was possible to really combine being an *out* woman (meaning not pretending to be a man) and sailing before the mast,[4] as a deck officer or engineer undisguised.

As of the 2010s, the UK's 3,000 Merchant Navy women were 13 per cent of the total 22,830 UK seagoing workforce. Worldwide, women made up a smaller

Old sea dog's lament

Give me a baboon to sail with,
Even a snake would be great,
They would both be a vast
    improvement
On a female person as mate.

'The end of life as we know it.' Jim Haynes illustrates the typical reactions that faced
a woman, Sally Fodie, when she first ventured on the bridge of a ship. (Captain Sally
Fodie, *Waitemata Ferry Tales*, Ferry Boat Publishers, Auckland, 1995)

proportion, about 2 per cent of the total maritime labour force. Seawomen in the
early twenty-first century are mainly on cruise ships, in hotel-type jobs. In the
UK's case, about two thirds of all its women seafarers are on such ships, not cargo
vessels.[5] Women are still mainly found doing these lowly paid 'chambermaiding'
jobs on ships.

WIFE, 'BOY', 'MAID' AND EQUAL HUMAN BEING

These women seafarers were working far from home, in a field marked 'men only',
or even '*ruggedly masculine* men only'. Yet they managed to break through into
operating the vessel and taking the decisions at the very top, rising from the lowly
domestic servicing of the ship's hotel operations. It is a complex story, but the first
women who went to sea for a living did so in the following three ways.

Sea Wives

First were the women who were 'out' as women: the seagoing wives of officers.
The 'plucky' wife of Martinique-bound Warrant Officer William Richardson was
one. William went to say goodbye to her one summer in the 1780s but 'found that

she had fixed her mind to go with me, as it was reported the voyage would be short and the ship would return … [However] in parting from her parents [she] almost fainted … but was still determined to go with me.'[6] In the King's (Royal) Navy wives sailed the oceans, including into battle. They did support work in crises from Africa to China, from the Baltic to the Mediterranean, from the East Indies to Central America. Invaluable auxiliaries and undervalued support workers, they were a bit like the sutlers and *vivandières* (sometimes called 'camp followers') who looked after armies on the battlefields of France and in the US Civil War by selling services and goods including hot food and nurture such as laundering. The Navy expected husbands to share food with wives; it didn't victual or pay them (except for some rare pensions). Naval men sometimes struggled to control this group, which wasn't organised under the same naval disciplinary codes. Horatio Nelson, England's inspirational naval leader, said that women on ship 'always will do as they please. Orders are not for them – at least I never yet knew one who obeyed.'[7]

Whaling wife Eliza Underwood was one of at most a thousand British wives on merchant ships, in the period from 1750 to roughly 1900, whose ships were sometimes called 'hen frigates' (interestingly, implying that the rest were cocks; today all-male RN ships are called stag ships). US and Antipodean wives avidly sailed. It's their accounts, popularised by New Zealand historian Joan Druett,[8] that today help us imagine the far less recorded situation of British wives. We certainly know wives had borrowed status, and they often took their offspring with them: 'The captain and his wife and children were members of the royal family of a tiny but very wealthy, kingdom,' explains historian Linda Grant De Pauw.[9] Some spouses wanted each other's company regularly, despite the privations. Cosying up in the best space on ship was cheaper than maintaining an additional home on land. Historians of whaling wives argue that when these women sailed they were not necessarily choosing a 'feminist' or 'boyish' adventure. Rather it was often a case of 'whither thou goest I will go', dutifully and no matter what the hardship.

Married to the Captain

Eliza Underwood (b. 1794, probably at Lewes, in Sussex) got her opportunity to sail because she married Samuel, who was already master of the London whaleship *Kingsdown* when they met. She had no children to tie her to home, and at that period captains' wives were increasingly sailing on whalers (at least in the US). By 1829–31 Eliza was sailing to the Sulu-Sulawesi Seas whaling grounds and visiting many islands in Indonesia. Her journal reveals her isolation, tolerance (of the seamen's limited domestic skills, for example: 'they would make sad charwomen') and remarkable tenderness towards her irate, seemingly mentally ill, husband. Tales of encounters with Muslims and exotic ports mingle with domestic rumblings: 'He does not much attend to woman's knowledge,' she remarked, but she didn't crow when her weather predictions proved better than his, yet again. And she was always concerned about his gout. She enjoyed collecting – and assessing the value of – rare shells, which she would later sell on in London.[10]

On very small ships wives got their chance to sail because they were useful. As auxiliary cooks and mates they supported the family business, when and how they could, particularly with informal nursing, laundering and bookkeeping. Unwaged and undervalued, their situation was similar to that of wives in family-owned corner shops who were incorporated into 'his work' for 'our survival'. Often they were seen only as assistants, or utilisable in crises, but in fact some were consistently doing non-peripheral tasks and sustained the entire family's economy.

Situations varied, especially by the late nineteenth century. But certainly on larger merchant ships of the mid-nineteenth century captains' wives offered emotional support to their stressed and socially isolated husbands. They negotiated a tricky path vis-à-vis agency (meaning their ability to act, to engage with the ship's social structure). Orcadian Elizabeth Young (later Linklater), sailing with her mother, Sarah, on the family's windjammer in the 1880s, observed:

Women on board a merchant vessel, other than passengers, were there on sufferance. They had no part in the working of the ship, and as far as he [Father]

Families went to sea. Artist's impression by Ron Druett. (Ron and Joan Druett)

was concerned they were non-existent. It behoved them to keep their thoughts to themselves, and conceal their feelings, and show what interest they could assume in the welfare of Her Majesty the Ship.[11]

Wives on these merchant 'her majesties' were far lesser queens. Only carefully and sometimes did they exert the limited authority which was conferred by their connection with the master. (On naval vessels wives' majesty was even less.) Sailing on merchant ships, the lonely 'aristocrats' in their antimacassar-and-harmonium-furnished floating parlours were usually only allowed to speak to higher-level crew. They were not integrated members of the hierarchical ship's company. Indeed, crew could resent master's wives who 'missioneered', although lonely boys sometimes quietly appreciated a bit of maternal coddling.

From the 1950s big shipping companies started allowing other wives to sail, as a way to retain skilled male workers such as engineers. By the early twenty-first century husbands of women officers, and same-sex partners too, could accompany them. Seagoing wives' stories appear only briefly in this book, which focuses on waged workers at sea, but their few accounts do illustrate what life was like for women on board.

The 'Boys' Aloft

If you weren't a master's wife then the best way to secure a job at sea was to crop your hair, don your brother's breeks, learn to chew baccy and sweet-talk the land girls. Women in the second category of seafarers, those pretending to be men or boys, were usually much more 'hands-on' than wives, not least because the usual position – cabin boy – was a role for minors who were expected to be Jacks of all (lowly) trades. Disguising yourself as a male was essential when ships were men-only; it got you the job and you were relatively safe from heterosexual attention. There were probably several hundred more cross-dressed women seafarers than the forty-nine listed in Appendix 3, but they remain unknown because they were never found out or because their stories didn't reach the newspapers and law courts.

Disguised as boys and men, these mould-breaking 'cabin boys' or 'lady sailors' are significant because they prove that manual seafaring tasks were not necessarily beyond women. The cabin boy's role was something of a cross between today's steward and a general-purpose rating (GPR). They did 'masculine' work on deck, including handling the sails and the hated task of cleaning out ship's pig sties as well as some relatively unskilled domestic work such as serving food. Their status varied. It's thought that some officers and older crew abused them pitiably as runts while others 'mothered' and protected them. Rowlandson's famous 1799 aquatint is the classic image of a cabin boy, clearly not a macho and empowered figure. Derring-do accounts of women-'boys' don't mention the distasteful tasks nor that some 'boys', like real boys, were targets of sexual bullying.

The archetypal cabin boy. This really is a boy, even though he looks so girlish as he mops the deck. Etching by Thomas Rowlandson, 1799. (National Maritime Museum)

Female 'boys' began sailing well before 1750. And some women were still getting away with it in the late nineteenth century. Subterfuge like this was easier to pull off in the Merchant Service than in the more strictly controlled Royal Navy. Generally the popular reports about them are upbeat. Admiration for their daring was easy because they were exceptional, not a thorough challenge to a segregated career. Cabin 'boys' adapted a rolling gait; learned to swear, spit, sozzle and be lion-hearted stalwarts. In other words, they manned up, yet retained prized 'feminine' characteristics such as cleanliness and obedience.

Cunard steward Thomas (alias Mary Anne) Walker's 1860s story provides a bridge between the second category of seagoing women (those passing as 'boys') and the third category of openly female 'maids'; I'll call her 'Thomas' and 'he' because that became her own preferred identity.

Thomas could be seen as someone taking gap year after gap year. Like many such 'boys', he lived an uprooted life estranged from his family. For me, Thomas is the most real of the 'boys': he cleaned engines at London's King's Cross, a station that I use. He sang his autobiography to a tune still played on the radio, 'Champagne

Charlie'. I walk past the Hackney building in which he sought rehab, the Elizabeth Fry Refuge for women prisoners seeking reformation; Thomas's successors seeking a post-jail haven now go to the Elizabeth Fry Probation Hostel in Reading.[12]

Little is known about Thomas Walker's two years of stewarding on Cunarders. He would have been mainly crossing the Atlantic, taking emigrants to the US. Stewards were notorious chancers involved in opportunistic fleecing of 'bloods' (passengers). They worked ferociously hard and slept in over-intimate proximity in cramped dormitories. A balladier celebrated 'The She-He Barman of Southwark':[13]

> She Tom had been a sailor
> Two years upon the main …
> Three years she doffed the petticoats
> And put the trousers on …
> For years she plough'd the ocean
> As steward of a ship,
> She used to make the captain's bed,
> Drink grog and make his flip.
> She could go aloft so manfully,
> This female sailor Jack,
> But if she slept with a messmate,
> Why, of course, she turned her back.

From others' reports it sounds as if Thomas might have, had the term then been in use, described himself as an intersex person, meaning someone then called an hermaphrodite. Certainly when he was in jail (for swindling his boss) all the warders assumed he was a man, not least because his fiancée Rosina visited him. The stories of Thomas give us clues about the other cross-dressed women on ships. They may well have been on every part of the gender spectrum, from heterosexual women who camouflaged simply to get a job usually barred to women, through transvestites loving the part-time masquerade, to people who deeply felt they were actually male and trapped in the wrong body. For all of them, being involved in itinerant and marginalised worlds such as seafaring or bar work was a way to live a less trammelled life and find communities where social norms were less rigorously imposed.

Cunard Steward Thomas Walker

Thomas/Mary Anne Walker (c. 1842–after 1880) was the daughter of a pub licensee in Westminster, where she began showing 'a fondness for wearing male attire … and ultimately she took to the entire paraphernalia of dress adopted by the male sex'.[14]

Leaving home in his late teens, he did a range of casual portering jobs, then went to sea for several years. Unlike many recorded 'boys', his disguise was never detected on ship. Denouement only occurred after he'd worked ashore for a year or two, in 1867, when he was arrested and charged for minor embezzling.

Observer of working women Arthur Munby wrote:

> there she stood alone in the dock conspicuous and central: and to the outward eyes she looked … [a] brawny young man of four or five & twenty. A broad bronzed face, fullcheeked & highboned; well-cut straight nose, sharp eyes, determined mouth: the dark hair, short as a man's, and evidently worn in man's fashion for a long time past. Her head was bare, and so was her strong bull neck; about the way she wore nothing but the blue sailor's shirt, with the sleeves partly rolled up. Standing there with broad shoulders squared and stout arms folded on the dock rail, she seemed just such a fellow as one may see drawing beer at an alehouse or lounging about any seaport town; and it was almost impossible to believe that she was not a man … poor Thomas, who only said 'nothing , Sir' in a low tone when asked if she had ought to say, was committed for trial … [in] the crowd … one saw that she was of average woman's height and no more.[15]

Women workers were rare. Three women, at least one of whom is a stewardess, and the chief steward's staff crossing to Australia on the emigrant ship *Rippingham Grange, c.* 1900. (National Maritime Museum, N40880)

'Maids': 'Out' Women in Aprons

The third and main category of women seafarers are stewardesses, who like Thomas Walker did 'women's work', but were 'out' as women, looking like nurses or maids in their pinafores. Like pirate Mary Read, they were paid workers in their own right. They were the breakthrough women whom shipping lines employed precisely because it was thought seemly that female passengers were looked after by women. Although stewardesses were formally positioned as more subordinate than the captain's wife initially, they too tended to be married to a man on board, the steward. Such women were seen as 'assisting' their steward husbands rather than being the independent employees that they were by the 1830s. The earliest ones were somewhat like the disguised 'boys' in that they might occasionally have heaved the ropes in a gale. Everyone pulled together for the ship's safety.

A hundred years later stewardess Denise Meldrum was one of the many women doing such domestic and emotional labour (that subtle labour described by Arlie Russell Hochschild, where transport workers, particularly airline cabin crew, help to soothe travellers and assist them to manage a range of emotions).[16] When we talked in her later life, Denise definitely did not see herself as being 'in service', like a lowly housemaid. Most of the interwar stewardesses I listened to were proud of their agency in a job as combined hostess, nurse and experienced guide for novice travellers. They frequently summed it up as 'We were there to look after the ladies', whom they saw as needy visitors rather than temporary bosses.

Denise Meldrum: Doing Women's Work

Denise (1911–2003) sailed on Canadian Pacific ships such as the *Duchess of York*, *Duchess of Richmond* and *Duchess of Bedford* from 1928 to 1937. A Liverpool-based stewardess, her career was mainly spent on the Liverpool–Canada route, to Montreal and St John's, Newfoundland, as well as West Indies cruises and whoopee cruises from

A dynasty of women who went to sea, sometimes pragmatically. Denise Meldrum (1929), centre; her mother Elise Meldrum in 1927, and daughter Denise Donnelly, later Reed, c. 1978. (Denise Reed)

New York to Bermuda. Denise got her opportunity because she was the daughter of a company employee, a catering writer on ship. After his death, the company offered Denise's mother Elsie work as a stewardess, which she did from 1926 to 1936. When Denise was 17 the shipping company encouraged her to lie about her age (stewardesses were supposed to be 25) and she sailed as nursery stewardess and then stewardess. Some stewardesses joined for the adventure or the money, but many did this job by default and happenstance. Movingly, Denise said she sailed mainly because 'I was miserable on land so I thought I might as well be miserable at sea.' She married twice, both times to seafarers, and had two children; her daughter Denise Donnelly became a ship's nurse (see Chapter 6).[17]

Equal Human Beings

In the 1970s, the fourth category of women seafarer began. These new seafarers achieved a breakthrough: they did deck and engine work even though they were known to be women. Women officers were so unusual that initially crew called them 'Sir' because they didn't know what else to call them (the correct address is 'Ma'am'). At the time such women seemed to herald a non-gendered future. However, for some traditional male seafarers such 'interlopers' on the ship's navigating bridge were an unbearable intrusion, even a disaster and traumatic revolution.

Twenty-first-century women are increasingly taking the path to the role of captain, via positions as senior officers, in both the Merchant and Royal Navies. Unlike captains' wives like Eliza Underwood, they have authority in their own right, although to some seafarers from other cultures a woman in authority seems an anomaly and a contradiction in terms. But captains such as Inger Klein Thorhauge, master of the *Queen Elizabeth* in 2010, are deeply and genuinely respected. No woman deck officer could now be regarded as a junior partner who's 'just allowed to help out a bit when we're short of men'.

Inger: Captaining a Major Cruise Ship

Captain Inger Klein Thorhauge, formerly Klein Olsen (b. 1967) in 2010 became the first woman to command a Cunard vessel. She began by sailing as a stewardess in the late 1980s, as a way of travelling: 'I hate cleaning,' she says. When a friend told her about cadetships, she let the new career 'begin to happen'. 'Why not? At least I'm not cleaning!' She attributes her rise not to her background in a seafaring community (the Faroe Islands) but to her liking for thoroughness. Sponsored by DFDS/Scandinavian

Seaways, she went to pre-sea training school at Kogtved Søfartsskole, followed by three years on a range of ships from ro-ros (roll-on, roll-off cargo vessels) and ferries to a dredger. Although she'd had no dreams of becoming a captain, at the end of her three years she took her master's certificate at Svendborg Navigational School, then rose to become second officer, first officer, chief officer and staff captain. Her ships included the *Vistafjord/Caronia*, *Seabourn Sun*, *Seabourn Pride* and *Queen Victoria*. Then in 2010 she became the first woman captain in Cunard's 170-year history; she is now captain of the *Queen Elizabeth*, and a role model for aspiring women. Inger says, 'It's important to show it's possible for women to become captains. The door is now open.' When not travelling she lives with her husband in Denmark.[18]

Captain Inger Klein Thorhauge commands her ship. (Carnival Group)

THIS SHIP OF MINE

If you're a seafarer your ship is your home, your workplace and your badge of honour. Many felt and still feel acute pride at being associated with vast icons of imperial majesty and modernity, such as the interwar *Queen Mary*. While some women seafarers savoured high style, surroundings like Hollywood sets and brief encounters with illustrious passengers, others simply delighted in the sea, even on plainer ships. Maritime life just 'got to' some women – as it did to men. Poet John Masefield, that famous fan of the sea, even relished a 'dirty coaster with a salt-caked smoke stack'.[19] The women felt the same about their vessels, be they chic or ugly. Sara Miller (b. 1958), one of the 1970s intake of deck officers and still a recreational sailor today, explains the pull:

> The best thing about the sea is the ships. I love their creaks and groans, the smell of rust and oil, the flaked paint. I like the way seafarers just get on with their lives. One of my favourite times was always when we let-go the last tug and were heading out to sea once more. I have always loved a horizon of 360 degrees of blue, grey, green, white flecked ocean topped by an ever changing sky … my years sailing on a small boat were even better as you are so close to the sea that the blowing of dolphins at night make you jump, as do flying fish hitting you! I miss the night watches most of all, especially if they included stars and sunrise.[20]

Sara Miller teaching a cadet how to take a sun sight with a sextant on the *Galconda*, 1983, pre-satellite navigation. (Sara Miller)

Many seafaring women love – and they don't use the word lightly – their different kinds of sailings. Cook Maud McKibbin felt lucky to be on a cargo ship tramping (sailing to any obscure port where cargo needed to be picked up and delivered) in the 1950s. 'That was the beauty of … [tramping]. It was so exciting to not know where you were going next.' Closeness to nature delighted them, especially in tropical seas under clear skies. When Maud's shipmate Freda Price was en route to Ceylon (Sri Lanka) on the *Langleeclyde* in the 1950s:

> I loved … [taking] our bench cushions from our cabins and … sleep all night outside. An awning was put up for us. It was lovely to lay there and see the stars and the ship gently moving, the engines just a dull thud … and the sea sounds all around you. Sometimes … I'd walk up to the bows and see the dolphins … leaping in front of the bows. They were all outlined in phosphorus … like thousands of jewels falling all over the place.[21]

British women work or have worked on ships which vary enormously in their power, cargo, size, ownerships, routes, smartness and seaworthiness. They range from prestigious battleships to tiny colliers, from liners to small tramp steamers, from barges sailing coastally to chic Scandinavian ferries, from state-of-the-art cruise ships with on-board surf simulators to fisheries survey ships, from heritage brigs to family tugs. There are pazzy (passenger) boats, windjammers, very large crude carriers (VLCCs), Post-Panamaxes (ships that are too vast to go through the 180-foot wide Panama Canal), and many dodgy rust-buckets.

Today the categories of merchant ship are, in descending order of proportion of women personnel aboard: Ferry and Passenger; Deep Sea Liner/Bulk; Offshore Support (taking food and equipment out to oil rigs); Short Sea Bulk; and Royal Fleet Auxiliary (which supports Royal Navy vessels, particularly with fuel). Specialist or scientific survey ships are especially popular with women because they can join in oceanographic research and work with female scientists.

Britain's two navies, Royal and Merchant, offer two different sets of opportunities for women. Their flags are a key symbol – they sail under the White Ensign and the Red Ensign ('Duster') respectively. Each has their different purpose and corresponding shipboard culture and organisation. It is useful to remember that women associated with the Royal Navy only worked at sea after 1991, apart from a handful of early but significant exceptions. Like the men, they are called sailors. Women were employed at sea in the Merchant Service from at least the 1820s, and are officially called seamen.

The UK's Royal Navy (RN), sometimes referred to as 'the Andrew' and 'life in a blue suit', is essentially part of the nation's armed forces provision. Its seafarers are not civilians. Typically the Royal Navy had and has a hyper-masculine and heroic image. Firm discipline is imposed. Such ships' crucial fixed equipment includes missile launchers and surveillance equipment, in contrast to cruise ships' expensive jewellery boutiques, hot stones salons and climbing walls. In the RN voyages are about protecting national interests and potentially involve combat, rather than being for direct profit. Personnel know a voyage may end in their death through enemy action. They don't join for the tips – there aren't any. But they are often attracted by the promise of travel, like their Merchant Navy counterparts.

Until the early nineteenth century several thousand women sailed in naval warships as wives. There was also a handful of women in male disguises who sailed. Exceptionally a few nurses were at sea from the late nineteenth century, especially as members of the Naval Nursing Service from 1884. In wartime in 1917–19 and 1939–45 the (all-male) Royal Navy was supported by the Women's Royal Naval Service (WRNS). The WRNS ('Wrens') was created as one of the wartime auxiliary services, just as the Army and Air Force had their women's auxiliaries. 'Free a man for the fleet' was the WRNS's slogan, and its motto was 'Never at Sea', even though recruitment posters temptingly suggested otherwise. 'Jenny Wrens', sometimes cosily referred to as 'sailors' little sisters' (even if they were actually tall, terrifying and very senior martinets), were considered to be *of* but not *in* the Navy, even though they *felt* they were *in* the Navy, not just in the naval *services*.

Finally, significant numbers of Wrens were allowed to sail in 1991 and were all absorbed into the Navy in 1993. They didn't go to sea because they had 'women's skills', like the stewardesses in the Merchant Navy. Rather, they were employed because of personnel shortages. Hands were needed for tasks that were not gender-specific, such as stores management. Naval Services initially excluded women from many jobs, especially submarines. By 2015 women were barred, on health grounds, from only two fields: the Mine Clearance Diver Branch and the Royal Marines Commando. Today the RN's 3,000-odd women 'in blue suits' are there as ostensible equals to their male counterparts.

RN people are employed on continuous service, not per trip. A full career is eighteen years. Unlike their high-turnover Merchant Navy counterparts, they can't easily leave and they don't expect to cherry-pick roles in their career. The decisions that dictate where they sail and when are political. Deeply serious about its role as the nation's seaborne defensive force, and closely associated with organised national identity and patriotism, the ultra spick-and-span RN can be seen as the cultural opposite to the Merchant Navy, where today uniforms are sometimes only required in passenger areas. RN ships are mainly staffed by UK and former Commonwealth citizens, with Hong Kong Chinese men dominating the laundry.

The Merchant Navy (MN) – the navy that is mainly the focus of this book – is composed of commercial ships run by private companies for profit. Their purpose is the carriage of cargo, including human cargo. All the diverse ships and those who staff them are part of an economic, not military, system. Crew are civilians (Appendix 4, 'Between Navies', explains some of the grey areas and overlaps). Iron discipline is gloved in velvet. Those on cargo ships particularly pride themselves on sailing with seemingly nonchalant cool: no 'over-staffing' and unnecessary red tape. Originally the 'Merch' was called the Mercantile Marine or Merchant Service. Then in 1928 King George V conferred the title Merchant Navy, because of its contribution to the First World War. Today MN ships are polyglot and multicultural spaces: as many as fifty different nationalities might be on board. Staff are often employed by different agencies and concessions, so there isn't the same organisational coherence as in the RN. It's difficult to talk about a 'British ship' in the Merchant Navy today. British-owned does not necessarily mean British-registered and certainly not British-staffed.[22] On flagged-out merchant ships (meaning the many ships registered in other countries to avoid legal restrictions on pay and conditions), most shipmates tend to 'forget' nationality or race some of the time. The exceptions are when, for example, Filipina cabinmates take UK crewmembers home and show them a different way of living life; when at Christmas time on a small tanker the British crewmember is the only Christian aboard and has no one with whom to pull a cracker; or when male crew from unenlightened cultures demean women.

British seawomen sailed across all the world's oceans but especially the Atlantic, increasingly so as women emigrated more. For some seawomen on liners the Mediterranean, Pacific, South China Seas and Caribbean became almost as familiar as London's Oxford Street. The oceans they knew depended on the company they were working for. For example, Cunard focused largely on Atlantic crossings. P&O's contracts were usually for Pacific travel. Very few women were in a position to choose their vessels (which effectively would mean choosing where they went).

The knock-on effect was that their destinations were imposed by employers focused on an efficient deployment of hands, not sweetly enabling dream trips. Muriel Arnold, a 1960s assistant purser on Cunard's *Queen Mary* and *Queen Elizabeth*, explained the routine: 'We had no say as to which ships we were appointed … We received our instructions to transfer … by memo in a little pale green envelope brought on board on arrival in port. We grew to love and hate these little pale green envelopes.'[23]

Stewardesses in the interwar years might sail on the same ship, with the same companions, to the same destinations for ten years or more; it was as routine as a hotel job on land. So they welcomed the odd round-the-world cruise, which usually happened just once or twice in the careers of the most trusted and personable veterans. Fulfilment-focused women changed companies in order to try new routes or improve their workplace satisfaction. Others worked on ferries so they could get home more often and thereby continue to give practical support to their families every few days. When Union Castle stewardette Sha Wylie switched to ferries from the South Africa run she found it 'interesting that it did not have the same cachet as deep sea. Nothing can top that!'[24]

Today a lifetime of loyalty is not expected. Most staff are employed by international agencies, some of which are at the cavalier end of what was once a paternalistic spectrum. Opportunistic employment agencies stress, 'come and have the time of your life' on fun palaces and floating Center Parcs, which astute critics see as 'sweatships' (by analogy with sweatshops).[25] However, workers on cargo ships and tankers ('proper ships') sometimes refer to passenger-ship staff as 'working vacationers', 'not proper seafarers'. The RN tends to be even more superior about those they see as mere trippers and sea amateurs, sailing only for a jolly jaunt, for example dancers and wine waiters.

WOMEN'S LIVES AS FULL-TIME SEAFARERS

Seawomen varied widely, especially in the different periods, as the next chapter shows. They varied in whether they were from seafaring families, in their gentility and in their previous jobs. Their age, marital status, previous mobility, family ties, sexual orientation, sense of agency (which includes their degree of reflexivity) and their level of education all differed. Necessarily, they had robust constitutions, were used to working hard, getting along with others, being adaptable and self-reliant and enterprising about thinking up solutions. Seawomen who were mothers, or carers for parents quietly juggled two sets of responsibilities: home and work.

Women had to be able-bodied or good at pretending to be. Seafaring jobs were very active, and the ethos was 'keep up or get out'. You hid your varicose veins and alcohol addiction. The common maxim was not 'Be good', but 'Don't get found out'. Women did their jobs carefully, aware that they were being watched.

Until the late 1980s women had far fewer promotion opportunities than men did. If they did succeed, the gossip network (nicknamed 'the galley radio') often claimed that they were sleeping their way up to the next rung. Anything *one* woman did was seen as typical of *all* women, so they had a responsibility to be visibly blameless, indeed exemplary. On ship women's behaviour differed from men's. This was subsequently recognised by shipping companies who issued captains with dossiers on how to deal with female staff. Broadly, women tended to work with more alacrity, to be less involved in fiddles and to be better at communicating and getting on with others – although seafarers by necessity are usually very skilled at that. Some of my modern interviewees think women are better at foreseeing problems, but it was hard for women to take early corrective steps if males pooh-poohed this as unnecessary fussing. When women are firm, men often feel patronised; men called women bossy and inappropriate. This meant that authority was harder to exercise.

Women behaved differently to male shipmates when ashore in those longed-for destinations for which the trip was undertaken. It wasn't quite a case of shops vs brothels, but priorities certainly differed. Freda Price, who was sailing in the

1950s, points out that on that tiny half-day in port 'you must make the best use of your time off … We used to laugh, because [male] sailors on the whole didn't explore the places they went to. They mostly judged the place by what the beer was like! We girls, though, were more interested in seeing all we could.'[26] And women had to be more wary ashore, especially in countries where local men saw white women as ultra-desirable or loose. So even recreation brought women different stresses to seafaring men.

Fertile Bodies

Health problems, such as sprains after falling during rough passages, may challenge any seafarer. But the additional physical difficulties faced by women working at sea include that they may have a greater tendency to be seasick, according to one 2002 study. Marine technologists Stevens and Parsons found 1.7 women were prone to *mal de mer* for every one man who so suffered.[27] Indubitably, from the early 1800s to the 1950s, women were also hampered by the stiff corsets that constrained their movements. Women also usually tend to be shorter and have a smaller handspan and less grip. Upper-body-lifting muscles are less developed in women (which is why female tree surgeons and rock climbers today train specially, which suggests the early women who went aloft might have had initial problems).[28]

Reproductive systems have more impact on women than men. Seawomen had to cope with periods, pregnancy and problems such as prolapsed wombs in challenging circumstances. Women's unavoidable practical difficulties were made more complex by shipmates who reacted to them with insufficient wisdom, for example scorning or over-stressing the impact of pre-menstrual tension (PMT) – you're seen as narky because it's that time of the month, not because you're legitimately angry. Old fears

Are women more prone to seasickness? This device to help alleviate seasickness clearly assumed women were the main sufferers. (*Illustrated London News*, 1878)

about 'dark mysteries' of the womb and all the symbolic meanings of women's power to reproduce were slow to wane, especially in these male-dominated communities.

Menstruation affects a woman for as much as a third of every month for most of her working life. Of course menstruation has different impacts on different women, but periods are more obtrusive at sea than on land because there's so little rest time and no spare back-up workers. In the interwar years kind colleagues and supervisors sometimes allowed sufferers an hour's secret lie-down. More recently women, particularly those doing 'men's jobs', felt obliged to cover up the extent to which they were taxed by a heavy or painful period. After 1968 the contraceptive pill brought just light breakthrough bleeding, not the full loss that follows ovulation. For convenience many women in competitive yachting and the armed forces take the Pill continuously.

Seawomen struggled with getting adequate sanitary protection and discreetly disposing of it too. Traditional aids such as cloth, menstrual sponges, torn-up old uniform, as well as the cotton waste that engineers use as wipes, have all been harnessed when no fresh supplies of sanitary towels or tampons are available. Until the 1950s women usually made their own napkins by wadding old sheets into a pad about 12in long and 5in wide (30 x 12cm). They stitched a belt to hold the rag in place, attaching a strap to a sturdy tape or wide elastic around the waist. US whaling wife Mary Stickney on the *Cicero* in 1881 recorded in her journal, 'commenced to work on napkin strap'.[29] After use the napkins might be soaked in a bowl of salt water (which was inconvenient in a small cabin), rinsed, somehow dried discreetly and reused, or disposed of overboard.

The advent of tampons helped. Deck officers have recently said it's problematic to be on bridge duty when your flow is heavy, since toilet breaks are usually avoided on watch. Anxiety was greater for women wearing white tropical uniforms, because the blood would be so evident. Most women simply got on with the job and said nothing. The best-appreciated male shipmates were those with wives who also suffered disabling periods; they were quietly supportive. More irritatingly, even today some Royal Navy men fear women might impair operational effectiveness by being hormonally erratic or under par.

Pregnancy can be a major problem rather than a joy to a woman seafarer. At worst, it can mean the end of a career. Certainly she has to fight to be trusted as reliable. A mother may have to take a job not of her choice in order to survive. Today UK law stipulates a seafaring mother-to-be legally must be given only light tasks and put ashore no later than twenty-eight weeks from conception, even if there's a doctor on board. This is not least because a vessel's turnaround time in ports is too fast to allow women to go ashore for ante-natal checks.

Maternity and paternity is a well-discussed management issue in the RN, which has clear guidelines and policies available on the internet. During long deployments a mission could be compromised by the need to get a pregnant woman ashore quickly. Pregnancy has been used as an argument for excluding women, as well as viewed as women's unfair way of getting out of an unpopular deployment (voyage). However, by at least 2010 it was accepted that pregnancy is just one medical condition like others which can necessitate a flight home. In 2014 Army women circulated the useful slogan: 'Women get pregnant. Get over it!'

In the past, merchant ship wives in their final trimester were sometimes put ashore: Anne Bonney went to Cuba for friends' support with her delivery. Mary Rowland's husband Captain Henry Rowland wrote in the log of the *Thomas W. Rowland* off Aboco in the Bahamas in 1857: 'The Capt Wif gave birth to a child.' In fact, he delivered the baby himself. Sometimes other wives helped in port, as they did for Mrs Whitman on the whaler *Moses Wheeler*, at the Chincha islands off Peru in 1859.[30]

In the late nineteenth and early twentieth centuries apparently few seafaring women became pregnant. This was probably because so many were old enough to be prudent about the job loss and tarnished reputation that would follow. The 1970s brought not only effective contraception and the liberalisation of sexual attitudes but also an influx of women who upheld their right to combine career and procreation. Gaining maternity rights has proved very difficult as seafarers often can't put in a long enough period of continuous employment to qualify for benefits – it's too spasmodic a job now. And after giving birth some don't get their old jobs back.

New jobs can be hard to find, too, because employers fear the mother will keep taking time off to look after the child's crises. Ships now carry morning-after pills. Campaigners for women seafarers' rights are concerned at the large number of seawomen racing ashore for terminations. Today pregnancy is a human resources planning matter because so many women are now high-level workers with special qualifications, such as directors of the ship's hotels service, engineers or even captains. Maternity cover has to be found.

Employers' *ideas* about women's reproductive aspects are as important as actual pregnancies. Although in the UK it is illegal to discriminate on the grounds of gender, employers are still wary of investing in employees that they see as having 'a limited shelf-life'. It's easier to employ a man or someone determined to foreswear children, think some companies. But this disregards most women's actual desire to ensure that motherhood in no way affects their professionalism. Most firms feel that it's a good enough payback if *any* trainee stays for seven years.[31]

Wanting children continues to be one of women's main reasons for leaving a sea career. Seafarers' organisations argue that employers can retain trained staff if they make it more possible to combine parenthood and a career – say by arranging for shorter periods at sea or longer leaves and subsidised childcare. 'Don't ditch the woman. Meet her needs instead, for your own good,' they argue.

That Othered Species

It's controversially believed that women think and act very differently from men, because of hardwiring and socialisation. Be they really from Venus, not Mars, or not, women at sea were treated differently to their male counterparts. That distinction is starkly expressed in images of shipwrecks: women are the barefoot helpless waifs (in clingy wet nighties) who are carried to safety ashore (their right place) by rugged, bearded selfless heroes.

Women, even low-ranking ones, were treated as ladies (meaning distinct from, and more genteel than low women and from men), not as shipmates in a (superficially) gallant culture. Ship's hairdresser Robina Herrington tells a story which illustrates the great gulf that many women experienced. When in 1958 she went to the seedy backstreet Board of Trade office in Liverpool before joining her first ship, the *Media*, to sign on as 'a British Merchant Seaman', she found rows of 'rough-looking' seamen waiting but was beckoned ahead of them all. 'I felt every eye on me. The man behind the desk said, "You don't want to sit with all of them, do you?" He was right.'[32]

That pattern of treating a woman as a lady died away in the 1970s as the Women's Liberation Movement and the sexual liberation culture changed people's ideas about what a female was and how she should be treated. Although chivalry somewhat disappeared, other forms of discrimination didn't. Seafaring women started out on the back foot and remained disadvantaged throughout their career. Since the 1980s a number of seafarers have told me that men long at sea can be oddly behind the times in their social attitudes and behave with a puzzling kind of well-intentioned but wrong-headed chivalry not found in other occupations. Men, particularly those who went to single-sex schools and haven't lived ashore much, still don't know whether to treat a woman as a lady, a shipmate or someone of broadly the category you have paid sex with. Others aver that the great freedom to kick over the moral traces on passenger ships means that women at sea were among the earliest to experience the kind of equality expressed through having many partners.

After reflecting upon many modern women's stories it seems to me that women seafarers have – and probably have long had – a major second job to do on board: dealing with preconceptions and prejudices. As in many worlds, this included the problem that if long-standing habitués didn't have the power to obstruct the women formally, then they dealt with this threat by informally punishing the incomer for intruding, almost as a way of mentally keeping safe.

Such self-protective attitudes became mixed up with genuinely kind, selfless concern that a woman shouldn't be sullied or put at risk by being on the threatening sea. Males who have long done a job in a male-dominated world not only have the power associated with that established regime, but all the power that men in society generally have over women too. Stereotyped ideas about women (also held, surprisingly, by some female human resources staff in maritime offices ashore) have been a hindrance to seawomen trying just to get on with their work. This has meant that sometimes xenophobic preconceptions stymied possibilities and growth. Getting a job in merchant shipping at all, let alone keeping it, has been a challenge. Typical fears include that women will 'cause' sexual rivalry, expect deferential treatment (such as jobs that don't damage polished nails) and that they won't be physically or mentally strong enough.

Diehards argue that women aren't 'natural' at sea. Women's responses include that, as emotionally literate professionals, they can handle matters well, that they can learn and that, anyway, in a team people mutually compensate for others' deficiencies. Rather than seeking casual relationships at sea, women usually avoid them. Men leave seafaring careers too; no statistics show that women are more likely to 'waste' expensive training in that way.

Modern researcher Michelle Thomas found 'the industry seems unable to see behind the stereotyped perceptions to the value represented by women … the employers with the most negative views actually had little or no experience of employing women at sea.' By contrast, 'some employers said they thought women performed better than men. They may be more determined to succeed as a result of the difficulties and prejudices they encountered during training.'[33] Companies also like having women employees because they are there because they want to be there; they wouldn't stick out the situation otherwise. It's repeatedly said that, as in other male-dominated industries, women 'work twice as hard to prove themselves', but even then are sometimes mis-seen as only half as good.

Once a seawoman has been awarded the job, she faces sticking it out, living with her male shipmates' attitudes and expectations. It was hardest of all for women doing non-traditional jobs in deck and engine work in the 1970s to 1990s. Sexual violence and harassment generally follow entrenched gender patterns. Men attack women, not vice versa.[34] This is a severe problem on ships (although some seafarers think it is now lessening). In 2011 Nautilus International found that of the women they surveyed 40 per cent had suffered sexual harassment at work, compared with 2 per cent of men (men are usually harassed by other men, not by women).

Rates of harassment at sea were double those found in other British or Dutch workplaces. 'Why should this be? It could be connected with the pressure of being in a confined shipboard environment for extended periods, or it may be that old-fashioned prejudices are still tolerated more at sea than on land,' thinks the union.[35]

It's also worth adding that, depending on the period and the nature of the shipping, seafaring men, particularly those from developing countries, may have lived for a long time in male-dominated and even femiphobic (meaning irrationally fearing or obsessively hating women) situations. On non-passenger ships they've typically met very few women other than sex industry workers in foreign ports. On passenger ships recently they've enjoyed those women holidaymakers who see tanned men in uniform as exotic beefcake to be consumed with booze, as part of the holiday party.

Professional seawomen and casual ancillaries therefore sometimes have to face ignorance and out-of-date ideas about women's capabilities; unwanted gallantry that they feel is insulting; refusal to accept a woman's authority; and shipmates who mistake a woman's friendly collegiality for sexual availability and interest. One woman ship's master ironically uses 'seatotty' as her email address. There are other, complex factors which come into play. One is that ships are hyper-sexualised spaces. Sex is what some people do when bored or lonely. Colleagues working away from home imagine adultery isn't really adultery. In film industry parlance it's NCOL, 'not counted on location'. Another problem is the enduring background cultural problem of men expressing anger (often from complex causes) at the nearest available woman. Both sexual and aggressive tensions can be worsened on long or difficult voyages.

In the 1970s deck officer Sara Miller felt sorry for the men who initially hated her as that figure, 'Woman Interloper', but then developed romantic crushes on the nice friendly person they realised she was. They slid poems under her door, proposed marriage and hung about chatting when she was on the bridge trying to do her job. Introducing women to male-dominated situations (especially cargo ships), said the International Labour Organisation back in 1980, 'calls for skilful managing and effective psychological preparation' to deal with male reactions that could involve 'thinly veiled resentment'. If women did 'men's jobs' well, alongside men, that tended to 'tarnish' men's 'carefully-cultivated "macho" image and foster … hostility'.[36]

Some men imagined that successful women were showing them up, even deliberately. So women could be damned if they did well (as competitors) as well as damned if they didn't do well (as inherently never up to the job).

In what can be a ruthless shipboard world, vulnerable people (including shy young men, and some women) fought – and fight – social and psychological battles. These wars can be violent and even result in punitive rape – about which the victims keep silent to keep their job. Targets bear this bullying and hostility far from family support and – in modern cadets' cases – when they are as young as 16. Such destructive discrimination is much harder to bear than on land because victim and perpetrator are cooped up together in a residential workplace for weeks or months.

Targets endure not only pressure to have casual sex but also additional complications if the rebuffed wooers are senior enough to scupper promotion prospects. Impossibly randy captains have become so hostile after being turned down that women have had to leave the ship and even the company. In these gossipy floating villages a good name, once lost, is lost forever – however erroneously and even though the target rejects the double moral standards involved. If you become pregnant or infected by sexually transmitted disease after a rape and are too far from shore to get appropriate treatment, these physical difficulties are piled onto the emotional distress.

In some ways seawomen's situation is easier today than in the past, even in the hyper-sexualised twenty-first century. Since the 1970s women have gained greater feminist awareness of women's right to say no, good contraception, sometimes morning-after pills and more readily available terminations. Men are less outspokenly sexist. Because many people from alcohol-prohibiting cultures are on board there can be less booze-fuelled promiscuity nowadays. If the worst happens, the increased availability of mobile phones means that if you're in signal range you can get support by email and text, rather than waiting to blurt it out in a public phone booth at the end of a pier. And many organisations are now supportive of women seafarers' rights.

From at least the eighteenth century seawomen learned to handle the widespread gender discrimination, and the power relations that fuel it, according to their various situations. Seagoing wives had some respect and protection from crew and other officers by virtue of their husband's superior position. 'Boys' were protected by their disguise. If discovered to be women they had to face hostility from any shipmate who felt cheated, or pay for silence with sex. Early women workers who were unprotected by marriage to shipmates must have had it hardest. But stewardesses in the early twentieth century were somewhat helped by being older than most crew, and fierce about their dignity and morality. Strict chief stewardesses could terrify mere importuning male predators. For much of the early twentieth century mixed-gender socialising was formally prohibited on ship (though actually the rules were often ignored). Women weren't allowed to drink in the ship's bar, the Pig and Whistle, or to visit male crew areas or work alone in a cabin with a man.

As well as these practical arrangements, with various degrees of consciousness women adopted some of the identity management strategies recently discussed by Momoko Kitada, an expert on gender at sea.[37] The 1960s and 1970s pioneers going into 'men's jobs' sometimes felt they had to decide whether to consciously 'butch up' and become 'ladettes' to win acceptance. Often they tried it, then stopped because it felt like self-betrayal, was too tedious an act to keep up or became unnecessary as people's knowledge of each other became more realistic during the voyages.

Some women became very private and dated very warily at sea, in order to keep their good name. Many thousands were circumspect and conciliatory with male colleagues – perhaps too much so for their own good. Some ignored the problem and their own distress. Brave ones banded together and spoke out, usually fruitlessly: one such team was told by head office, 'Oh, no, that can't have happened. None of our captains would behave like that!' A few women exploited their sexuality to gain boons and promotion; such eyelash-flutterers offended other seawomen. Many laughed, shrugged that 'men were like that' and tried to not let it undermine them.

At least one cracked under the pressure, and some wrote fiction about it afterwards as therapy.[38] In general, seawomen handled all the gender-based situations at work by being hugely determined to make their career work, developing the crucial ability to 'banter' (that term that can so often be code for 'trade insults'), adopting a tolerant attitude (protesting far less than they would in a shoreside job and accepting teasing), getting tough (or at least putting on that protective shell when on ship –

'I never wear pink at sea,' said one) and behaving with the utmost discretion. Above all, they became people who pulled their weight and did their work so well that eventually they were trusted as 'good sorts'. Their shipmates even 'forgot' these team-mates were women (which the men saw as a compliment).

Many, of course, had good and fair relationships with shipmates which even ended in marriage. Broadly speaking, these marriages seem to have worked best if the women then stopped going to sea, at least for a time. In some partnerships today, a supportive house-husband looks after the children, perhaps part-time, while the woman goes to sea, even deep sea.

Seawomen varied personally, and on different ships and in different jobs, but also at different times in history.

2

DIFFERENT TIMES, DIFFERENT POSSIBILITIES

Looking back from the twenty-first century at the broad story of how women were affected by what was happening at different times in the maritime past is a helpful way of preparing for the remaining chapters which focus on different occupations on ship. Changes in technologies and attitudes brought increasing possibilities to women's lives as they ventured across the farthest oceans. Appendix 2 gives the chronology of key landmarks in the history of seafaring women, and also includes related developments in other countries, and this chapter tells the story behind those landmarks.

NOW WE ARE CAPTAINS: THE TWENTY-FIRST CENTURY

Once there were grand palaces of shipping, headquarters of shipping firms that were household names, dominating the business streets of major ports such as Liverpool's waterfront quarter and London's Bishopsgate; the only women in sight were the cleaners. Powerful men in these mansions controlled the lives of the empire's few seafaring women, who were all stewardesses. But today it's almost impossible to talk about centres and control because so many merchant ships are now registered overseas,[1] and much that happens is opaque or barely visible to people in the UK.

By one measure the British Merchant Navy has just 1,504 large vessels of 100 gross registered tons (grt) or over. This amounts to 27 million grt,[2] the equivalent of 2,700,000 10-ton African elephants. By global standards, however, Britannia no longer rules the waves but stands at number ten in the hierarchy of world shipping. The total world tonnage is 1,111 million grt.[3]

And what of the lives of the women who work in this vast opaque business? Seafarers everywhere face a situation of long hours, uncertain employment prospects and worryingly under-regulated and under-staffed vessels. Newcomers tolerate it because they accept the maxim that you work hard and play hard, although they find it very distressing to be so out of mobile-signal range that they can't do that now-central activity of life: text and access the internet. An anonymous Facebook user recently posted this summary of what it was to do 'a dream job' on a cruise ship. Her story went viral. At the last count over 30,000 people 'liked' her list because it felt so accurate. She wrote:

> Days of the week become countries; Taking a bath is considered a luxury; You have to be a contortionist to shave your legs; When you talk about how to spend your 'hours off' not 'days off'; You have to turn on the TV to see the weather outside … You haven't had 10 minutes alone since you walked onboard; Arriving at a new country usually consists of finding the free wifi … Being solely responsible for tens of thousands of dollars with no sweat; Happy hour can be every hour; Working less than 10 hours is considered to be an easy day … Partying with your bosses; It's been 4 days since you've stepped outside; You've just spent a 13-hour day with the same people, so you go to dinner and happily spend the rest of the night with them; … You can survive with 3 pairs of jeans for 6 months; Seeing the captain at the gym is like seeing a movie star at a grocery store. You smile even if you're having a bad day; When you're in the real world you stop yourself from saying hello to random people walking past you; Walking across the hallway and knocking replaces the need for a cellphone; If you get a job on land you'll feel naked without a name badge; You're so far from home but seem to be surrounded by your family.[4]

Most of that is true of men *and* women. But women are fewer, have fewer job options and are less likely to be at the top. It's impossible to obtain accurate statistics about the number of UK Merchant Navy seawomen there are on ships today, only snapshots from oblique angles which don't quite match up. But indicative figures for 2014 show a total of 2,708 women. They are 13 per cent of the 20,840 UK people called 'active at sea', meaning in work or seeking employment.

In terms of rank, approximately 870 are women officers (32 per cent of all the officers). Lower down the scale 1,838 are ratings (13 per cent). A rating is someone who is not a commissioned or petty officer.[5] Women today still find it easier – and sometimes more attractive – to get jobs in 'people work' rather than technical work, therefore most of the merchant seawomen are on the seven British passenger ships and sixty-six British passenger/cargo vessels, as well as on the many flagged-out passenger vessels with their polyglot crews and a strong British connection.

In the Royal Navy there are slightly more women (3,150) than in the MN. But they are a lower percentage of the total (just under 9 per cent of a 33,000-strong workforce). Most of these RN women work in medical, dental and logistical roles, though virtually all seagoing roles are currently open to them. Two women were commanding frigates by 2002.[6] Several went on to command warships. All-male vessels still exist, mainly because it would too costly to convert old accommodation. But women are aboard most of the RN's seventy-eight commissioned ships. These include six guided-missile destroyers and thirteen frigates. In 2014 the first three pioneers were allowed to sail on some of the ten nuclear-powered submarines.

But women are not yet permitted on the fifteen mine counter-measures vessels. The Royal Fleet Auxiliary (RFA) also employs women on the fourteen merchant ships that service RN ships with fuel and food. Roughly 10 per cent of RFA staff are women. They mainly do stewarding work. Appendix 4 summarises the situation.

Today's RN has remarkably good equality policies in place and makes sure they are implemented. Many RN women think *their* navy has a better record on this than the MN. But Merchant Navy people tend to think Royal Navy traditions are still restrictive and that the commercial shipping world is a more open one, which women can access more easily. Centuries of men-only, war-focused seafaring have left subtle legacies in the RN, although by the early 1990s hostility has waned substantially. Navy men have two big fears about women: that women won't be physically able to carry an injured shipmate to safety; and that if it's necessary to sacrifice a colleague – by shutting a watertight door on them, for example, in order to stop the ship being flooded and sinking – this would be a problem. Either women will be too soft-hearted to carry out this action which will lead to someone's death. Or men will be too soft-hearted to shut the door on a woman. Skills training and education may change these concerns, which at present cause some men to prefer to sail on stag ships.

Obstacles to women joining the RN include the fact that they don't know the Navy has vacancies for women: recent defence cuts have led to less recruitment advertising. A key reason they don't stay on, let alone for the twenty-nine years it takes on average to become a rear admiral, is that being liable to service at sea conflicts with some women's desires to start a family. In 2011 Commander Ellie Ablett set up the Naval Service Women's Network 'to show women … how they can … still have a personal life and a great career in the Royal Navy'.[7] (The network grew from a climate in which merchant seawomen set up the US Women's Maritime Association in 1980, the New Zealand Women's Maritime Association in 1995 and the German Verband Frauen zur See eingetragener Verein in 1998. They recognised that sharing information and support was crucial.)

We will look at how this situation compares to that of these seawomen's predecessors.

1750–1800: I SEE NO WOMEN … OR IS THAT ONE?

Around 1800 Britain possibly had fewer than 200 women working at sea, out of a maritime workforce of 118,000. There were 16,000 merchant vessels. Most of these women were in very early stewardessing roles, probably as wives of the ship's steward. They benefited from passenger tips and their husbands' largesse rather than being directly employed by the shipping company. A few were women disguised as cabin boys. Some of the other (unwaged) women sailing were masters' wives, such as Frances Barkley. She is recorded as the first out woman to circumnavigate the globe. Frances's 400-ton *Imperial Eagle* in 1787 was the biggest ship thus far to enter Friendly Cove harbour, near Vancouver Island.[8] By contrast, today P&O Captain Sarah Breton's *Arcadia* is 86,799 tons. Although there were many more British ships then than in the present day, they were not only smaller, but they carried far fewer passengers (for women workers to wait upon).

Probably most of the women who were out as women managed to go to sea in association with a man of some status on ship. Fragmentary information suggests that usually these women lived near ports. From girlhood they could get to know seafarers, learn about seafaring life through their stories, and go aboard ships on visits. Proximity brought not only introductions to potential sweethearts but enabled disguised women and seagoing wives to fit shrewdly into shipboard life.

Novelist Jane Austen readily understood naval culture through her naval brothers. Famously this enriched *Persuasion* (1817) with its admiral's wife Mrs Croft, probably the most famous and knowledgeable naval wife who never existed. In the King's Navy, with its 755 ships in 1799 (which were mainly at sea only during engagements, not full-time) wives were unofficially allowed to be on board. Mrs Croft was one, and loved it. Captains 'issued' women to lower seafaring men as rewards. Wives 'were the anodynes which made naval life bearable for the men in wartime'.[9]

Looking at cross-dressed sailor 'boys' in the eighteenth-century Royal Navy and Marines (the Royal Navy's soldiers), the historian Suzanne Stark argued that: 'It is difficult for us today to appreciate how casually recruits were accepted into the Navy.'[10]

Indeed, some people wanted to get out of the RN, not in it. Press gangs were under economic pressure to provide likely looking men, so plausibly disguised women could very occasionally and briefly get away with it. However, it cannot have been *that* easy, because there were medical examinations, albeit cursory. An unmarried out woman would not have been employed because of assumptions that she would not be strong enough to handle the sails, and because men would be competing for her sexual attention; sexual rivalry would have divided the shipboard team.

Suzanne Stark scotches the hackneyed idea that any woman cross-dressed and joined up because she was following her man as 'patently absurd'. 'Most sailors' sweethearts came from seafaring communities and would have known that a woman could usually go to sea with her lover in her own right [as a 'wife'].' There was no need to adopt male disguise and join the crew as a working member. Any be-trousered sweetheart-pursuer would also have known that, even if she was assigned to her lover's ship, officers might switch her to another vessel at any time.[11] But certainly the fact that Frances Barkley's French counterpart in pioneering her way round the world, Rose de Freycinet, had to be stowed away cross-dressed by her husband on his military-scientific world voyage in 1817–20 shows that some subterfuge was needed to sail on some early ships.

1800–1850: FROM SAIL TO STEAM AND THEREFORE OPPORTUNITY

This was the period when passenger ships included slave, convict and, increasingly, emigrant ships travelling between Africa, the southern US, the Caribbean and the Antipodes. As the empire grew, so industrial exports – and the number of colonial administrators – increased, so that the British merchant fleet had 22,654 ships by 1840.[12]

The most hopeful sign for women would-be seafarers was that 771 were steamships, not sail. Steam enabled a pleasanter, safer, faster travelling style, which meant that more women passengers would travel by ship, so there'd be more jobs for the stewardesses assigned to their care. The fair sex could enjoy hot running water, and even single-sex public lavatories, complete with vestibules, boudoirs and washbasins. Scores, though not hundreds, of seawomen may have been sailing by this time, all as stewardesses.

Margaret S. Creighton, a leading historian of the gendered seas, has described nineteenth-century sailing ships as 'Hislands; the global ocean has seemingly been inhabited by an unvaryingly single sex. And like the cowboy, the historical sailor has been an icon of ... "manliness:" tough, undauntable and thoroughly undomestic.'[13]

Through such vivid images we can imagine that women sailed with would-be John Wayne-type figures, and that naval men in particular travelled as brave warriors going to war with the ocean or the enemy on (or 'in' as they say in the RN) their noble sea steeds. She points out that relations between the women and men on these Hislands was no simple matter.[14] Similarly women in the early Wild West, who were complex flesh-and-blood creatures – not just stereotypical bold saloon bar workers, strict teachers and patient homemakers – found relationships with frontiersmen hard.

Ships varied. Wives, particularly women from US ports such as New Bedford, were increasingly on whalers, which might be seen as uber-Hislands full of testosterone-fuelled roustabouts on a mission to bravely lasso sea behemoths. It appears there were no women crew on slave ships. Mainly this was because it would have been considered unseemly for females to see naked black people being treated as animals, though I suspect the occasional captain's or doctor's wife sailed on slave ships.

Women seemingly weren't employed to work on the no-frills ships transporting convicts to the penal colonies. However, passengers were often paid to do shipboard tasks of the kind a stewardess might do. This included trusted convicts on convict ships, as well as 'superior' women on emigrant vessels. On ships taking out troops, wives of the lower ranks might offer ad hoc service to officers' wives, not least because elite people at that time were used to having servants.[15] There were many naval wives, to whom naval captains would turn a blind eye. Twenty-two nationalities fought together on the British side in the key naval battle of Trafalgar, so a number of the women will have been black and non-British (particularly wives of ex-slaves from Nova Scotia).

After 1815 wives had far fewer opportunities to sail on RN ships because the British war with France had finished: fewer seafarers were required, and hence there was a knock-on effect on the number of wives who could sail. By the 1820s, new recruits were becoming subject to greater scrutiny, which meant that women disguised as boys could no longer pass easily.

1850–1913: WOMEN NEEDED – FOR HOUSEWORK AT SEA

The introduction of steam propulsion was the factor most affecting ships, and consequently seawomen, in this period. The Merchant Navy's tonnage was 11 million by 1913, by comparison to 2 million in 1815. With 20,938 ships, the British fleet was the largest in the world. The sailing fleet had dwindled to less than 2,000 tons.[16] 'Proper seamen' derided the increasing number of comfortable steamships as 'floating tin kettles' and averred 'sail's a lady, steam's just a bundle of iron'. But steam meant more stewardessing jobs, although ships were still seen as no place for a lady.

That gender divide was evidenced by the famous incident on the troopship *Birkenhead*, carrying soldiers and their families out to fight the Eighth Xhosa War. It sank near Danger Point, Gansbaai, off the coast of South Africa in February 1852. Soldiers chivalrously stood firm on deck, as ordered, to let the women abandon ship before them – fatally for the men. This established the noble-minded 'Women and Children First' protocol. Historian Lucy Delap has discussed the way the 'Birkenhead Drill' was subsequently held up as epitomising the most glorious British (masculine) behaviour. Today's survival experts reckon that prioritising can be counter-productive: it holds up evacuation. And macho actions aren't always useful because they can be too hasty and irrational.[17]

Census enumerators found that the number of seawomen (whom they called 'stewardesses etc.') grew from at least seventy-six in 1851 to at least 420 in 1901. Actually the number is likely to be treble that.[18]

And a new job had emerged. The 1875 Merchant Shipping Act stipulated that a matron, with authority, had to be carried on all ships taking mixed-sex groups of emigrants overseas. By the end of the nineteenth century a few women were also working as ship's nurses and had officer status of a kind. As Britain still had the biggest fleet in the world it's likely that Britain also had the most seawomen at that point, although the US and Scandinavia had increasing numbers too.

The period 1869–75 saw the last of the women seafarers disguised as men (or at least those who were detected). From Tom Stewart in 1860 to the last one, William Armstrong in 1873, only five were discovered on merchant ships in this period. It was probably less easy to get away with it: crew undressed more frequently as habits of cleanliness developed, and shipmates may have regarded each other with more astute eyes. The possibility of 'nature's agreeable blunders'[19] (i.e. women) doing deck work in their own right was emerging.

At least two US women, Mary Miller and Mary Coons, had gained their masters' tickets and were about to dilute the Hislands. More wives accompanying masters were recorded than ever before. They were mainly on small coastal vessels, often under sail. Probably numbering in the low hundreds, they're mainly visible through tragic accidents reported in newspapers. In the RN lower-ranked wives were travelling less. Even the wives of commissioned officers were restricted in the way they were allowed to sail. Historian Suzanne Stark found that the 1879 Queen's Regulations and Admiralty instructions were very firm, formally. A wife was not allowed to live on board unless the Admiralty had expressly authorised it, or in an emergency, when the Commander-in-Chief was allowed to authorise it.[20] Actual practice was sometimes different.

1914–1946: WOMEN SAILING THROUGH WARS

Just before the First World War the British merchant fleet comprised 9,488 ships. Britain owned 40 per cent of the world's shipping and carried 50 per cent of the world's trade.[21] Possibly a handful of very small ships were commanded by women. In 1904, 224,000 seafarers were working on British ships. There were at least 1,700 seawomen at that point, I estimate, and they were overwhelmingly outnumbered.[22] War put many of these seawomen out of work as few female passengers were allowed to sail; civilian voyages were seen as unnecessary. And there was no official thought to move women into men's sea jobs. Presumably it was thought too dangerous and that female casualties would be bad for public morale. About twenty to forty stewardesses were in harm's way in the First World War, including at Gallipoli. A total of fifty-three British seawomen from eighteen ships died in the First World War, 3 per cent of the female pre-war maritime workforce.

The RN offered even fewer opportunities for women during the war. Women's Royal Naval Service members didn't work on seagoing ships, although they might work on moored ones; a few sailed as passengers to overseas postings in 1918. Just under a hundred naval nurses sailed on hospital ships. War's end in late 1918 brought changes to ideas of how women passengers were to be cared for. Associated with that came the rise of the first seawomen who had officer status: conductresses. The increasing luxury of ships and the start of cruising meant several service jobs for women were emerging. They included shop assistants and masseuses as well as social hostesses, travel agents, swimming pool attendants, manicurists and even visiting entertainers.

Meanwhile to the east women were moving into 'men's jobs' on ships. Scandinavian countries accepted women wireless operators and the Soviet Union's merchant fleet employed women in a range of non-traditional tasks, including deck work. Newspapers adored stories of such pioneers, especially if they were tiny and 'girly' and if they were patriotically and temporarily doing their wartime bit.[23]

Britain's first women marine engineers were struggling up the ladder too. For all that, in the Second World War Britain didn't usher women into 'men's jobs' at sea. Again, many hands were needed as men went to the Front or died. Seagoing hands could have been women's hands but this was still unthinkable.

Similarly, US seawomen were not allowed to work at sea after December 1941. A delegation to the head of the Maritime Commission and War Shipping Administration argued 'for the right to go to sea, since among other reasons, one Russian skipper was a woman. Admiral Land finally told these ladies of "mixed nationalities including a couple of coloured women" that the question of their morals must be considered. The blonde leader replied, "Damn you, Admiral. You take care of your morals and we'll take care of ours."'[24]

British merchant shipping women only started sailing again in late 1945. They mainly got their opportunities by being old hands from pre-war days who were available to assist war brides heading to the US, Canada, Australia and South Africa on troopships.

1947–2010: DOING ALL SORTS IN FLOATING HOTELS

The Second World War had decimated the British merchant fleet, which in 1939 had numbered 9,488 ships.[25] But by 1947 numbers had climbed again to 8,813 ships, despite the war losses. Pre-war stewardesses came back, working on the 322 passenger ships, including ferries and ships carrying assisted emigrants to Australia. A new job choice for women was emerging: purserette or lady assistant purser. And the 'ette' or 'lady' attached to the job title 'purser' very slowly fell away. By 1951 the number of women seafarers had risen to today's figure of over 3,000; they were more than 1 per cent of British ships' complements.

Women in search of sea jobs were affected by the way commercial flying took passengers away from shipping. To counter the decreased demand, shipowners turned increasingly to cruising, creating ever-cheaper voyages. Ships that were transformed into floating shopping malls and casinos needed women staff, including a range of hairdressers, beauticians, shop managers, bank staff and entertainers who were employed by concessionaires; a ship's complement was no longer just 'our community'. In the early 1950s Buries Markes and the Medomsley Shipping Company were two decades ahead of other firms in allowing women into catering jobs. And the growth of schools cruises in the 1930s brought increasing numbers of women to look after the children, including doctors. However, numbers of women laundry workers decreased as Hong Kong Chinese men replaced them, ships offered launderette facilities, and new easy-care fabrics such as Bri-Nylon took over.

In the late 1960s the unthinkable happened: women took up deck jobs on merchant ships. It seems to happen particularly if employers were small, family-owned companies where people were assessed on the basis of their competence not their gender. This was probably the stage when women in dark-blue trousers and boilersuits, rather than dresses, appeared on ships. Symbolically it was a revolution, but only a partial one as these early women pioneers were required to wear uniform skirts in more formal situations. For the first time, passenger ships were becoming places where it was normal to see other women in your working day. They even bore gold insignia designating rank on their pristine navy-blue sleeves.

At the same time as seawomen's formal position was improving, the situation for all British seafarers, irrespective of gender, was deteriorating. Between 1975 and 1993 the merchant fleet declined by 75 per cent, a steeper decline than in any other nation. By 1993, 80 per cent of British ships were flagged overseas and the number of seafarers on ships registered with the British Chamber of Shipping dropped from 80,000 in 1975 to 19,000 in 1993.[26] Efficiency was increasing (notably when cargo began to be transported by container), so fewer deck personnel were needed.[27]

Only 167 of the 3,211 ships were passenger vessels and ferries.[28] The growth in flagging out from the 1980s meant a very drastic decline in opportunities for British seafaring women and men as cheaper workers from the Philippines and South Asia took up the lower-grade jobs. By 2001 only 368 trading vessels were registered in the UK, just 3.6 million grt.[29] However, the demand for highly skilled deck and engineering officers remained high, so skilled British officers of any gender were (and are still) sought after, though their numbers are still low.

By the late 1980s if you were a woman doing scientific, engineering or technical work on ships you had extra opportunities because of the rise of heritage shipping. Historic tall sailing ships brought scores of chances to voyage as a volunteer, worker or guest. Just as women are more easily allowed to become train drivers on *vintage* railways,[30] so women found much more freedom on sail training ships. A two-week trip often tipped women into choosing the sea as a career. After the 1980s some of these ships were partly officered by women.

In 1991 women in the Royal Navy started going to sea. At that point the RN had 177 ships (including forty-seven destroyers and sixteen Royal Fleet Auxiliary ships), compared with 272 UK-owned and UK-registered merchant ships.[31] British naval women made it to sea eight years after Australian women had been given that right in 1983 and twelve years after US women were allowed to sail on support and non-combatant naval ships. The Royal Netherlands Navy had paved the way in 1981 with the first women in any European navy. Indeed, Hr Ms *Zuiderkruis* became known as the 'womenship'.[32] Similarly the UK's *Brilliant* was nicknamed 'the Love Boat', as if an entire ship changed its identity when a few women worked on it. In 2014, three years after the US, UK RN women were allowed to serve on submarines.

Were the 2000s the start of the run-up to a golden age, where gender no longer matters and ships are 'Ourlands'? It's hard to say yet. Most professional seawomen today would probably look nonplussed at such a fanciful idea. But certainly the period 1970–2010 has been the most accelerated of all in the development of work at sea for women, as well as a time of terrible erosion of labour rights. For men, too, 2006 was a key year of achieving some justice, after the Maritime Labour Convention 2006 was passed. It meant that those countries that signed up to it agreed that seafarers had to be properly waged; they couldn't just be expected to rely on tips (as some stewardesses had to) or commissions on selling products (as in most hairdressers' cases).[33]

Women seafarers' joyous nostalgic stories on Facebook today makes clear that the 1970s, 1980s, 1990s and even 2000s were a time to celebrate, even though progress still remains spasmodic and slow. In the days of the disguised 'boys', it would have been hard to imagine that women, some of them disabled and elderly, would do 'male' jobs on heritage sail training ships.

Nowadays, be-trousered but not in disguise, they stride the deck and climb the shrouds, free from the daily fear of expulsion as members of the not-allowed species. Women seafarers' occupational progress is also a story of a more personal and profound quest for adventure and new identities; the right to go aloft is a metaphor for the right to risk, explore and be 'unfeminine' and enjoy the transformations that travel can bring.

PART ONE

THE VESSEL

3

FROM 'BOY' TO CAPTAIN: WORKING ON DECK

Second Mate Deborah Harrison was attacked by pirates in one of the worst piracy incidents then known. It was Friday 9 January 1998. Deborah worked on a Shell tanker, the MT *Isomeria*, which was anchored at Brazil's Mosquito Island terminal, discharging liquid propane and butane gas. A little boat powered out from the *favelas*, eluding the bay's night patrol. To the far-off sound of samba, reported a newspaper, four pirates armed with the usual Uzis climbed aboard the *Isomeria*, took over, and held Deborah and a (male) cadet hostage.[1] They held guns to her head and stomach to make her open the ship's safe. 'We'll kill you if you don't,' they threatened her. Armed police zoomed up. For ninety minutes a gun battle waged.

Pirates used Deborah as a human shield. Maybe these hoodlums believed gallantry would make the crew more compliant, or that a woman was an easier target. In the fight a misdirected bullet struck her in the chest: 'I just remember looking down and seeing a large red stain starting to appear on my boiler suit … I remember being somewhat bemused at first as I was still moving and it was not like in the films where they are coughing and spluttering on the floor.'[2] Luckily her vital organs weren't hit.

She survived, to raise serious concerns internationally about the dangers of piracy and about the unproductive ways that pirate attacks were sometimes being tackled, and to win the Queen's Commendation for Bravery.[3] Deborah, who at 13 had decided that she wanted to go to sea, added the award to her list, having won the Victoria Drummond Award in 1987 for being the first woman to get a dual Class 2 qualification in both deck and engineering skills.[4] Her courage has many precedents in seafarers' history.[5] Maritime crime is only one of the challenging situations faced by women doing deck jobs today. Dealing with colleagues', stevedores' and employers' social attitudes is also a major issue.

DECK WORK

People who work on the deck (also called 'navigating') side of the ship, as Deborah Harrison still does, are responsible for the safe navigation of the vessel. They take it where it's intended to go, and ensure that its cargo or passengers are loaded and unloaded correctly, stowed appropriately, and looked after properly. Deck officers, together with the engineers and lower-grade maintenance workers (called deck and engine 'hands'), are responsible for the ship as a vehicle, rather than as a hotel.

Maritime statistics are kept in different and limited ways by different organisations, so a definitive picture is impossible to obtain. However, the approximate position in 2014 in the UK, according to three different non-matching sources, is as follows. Over 367 women are certified to do deck officer jobs: 1.8 per cent of all Britain's 20,000 deck officers are women.[6] At least 122 women out of the 3,645 people with master's certificates are women.[7] (The word 'master' is used interchangeably with 'captain' and seemingly troubles few women.) Captain Barbara Campbell, one of these trailblazing women qualified to command, is master of a large square-rigged sailing ship.

Captain Barbara: In it for the Long Haul

Captain Barbara Campbell, formerly Sampeys (b. 1957), says, 'I am not aware of any other female deck officer who has worked at sea, continuously, for forty years.' Gender seems to be far less an issue now than it was when she started out, she finds. As a girl she sailed dinghies and read about Nancy Blackett, Arthur Ransome's boatie heroine in *Swallows and Amazons*, but had no dreams of becoming a captain. In 1975 Barbara joined P&O as one of their first female deck cadets and trained along with fellow cadet Sara Miller. She gained her foreign-going master's certificate in 1986. Ten years later she joined the Jubilee Sailing Trust, became the first female master with the Sail Training Association, commanding a ship reminiscent of the brawn days, the 150-foot, three-masted *Malcolm Miller*. She later returned to the Jubilee Sailing Trust (JST) as master of the square-rigged sailing ships *Lord Nelson* and *Tenacious*. She comments, 'The shipboard camaraderie is outstanding, particularly on challenging voyages such as the recently completed circumnavigation on board *Lord Nelson*.' In 2004 Barbara, the Princess Royal and Captain Wendy Maughan were warmly inducted as 'brethren' of Trinity House. They were the first three women in an organisation that has protected mariners and shipping since 1514.

Ship's captains are officially 'master under God'. With four gold stripes and an autocratic bearing, such patriarchs used to rule their off-shore kingdom. Today *Queen Elizabeth* captain Inger Klein Thorhauge doesn't see herself as the matriarchal

Deck cadets Barbara Sampeys (left), Sarah Stuart and Sara Miller (right) climb the gangway of their second ship, P&O's *Strathmay*, Sydney, 1976. (Sara Miller)

equivalent of the 'old man' but simply a member of the interdependent team who run the ship, in which her role happens to be captain.

The main reason that so few women are captains at this point is that they were given a very late start and that it takes anyone at least ten years of training and fifteen years' experience. Promotion is a matter of waiting, not so much to step into dead men's shoes, but for older captains (who, yes, are male) to move to shore jobs or retire. However, Inger is one of the many women deck officers of her generation who feel that old sexist ideas mean it takes women a bit longer to progress. 'And there'll always be someone at headquarters who thinks women shouldn't be at sea at all,' she thinks.

Below captain level are fifty-three women who have their British chief mate's certificate (just 1.8 per cent of the 2,930 people so certified). A further 192 women (4 per cent) are on their way up as officers of the watch (OOWs), which include second officers and third officers.[8] It's said that the only people allowed to make jokes about women drivers – such as 'they need wing mirrors to reverse into the dock' – are the women actually driving the ship. And they grow so tired of hearing such 'witticisms' early in their careers that they are not likely to prolong the tedium by repeating such jests. Below the OOWs are, depending on the shipping company, vessel size and type, about six deck cadets, who have to complete a three-year apprenticeship. Like any tyros, cadets are the butt of jokes, but can also be objects of protective concern. Sometimes this can be a bit too gendered for women cadets' liking.

Below officer level in the deck department are the chief petty officers. These include the boatswain/bo'sun (sometimes called the 'deck foreman', which explains well their role of organising lower crew), carpenter and plumber. Bo'suns reputedly ate razor blades for breakfast: it was once a job for seemingly hyper-masculine males, even bullies. The old nickname 'deck ornaments' indicates the attitude some lower-ranking men had towards deck officers' privileges. Masculinity was equated with 'real' authority.

Very few women indeed are bo'suns, carpenters or plumbers, other than the occasional volunteer on a sail training ship. Lou Price was one of the rare ones, on the heritage ship *Lord Nelson* as bo'sun's mate. She went on to join Maersk as a deck cadet.[9] In 2000 Kendra Savage in the US became one of the most high-profile women bo'suns on the internet. She's described as 'a pleasant fair-haired lady', not one of those legendary 'fearsome folk who can bite the necks off bottles, with every finger a marline spike'.[10]

Below these chief petty officers are petty officers such as the crane operator and quartermaster. Lower down the hierarchy again are ratings, meaning people doing the crucial drone work of the ship. Women are better represented at officer level, not rating level. A few women deck ratings work on ferries; very few ratings indeed are on cargo ships. Possibly this is because they would have to share a twin cabin, and companies would be legally required to provide a separate changing area for women (boilersuits and boots aren't allowed in cabins; everyone strips off in a shared changing room) or else firms permit women to change in their own cabin, as in Fiona Rush's case.

Today the rare women doing lower-level jobs mainly do so as working volunteers on heritage sail ships or as paid workers on yachts. Some then move to what professional seafarers regard as 'proper' ships and work towards qualifications.

To the side of this hierarchy were the radio officers, a job now morphing into electro-technical officer (ETO), as well as, on cruise ships, security staff and safety staff.

In theory a UK shipping company should be open to employing you if you are suitable. In fact, fear that females waste company money by leaving to have babies, and misogyny, are obstacles. What helps women overcome such problems?

The same as in most seafaring jobs: effective role models and mentors; relatives already in the industry/company who can act as an advocate; luck – you're in the right place when a job comes up and no man is available to do it; and having the right sort of persona – a mix of no-nonsense but affable.[11] Once you've got the job, matey colleagues help. On the way up, women deck officers have to work hard to prove their undoubted suitability for promotion. Some feel that the glass ceiling is still there. It's hard to breach this solid if invisible barrier if, however well-qualified and experienced, you are a member of a 'minority' (although women actually form a slight majority in the population overall: 50.8 per cent of the UK's 63 million population).[12]

Women captains are crucial proof that women who have worked their way up can do the job, and they lay a vital trail for their successors. Captain Lis Lauritzen (b. 1971) of Royal Caribbean's *Vision of the Seas* thinks the situation has improved since 2000, although some passengers still expect the captain to look like Cap'n Birdseye. 'When I make the announcement for the guest safety drill, people always believe that I am a big lady because of my deep voice. Then when they actually see me they say, 'My goodness, how is it possible that this tiny woman can run a big boat like this?'[13]

Doubts whether a woman can command are lessening in the Royal Navy too. The idea of women in combat situations is still highly contentious, but in 2012 Commander Sarah West became the first woman to command a large warship. Today Britain's Royal Navy has forty-eight women with the rank of commander or higher.[14] It's expected that a woman will be made a full admiral by 2025. In the US and Australia women have already been made admirals, but tended to work on land. (In 2011 surgeon Robyn Walker was the first woman admiral in the Royal Australian Navy; in 2014 Michelle J. Howard became the first US seagoing woman admiral, following computer scientist Grace Murray Hopper.)

First Major Warship Boss: Sarah West

Lincolnshire-bred Sarah West (b. 1972) became the first Royal Navy woman to command a major warship, HMS *Portland*. The factors that helped her rise to this position include a maths degree from the University of Hertfordshire, a course at Britannia Royal Naval College from 1995, and a lot of experience in large-scale naval planning, mine clearance, weapon systems and underwater warfare. She has commanded four small ships, co-ordinated the evacuation of British citizens during the 2006 Lebanon War and been involved in the Iraq War. The Navy's improved readiness to accept women as her career began also made these achievements possible. Women did still face consternation and even outright hostility from some men, although this has waned as women have proved their value. In 2014, Commander West was removed from command for a breach of the Code of Social Conduct. The code is 'a guiding set of principles for a wide range of social behaviours which have the potential to adversely affect the management of a ship or unit'. Contrary to press disinformation she remains a member of the Naval Service, but at the time of writing is not at sea.[15]

Sarah West when a lieutenant commander and in charge of a mine counter-measures vessel. (Ministry of Defence, NE110397028)

1750–1800: ON THE DECK OF SAILING SHIPS

Two women admirals were sailing way back in history, or so the myths go: Artemisia, Queen of Halicarnassus in 480 BC and Keumalahayati/Malahayati in sixteenth-century Aceh, Sumatra. Both widows achieved their roles because they were high-status authority figures. Artemisia owned ships; Malahayati had extra expertise as she'd studied at a military academy and was an admiral's daughter. Lower down the social scale women in China sailed with their children and husbands on pirate vessels in the 1790s: Dian Murray found that there were thirty-four women and children with the 1,422 male pirates in Chang Pao's squadron in that period.[16]

By the eighteenth century ships resembled the ships of today in that essentially the same tasks had to be done: loading/unloading, steering, vehicle management. There was also a similar hierarchy of roles, though proportionately many more people did that work – and they did it differently because ships were propelled by sail and had fewer and less-sophisticated navigational aids. Some modern women captains say they couldn't have done their job then because it would have been physically much harder.

Probably fewer than 300 women sailors in a whole population of 6 million were sailing at this point. Around 1792, just before the start of the French Revolutionary Wars, Britain had 118,000 merchant seafarers. Parliament was shortly to seek a Royal Navy that would be 120,000 strong. So in theory maybe 200,000 deck opportunities were available. But, as we saw in Chapter 1, only a few women dressed as boys sailed. The idea of an 'out' woman doing the work was unthinkable, even when cross-dressed women's competence proved that women could do far more than they were believed capable of, and at a time when girls were increasingly leaving home and finding casual jobs of all kinds.

Most newspaper reports about women disguised as male deck crew mentioned them carrying out many and diverse low-grade tasks each day including climbing the masts to furl the sails, cleaning and serving food. Seafarers then did not have specialised jobs. The majority of disguised women were probably, like Sarah Davies, working on ordinary trading vessels.

Sarah the Sailor

Sarah Davies (c. 1725–?), the daughter of a Bristol tide-waiter (customs officer) left home cross-dressed in the early 1740s. Newspaper articles say she 'found herself' apprenticed to a ship's captain. As 'John Davies, sailor', she went to Jamaica. She sailed on several ships for five years, seemingly doing general ship's work. But in November 1751 her ship foundered in the Bay of Biscay. 'John' and thirteen other survivors were picked up and her gender was revealed. By that time she was visibly very pregnant, so at least one man aboard had already realised she was a woman. Would she have been allocated lighter duties or would shipmates have felt she should still pull her usual weight despite her pregnancy – and would she have accepted such concessions. If the father was an officer, preferential treatment would have been easier to get but, like any favouritism, embarrassing to handle.[17]

Wives travelling with the officers and petty officers would usually only do deck work in emergencies. It was almost certainly a mix of whatever was needed and whatever they had already learned from following their husbands' actions. Some husbands taught spouses skills such as working out compass bearings, perhaps as a precaution and perhaps because wives didn't want to be 'spare parts'. It also helped lessen senior men's loneliness of command.

Similarly in ships of what was then called the King's Navy, especially those in the many battles of Nelson's time (c. 1780–1805), any women on board were either wives or common-law 'wives' of warrant officers and artisans aboard, or more rarely young women in disguise. There was and is a recognised 'shadow stripes' phenomenon operating in the armed forces and Merchant Service: a woman is seen as having her husband's rank. So wives on these naval ships would have done the tasks suited to their husband's rank, except when it was 'all hands to the pump'.

Wives were a sort of reserve navy-on-demand. Suzanne Stark, their main historian, found that in an engagement the shortage of people meant that any hand, even that of an elderly wife, was pressed into service to pass the gunpowder. Records show wives standing resolutely by their assigned gun despite injury, loyally doing their duty in the culture of noble collective self-sacrifice.

1800–1849: WHALING IN CRINOLINES

When the nineteenth century began, British seafarers were sailing to the increasing number of ports in the growing and glorious empire. As outright naval war waned, ships from many European nations opened up remote locations in the quest for profits and scientific knowledge. On the vastly reduced number of naval ships any officers' wives (probably only a few hundred) would be emergency assistants in warfare. Otherwise they would do routine emotion labour rather than deck work. Women disguised as boys were still sailing, but less often because peace meant there was a far less voracious demand for hands, and new crew were more closely inspected – disguises would have been penetrated. The last three known Royal Navy 'boys' were 'Tom Bowling' and Lizzie/'John' Bowden in 1807, and 'William Brown' in 1815.

Instead, disguised women joined the Merchant Navy. At least ten were discovered in this period, including 'Billy'/Isabella Stewart in 1841.[18] Others may have sailed but never came to public attention. It's unlikely that any cross-dressed women deck officer existed, because they would have doubtless have been discovered long before they had the time (many years) to develop sufficient skills. Although some male deck officers were at least *trained* by women teachers of navigation ashore or used instruments made or repaired by Janet Taylor, women's place was seen as not at sea. Navigation teacher Sarah Jane Rees sometimes went to sea on her father's ship when he was shorthanded, and may well have applied her skills on board.[19]

Some whaling wives 'looked after' the ship while their husbands were away in the small boat chasing whales. But the principal daily role of wives of higher-ranking men on trading ships and whalers was 'emotional labour': supporting their husbands, and, at worst, protecting the crew from the harshest, even insane captains, as in Eliza Underwood's case when she sailed with her rage-filled husband Samuel on the whaler *Kingsdown* in 1829. By contrast, 'handling the old man and his temper' could be said to be the job of a chief officer today. There may well have been British women cross-dressers on whalers, like the US's Rebecca Ann/George Johnson, but none is recorded.[20]

Artist's impression of a pregnant captain's wife taking the wheel, standing on a box to boost her height, *c.* 1850. (Val Mitchell, 2015)

This was the period when the first woman captain came to notice: Betsy Miller. Master of the *Cloetus* or *Cletis*, a 197-ton brig taking timber from Ardossan to Belfast, Dublin and Cork, she was probably the very first woman ship's master in Britain, in those uncertificated days. Captain Miller had several crucial advantages that gave her the metaphorical seven-league boots that allowed her to step over the usual rules for women at that time. Her father owned ships and his family worked on them.

She had learned about shipping while ashore by acting as her father's 'ship's-husband' (clerk); his ships were small and so was the business, so she was not confined by any great international million-pound empire with established rules; she was the eldest child of eleven, so she was used to managing people; and she had no children or husband to keep her at home. And, like so many women, she gained her opportunity because there was no one else to help out in a crisis that would otherwise have ruined the family business.

Cap'n Betsy: The Very First?

Betsy Miller (1792–1864) was from Saltcoats in Ayrshire. She took over the *Cloetus* after her brother, its master, died in an accident in 1833 and her elderly father was too ill to help. A seaman who'd met her described how she worked and acted: tough. 'She took full command of the vessel and the work.'[21] Another said she was 'a strong, dominant, woman dressed roughly in a style in keeping with her work'. She wore a wide-brimmed straw hat, fastened down with a scarf passed over the crown and tied in the chin, making it look like a poke bonnet.[22]

Betsy ran the company for over thirty years and sailed intermittently for twenty-two of them, until stopped by ill-health just before her death. In this family business Captain Miller was assisted by her sister Hannah, who appears on record as a passenger and a stewardess but actually took over as captain.[23]

1850–1918: STEERING STEAM MARVELS

By this stage *out* women, unlike the five disguised ones discovered in this period, were coming to the fore even as owner-masters and as competent navigators, at least in other countries. US-born Mary Ann Brown Patten in 1856 challenged a mutiny on her sick husband's clipper and took the ship safely to its San Francisco destination, round Cape Horn in a storm. She was able to do so because her husband had taught her navigation and meteorology, as well as other skills such as stowage and rope work.[24] And by 1881 a kind of duplicate of Betsy Miller appeared, in Ireland: Kate Tyrell.

Captain Kate Sails

Kate Tyrell (1863–1921) was the owner and navigator of the *Denbighshire Lass*, a 62-ton schooner. In a family without sons Kate was close to her father and he gave her the ship, which she sailed between Connah's Quay in Flintshire, Bristol and Arklow, carrying brick and tiles, in the late nineteenth century. In her travels she learned that Russian and Scandinavian wives of crew also sailed. Kate was on deck on most voyages, in charge of the vessel, and happier there than on land. There's an interesting gap between the oral testimony of her actions and the Board of Trade records, where she wasn't even listed as crew in the 1890s. This suggests that other women deck workers, are likely to have been omitted from the formal records, which is why women's seafaring history is so untraceable.[25]

It was a period when women were increasingly doing deck work on family ships, particularly tiny cargo vessels under sail round the British coast. But seemingly there was no possibility of out British women becoming any kind of deck worker on the new steamships, not least because the technology was so new that that world was suffering from 'boys' toys' syndrome. Females were usually seen as unsuited to handling this prestigious equipment at sea. And by now deck officers were legally required to have formal qualifications too.

But women could do it – at least in the US. From 1887 pioneers included Philomena Daniel, 'the first female steamship captain', Mary M. Miller and Mary W. Coons.[26]

Another US-based woman still found it easier to disguise herself to do deck work at the unskilled end. In the 1890s Amelia/David/Timmy McKinley (b. *c.* 1880) sought work as a mess room steward (having already been in service since she was 13). The daughter of a deceased chief engineer on transatlantic ships, she found work on the Portland-bound steamer *Beignon*, where she signed on as an ordinary seaman and did a range of maintenance tasks.

'My first job was holding cork fenders over the side. Then I was put on cleaning brass work.' She later went to work on the steamer *Blaenavon*, carrying coals to Cagliari. 'They set me to work chipping steam winches … in Cagliari I used to help drive the winches and look after the brass work.'[27]

When Timmy was discovered to be Amelia in 1898 she was relegated to housekeeping work. But in the wider world, women – especially privileged ones – were handling yachts, planes, buses, carts, trucks and even their own limousines. Actor Minnie Palmer had in 1897 become the first woman car driver and Harriet Quimby in 1912 became the first woman pilot to fly at night.

All this rather glamorised and suffrage-associated mobility was pushed much further in the First World War when women were pilots, nurses on ships and ambulance drivers. It was officially unthinkable that women would be put in danger from enemy attack at sea. However, undoubtedly many women relatives on a few small coastal vessels stood in for the usual hands who had gone to war. After the Women's Royal Naval Service formed in November 1917 scores of women worked near ships or on moored vessels until 1920.

1919–1950: LIPSTICK ON THE BRIDGE?

An ostensibly light-hearted 1923 Cunard cartoon reveals how nonplussed some interwar people felt at the merger of two seemingly incompatible things: a woman and the bridge of a ship. This drawing suggested that if the person on the bridge belonged to the lipstick and perfume-wearing gender then she would somehow transform the ship into a boudoir, not a sensible workshop-cum-work horse. But brave women

'When ladies become "skippers"', *Cunard* magazine, April 1923. (University of Liverpool Library, D42/PR5/42)

such as 'aviatrix' Amy Johnson (1903–41) were visibly becoming experts in handling vehicles. So maybe it didn't matter so much that the most acclaimed autobiography of a pioneering woman skipper, Joan Lowell's 1929 *Cradle of the Deep*, later turned out to be a shocking fabrication.[28] Joan's story gave women a daring maritime model: she took the wheel on a windjammer, learned about biology by dissecting a mother shark and swam to safety with her pet kittens clawing her back.

Real seafaring heroines such as US Captain Ivy Wambolt (1910–76) followed. Captain Ivy herself simply commented to a newspaper that:

It was natural for me to go to sea … my father and my brothers all went … Following the sea is much more exciting than sitting at a pokey old desk. I get to go places, see things, and know that my ship is my own … I don't see how it is unusual for a girl to be a captain. It happens to be my job.[29]

Ivy was followed by Françoise Lemay 1937 and Molly Kool in 1939.[30] Both women were taking over their father's ships, after extensive sea experience and training by older males who'd trained and trusted them from girlhood. Other privileged women were *buying* access to deck roles and becoming proud Cape Horners on sailing barques (having sailed round Cape Horn was the apotheosis of seamanship: you had passed the ultimate test). Pamela Bourne (1908–84) was one of the daring young women who became working passengers aboard Gustaf Erikson sailing ships. Her first book, in 1935, led to other 'tom-boyish' women buying passages under sail too.[31]

Big international waves were made by the Soviet Union as its Merchant Navy opened up jobs for women in deck work. In 1935 Anna Shchetinina (1908–99) was acclaimed the first woman in the world to serve as a certificated captain of an ocean-going vessel. Captain Shchetinina was one of a steadily increasing number of women sailors, engineers and wireless operators in Soviet merchant shipping in the 1930s. They seemed to symbolise a future where women could do anything.[32]

So why couldn't there be Annas on British ships? The *Journal of Commerce*, the shipping industry's main mouthpiece in 1936, had the sage answer: ships were female. The article quipped that 'since two women rarely got on together it is too much to expect ships and women would make good shipmates.'[33]

A real obstacle was that few politicians or shipowners would risk overturning the gender balance to that extent. And they didn't need to. There was an oversupply of men ready to do such work. Anyway, there weren't separate toilets for women, nor the will to build them. It couldn't be done. Maybe the new technology had actually made ships easier to handle, but to allow women into men's kingdoms would upset the apple cart of masculine prowess. A woman's best chance of becoming a captain at this point was to be like Ivy Wambolt and female flyers: own her own machine.

In the Second World War the Women's Royal Naval Service re-formed, but again with the assumption that women workers would 'free a man for the fleet', not actually *be* at sea. By contrast, at this stage, in the Soviet Merchant Navy women deck officers were working deep sea, crossing the Atlantic and even doing the feared Murmansk run in the Arctic. British girls were certainly gaining sea skills, though, through the Sea Rangers (begun in 1922) and the Girls' Nautical Training Corps (GNTC), which started in 1943. GNTC girls worked towards maritime skills badges such as boatswain's mate, yeoman, oarsman and sail or power coxswain.[34]

1950–2010: UNTHINKABLE NO MORE

This was the period when women doing deck work gradually stopped being such an anomaly. In the 1950s and 1960s Patricia O'Driscoll was one of the very rare women sailing as a mate. She was on cargo-carrying sailing barges near London, not deep sea, but the skills and abilities she demonstrated made her legendary.[35] There are rumours of a woman on pilot cutters off Ireland in the 1960s or possibly even a little earlier. And no doubt wives served as deck workers on family coasters.

In China the coastal cargo ship *Fengtao* was officered entirely by women deck personnel from 1976 to 1980.[36] Denise Bradlaugh-Bonner was one of the first British masters of this period. She sailed with Arklow Shipping, commanding small ships such as the *Serenell* (1,000 tons) because as a woman master at the time she 'didn't think it was possible on *large* ships!'[37] She found 'the big problem for me was having no role model to follow as a woman – so I just looked at the good examples of Captains I had sailed with and tried to see things from their point of view. I think to be a good Master of ship is more about attitude than gender, and it is a difficult job for anyone to manage properly.'[38]

Amid great publicity, in 1967 Sheila Edmundson became the first woman deck cadet. Sheila was on the accelerated degree-entry trainee scheme at Plymouth Technical College, as opposed to being a cadet sponsored by a shipping line.

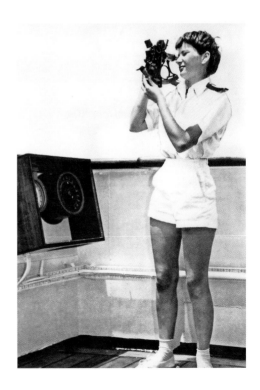

Deck cadet Sheila Edmundson taking the sights, c. 1970. (Eve Tar Collection)

Sheila Edmundson: The First of the New Tranche

Bedfordshire-born Sheila (b. 1949) said, 'Ever since I was thirteen years old I've thought about joining the merchant marine fleet ... I can't give any reason for it.' The media greeted Sheila's advent in 1967 as they'd greeted Mary Patton and Ivy Wambolt, wondering at her femininity as if it was somehow at odds with her competence: a 'nineteen-year-old English girl with a figure which would qualify for pinup honours, [who] wants to be the captain of a merchant vessel. A petite brunette ... Sheila speaks in soft tones,' it was said in 1968. However, her skipper, Captain John McVicar, loyally insisted – as many women's early skippers were to do – 'Even though she is a girl I have given her the same assignments as those given to apprentice seamen ... she has come through with flying colours.'

Her career is very much the subject of hearsay, as she gave no later interviews. It appears that she applied to seventeen companies before getting a job, and suspected she only got her first chance 'for the publicity the shipping company rightly guessed she would attract'. Afterwards she served on oil tankers, bulk carriers and general cargo ships. British colleagues respected her as gutsy but noticed she had trouble with Spanish deck crew who'd never before obeyed a woman's orders. In 1980 she got her master's ticket (it's claimed she was the first woman to get a foreign-going master's certificate), when Ellerman City Liners gave her champagne and flowers at the Victoria deep water container terminal; but she was 'obviously ill at ease with the public relations function' and enquired whether they'd do the same for a man. Seemingly she was never given command before she left the industry.[39]

Sheila's entry into maritime life in 1967 did not initially lead to other shipping companies following suit. When in 1970 Nina Baker tried to enter as a cadet she received replies such as 'no positions exist in our fleet that are occupied by young ladies and we are therefore unable to offer you employment.'[40] Most female applicants for deck work were usually just greeted by silence. Lucky ones were favoured with a Roneo'd sheet explaining that the jobs open to women were as nurses, assistant pursers or stewardesses.

Nina: Path-breaking in BP Tankers

Nina Baker (b. 1954), like Sheila Edmundson, is also seen as Britain's first woman deck cadet. (She was on the Ordinary National Diploma deck cadet scheme, rather than the accelerated degree-entry trainee route that Sheila took.) In her early teens she'd set her sights on working on deck at sea. Knowing she aimed to become an officer (not a rating), she began consciously preparing herself by joining a Sea Ranger unit and attending a mixed-gender school for her final two school years in order to become more skilled at socialising with males. Her other aids were persistence and her mentor, Vera Corner Halligan, the skipper of her Sea Rangers crew in central London. Fortunately, too, a man at the Shipping Federation decided to support her case and pushed her application towards several shipping lines. BP said yes in 1972 and she was their first woman, out of around 500 cadets. Subsequently, she gained her first mate's certificate and sailed with various companies until 1979. After that she left the sea, married and had two children. After working in academic life and as a Glasgow councillor she retired in 2014. Nina remains very active in pushing for women's rights to access science and engineering careers.[41]

BP's first woman deck cadet Nina Baker (right) helping to secure mooring ropes with one of the deckhands and another deck cadet on BP's *British Willow*, probably in New Zealand, 1972. (BP)

'Why should attractive girls in their late teens, with brains as well as beauty, forsake the 15-denier society that they were obviously bound to enjoy had they stayed ashore?' asked BP's in-house magazine in 1974, featuring its new female deck cadets. Nina's successor Claire Tomlinson, one of the first five women to begin the second mates' certificate scheme, ignored the interest in her tights and replied, 'I can't see anything strange in wanting to work on a tanker.' She and her colleague Anne Rutherford, it was reported, 'insist on being treated as two of the boys … [and off duty] the two most usual acts of chivalry – holding doors open, ladies first – are discouraged by both to the point of resentment.'[42] They made national headlines, and had to handle gender relations without having had any training and as well as trying to do their job.

The previous March Rosemary Daulton had earned her efficient deck hand certificate and became the first women deck hand in Irish shipping; she was on the *Irish Oak*. Rosemary had no officer privileges to ease her path, unlike Nina, and unlike Linda Forbes (b. 1957), Scotland's first woman deck cadet. Linda thinks what helped her own breakthrough in 1974 was that 'I had two brothers, I wasn't a girlie girl … and it never crossed my mind that a girl couldn't do anything. You don't expect to be put down for something you can't help [your gender].'[43] Her advent was greeted by newspaper headlines such as, 'Why a nice girl became a sailor', a pun on the 1909 music-hall song 'All the nice girls love a sailor.'

Never happy working at height, cadet Linda Forbes puts on a brave face and keeps a firm hold while boarding MV *Cape Race* on the Suriname River at Paranam, 1977. (Photo: Frank Lyke, Scottish Ship Management Ltd; courtesy of Linda Forbes)

Women's 'storming' of deck and even engine citadels was helped by the time being right; three factors were particularly important. First, the Suez Canal closed during the Arab–Israeli war in 1967, forcing ships to take the longer route around the Cape of Good Hope. Shipping companies therefore needed more ships, and more people to run those ships. Second, the 1970 Rochdale Report from a committee of inquiry into shipping recommended: 'Both sides of the industry should pursue a policy of widening employment opportunities at sea for women.'[44] This industry-specific move was further affected by a third factor, the climate that was emerging because the Women's Liberation Movement had raised awareness of injustice. As a result, the pivotal Sex Discrimination Act of 1975 was prepared. It lifted the barriers to employment opportunities throughout the British working world, including on ships, with the first case eventually brought and won by a would-be seawoman, Lucy Wallace, in 1979. Employers knew they had to change – and they did.

In 1976 the International Labour Organisation's Maritime Worker's Branch found increased opportunities for women occurring internationally, in a business that was in any case expanding. Researcher Theodore Braida calculated there were 32,000 women ratings and 1,100 women officers in the twenty-four developed countries he surveyed. At that time the Soviet Union and Finland had the most female ratings (12,000 and 3,000 respectively); the UK had the most female officers (255 by comparison to the USSR's 207).[45] In the 1970s women in Argentina, West Germany, Greece, Portugal, the US, the UK and the Netherlands started becoming more readily admitted to maritime college and industry training schemes.

Women went on to do well, especially in BP, Shell and Denholm Ship Management, the top three firms taking on women. Slowly and patchily the misogynistic culture changed. By the end of the 1970s women were respected and expected to progress all the way up to captain. BP Second Officer Joanna White even went to war, the only woman deck officer in the 1982 Falklands Conflict; she was on the BP *British Tamar*. Joanna seems to have been the first British woman deck officer to sail in a war, though this relative success is totally unsung.[46]

During the 1980s progress up the ladder wasn't easy. Decline in the shipping industry meant that every newcomer, but especially women, had a long wait to get command. Linda left because of the recession, and 'I think being a woman counted against me too. I'd have to have worked in the Persian Gulf and companies were concerned that working with Muslim stevedores might be difficult for a female,' she says.[47] Most Muslim dockers wouldn't, and sometimes still won't, take orders from a woman deck officer. This causes tensions and holdups if the woman has to capitulate and find a male officer to relay orders in her stead. It was easier for shipping lines to employ a man in the first place.

So the 1980s and 1990s were a time of women deck officers learning their craft and climbing slowly. The entry of many was hindered by a general decline in the number of cadets shipping companies were recruiting in the 1980s – part of a nationwide tendency to not take on apprentices and trainees, as manufacturing declined. In the maritime industry's case this pattern was reversed somewhat by government assistance from 1988. But by 1993 the cadet intake was still low. Lord Greenway told the House of Lords that at Warsash College 'We have only some 300 new entry cadets in the present academic year, compared with about 2,500 in 1975. Studies show that we need at least 1,000 fully trained seafarers a year to feed our marine-related professions and industries.'[48] Males, of course, predominated in the ranks of the trainees.

In parallel, in the world of the Royal Navy, women such as Denise St Aubyn Hubbard (b. 1924) were finding a way round the long-standing prohibition against women serving on naval ships. These volunteers joined the Royal Naval Auxiliary Service (RNXS) which existed from 1963 to 1994. In the mid-1970s Denise commanded a small warship on occasion. Inspired by Denise, Jenny Simpson in 1986 qualified to command inshore minesweepers, fleet tenders and fast motorboats, again as a volunteer rather than as a paid member of the Royal Navy.[49]

On rare occasions Wrens went to sea just for the day. In 1983 Wren Wendy Hinton, a radar specialist, worked on the frigate *Arrow* for three weeks. As usual with Wrens on ship: 'I don't sleep on board but have to come off overnight. Otherwise, I suppose with all these [170] blokes about I'd need a chaperone,' she said. By the late 1980s shortages of skilled men meant Wrens would have to go to sea and on long voyages, as a normal part of the ship's company. HMS *Brilliant* took twenty in autumn 1990. Then in 1993, all new WRNS recruits had to be prepared to go to sea and the WRNS was subsumed into the Navy, although they were informally still referred to as Wrens. Eight years on, in the spring of 1998, the first two full-time naval women captains of warships were appointed. Lieutenant Melanie Robinson

Cadets Alex Holmes (left) and Sue Diamond (right) enjoy their camaraderie on a BP tanker, *c.*1980. (Sue Diamond)

was on *Express*, and Lieutenant Suzanne Moore commanded *Dasher*, a 65-foot Archer-class fast patrol boat; at 54 tons it was about a quarter the size of Betsy Miller's *Cloetus*. I had the honour of going aboard Suzanne's vessel at the Dartmouth media event celebrating their success.[50] It really did feel as if times had changed: a new order was emerging in the RN, at last.

Slightly in parallel, in the early 1990s women were allowed to become seagoing deck cadets in the Royal Fleet Auxiliary. This is the branch of naval services employed full-time to support the Royal Navy by taking goods such as fuel and food out to RN ships deployed remotely. I suspect that these RFA women benefited from the RN's good equal opportunities policies and the relative acceptance of women in the Merchant Navy by that stage. However, even in 1998 when Susan Thomson (b. 1981) became an RFA cadet, there was still such hostility that her first captain drafted a resignation letter for her (but he later backtracked).[51]

At the same time, several MN women were becoming relief captains on ferries. This meant small ships and short trips, but it was a start. In the US, but not in Britain, the fishing industry contained successful women owner-captains.[52] In summer 1999 Margaret Pigeon was acclaimed as the first British woman to take command of a foreign-going merchant vessel. She commanded a China Navigation Company container ship sailing between the South Pacific and the US.

When the officers' union NUMAST (now Nautilus International) presented her with the Victoria Drummond Award, the union acknowledged the 'incredible hurdles' facing women and 'shocking levels of discrimination, prejudice, harassment and abuse' they dealt with. Margaret made the oft-repeated point that brains, not brawn, were what was needed now. 'It doesn't make any difference being female [whereas] in the days of sail you needed some muscle,' she made clear.[53]

The late twentieth century brought enormous changes to the industry, particularly the deregulation of the industry whereby ships were increasingly registered in non-UK ports. UK women deck officers wanting to break into the maritime hierarchy were fortunate that the world shortage of skilled officers exerted a subtle pressure on the industry to include female officers. Women were now more likely to become captains. But captaincy had become a more tedious job involving fielding blame and tolerating on-board executive meetings and many hours at the computer.

WOMEN AT THE TOP: FROM 2000 TO TODAY

This latest period in women's deck careers has provided many role models for new seafarers (see next panel). Internationally feted female cruise captains have been very publicly acclaimed. Captain Karin Stahre Janson says that passengers 'have on occasion burst into spontaneous applause on hearing that a woman is in command. If the odd grumpy male has been heard muttering about women drivers … they are generally brought to order by a jab in the ribs from their wives.' Grandmothers sometimes affectionately pinch her on the cheek and wish their granddaughters would follow her career path.[54]

Most women captains don't like their gender being commented upon. Their performance is still being scrutinised in a way which does not apply to male captains, even though the skill with which these pioneer captains of huge cruise ships handle their command has absolutely proved that gender does not determine ability. And the number of women deck officers who earned master's certificates of competency in the UK rose from thirty-seven in 2004 to eighty-six in 2013.

Because it's difficult for anyone, but particularly women, to get a job commanding ships, many women captains did – and do – freelance work ashore as well as at sea. The period 2000 onwards was a time when the first women captains did what senior male captains do: leave the sea (not necessarily willingly – some hit the glass ceiling and stepped to one side) and use their expertise in positions of authority ashore. Captain Fran Collins, Condor Ferries' first woman captain, became its executive director by 2014 – and her gender is now not remarked upon. Captain Emma Tiller became BP's first woman marine superintendent in 2007.[55] Some became pilots, the harbour-based people who navigate a vessel into a berth. Some joke that it's an impressive sort of concierge parking; it was previously a very male dynastic preserve.

'Belle Norris' began training as a maritime pilot when she was only 26, and described the climate in the 2000s when she stepped aboard:

> in addition to the usual 'Where is my pilot?' [the response that women pilots got] I also got the look we affectionately called the 'Holy Crap, who is the girl' look! The frantic look at the door waiting for someone else to come through it! It had almost stopped by the time I left and it honestly amused me. My regular skippers were a joy and absolutely made the whole job. Their trust and acceptance of 'the girl' is testimony to no one but themselves … [My presence meant] the idea of the *man* who brings their boats in was shaken up a little on [our river].[56]

Rachel Dunn is a pilot who in 2011 won the Victoria Drummond Award. Her acceptance by both the Admiralty and Trinity House suggests just how far the UK has progressed in making opportunities more equal. As she rejoices, 'Not every job brings you a billion-pound ship to move around.'

Rachel: The First Woman Admiralty Pilot

Rachel Dunn (b. 1966) from Hampshire went 'blind' into maritime life (none of her family had been seafarers) and it worked. When she was a girl who wanted to travel, her father wrote off to find out about pursers' jobs for her and her mother found a taster course at Warsash Maritime Academy. She became a cadet with Shell Tankers in 1984, gaining her master's ticket in 1993. She found, 'I've always been the first woman [in a role on a ship] and they didn't know how to react to me.' Her approach was, 'I'm here and this is how you get me.' She's firm: 'If people don't like what I do it's not my problem.' But she had to prove herself because men 'think a woman isn't there to work but to be the R&R' (the armed forces term for 'rest and relaxation').

In the 1990s Rachel met the man she would marry and left for Wightlink ferries, where she worked for sixteen years. Every hour she was involved in berthing and collision avoidance at Portsmouth and Ryde: 'ship handling is what I love.'

She'd always wanted to be a pilot. By now mother of three children, she trained and qualified in 2010. In 2014 she became an Admiralty pilot, again at Portsmouth, the first woman to do so. Rachel is confident that more women will become masters and pilots as time goes on.

Her husband is a Southampton-based pilot for merchant ships, and is so supportive that he secretly sent off her application for the Victoria Drummond Award, which she won. She's happy: 'It is the most fun job in the world.' There are still just a handful of women pilots and she's not yet met any of the others, so hasn't benefited from any sisterhood. She gives many talks in schools because people still say, 'Women don't do that.' 'Oh yes, they do,' retorts Rachel.[57]

Christine McLean (b. 1954), Lerwick's first woman port controller, uses her skills as master in the vessel control centres where pilots are based. At sea in the 1970s her cabin door had the sign tacked to it: 'women for now'. But now women are 'here for good'. Now that some captains are mothers, sometimes with daughters who are heading for the bridge, the new generation of young women seeking deck jobs should have ample mentors.

YLS POUNDING BRASS: SAVING LIVES

In parallel with these deck officers were women radio officers (ROs), sometimes called YLs (Young Lady Radio Officers). Whatever their gender, ROs were more informally called 'brass pounders' and 'sparks', because hitting the brass Morse key really did make sparks.

Women had long been involved in telegraphy ashore. When wireless developed and marine wireless was ushered in by Guglielmo Marconi, women such as Mrs Pereira in 1904 proved capable of operating radios in coastal stations.[58] Many women were avid radio hams and even built their own sets. Girls learned Morse and semaphore in the Guides too, after 1910. But in Britain females were seen as unsuited to wireless work at sea. The US disagreed and led the world with Graynella Packer in 1910, then Mabelle Kelso, the first woman in the world to gain a wireless operator's certificate. Newspapers expressed doubt: 'did a woman have the strength of mind to be an operator, especially in a crisis?'[59]

In the First World War women's alleged propensity to lose composure in a catastrophe was conveniently overlooked. In October 1917 thirty-eight women took and passed their radio examinations in wireless colleges in several ports, including Aberdeen.[60] It may be that the authorities were considering allowing women to sail on minesweepers but this never happened. In the WRNS women were involved in communications as signallers (thirty-two), pigeon women (five), telegraphists (five) and a range of wireless jobs (thirty-one), including valve sealers and operators. They were never at sea.[61]

Never to sail as an RO: Jessie Kenney trains at the Rhyl Wireless College, 1925. (Kenney Papers, University of East Anglia, KP JK.9 (2))

In 1923 a former right-hand woman of suffragette leader Emmeline Pankhurst, Jessie Kenney (1887–1985), was acclaimed as Britain's first woman to qualify as an RO. This ignored the previous thirty-eight wartime pioneers. Science-minded Jessie found herself stalemated. Looking for an opening at sea, 'I found myself up against very formidable obstacles. There was Marconi House, the Board of Trade, the Wireless Operators' Union, Shipowners and a mountain of prejudice to overcome.' Sir Godfrey Isaacs, the long-serving managing director of Marconi's Wireless Telegraphy Company, 'had made up his mind he was having no *women* wireless operators'. Instead Jessie decided to go to sea 'as a stewardess in the hopes that later I may be allowed to practise as a wireless operator'. She wasn't, ever. 'How often I looked up at the wireless cabin … How I had longed for the peace and solitude of the wireless cabin where after my labours I could study [science] in peace.'[62]

In the Second World War fourteen US women sailed as radio officers on hospital ships. British women were not allowed to transmit and receive on British ships, despite their training and the shortage. Wartime Wrens were in three branches of signals work: wireless telegraphy, visual signalling (including using Aldis lamps and flags) and coding, but were not seagoing on Royal Navy ships.[63]

Exceptionally, thirty fortunate Wrens were involved in coding and ciphering at sea after 1943. As both members of the WRNS but also nominal 'merchant seamen', Wrens like Joy Bennington worked on merchant ships such as the *Aquitania*, which took high-level military and political men to international conferences such as Yalta. Women encrypted and decrypted top-secret messages, which they then passed to 'Marconi men' in the wireless room to transmit, a task Wrens were not allowed to do.[64]

In the war at least twenty-two Canadian YLs, including the famous Fern Blodgett, put themselves through radio courses but then were refused a seagoing place in the Royal Canadian Navy. They managed to find openings with Scandinavian shipping firms. Fern sailed on seventy-eight of the *Mosdal's* ninety-eight Atlantic crossings and married the captain.[65]

Angela Firman (*c*. 1938–2005) was probably the first seagoing British woman RO. The daughter of a stewardess and a chief engineer, Angela took up the job at her Scandinavian father's suggestion. She attended the North East Wireless Training School at Bridlington, aged 18, then did a radar course. In 1959 she imagined she would find work on a British ship because, as she declared, 'There's no law against it, only tradition.' Unfortunately, tradition won. Instead she worked as an RO on Swedish vessels in the early 1960s.

Dallas Bradshaw (b. *c*. 1943) is in *The Guinness Book of Records* as the first female seagoing RO in the British Merchant Navy. Dallas arrived from British Columbia in 1962, did a two-year course at Rhyl and graduated in 1969. She then found there were no positions, even on Scandinavian shipping lines: 'I waited for about two years before I was offered a job.'[66] She finally became a 'Marconi man' on British cargo ships, including the *Duncraig* and *Avon Forest*. Forty years on, Dallas is still remembered remarkably respectfully.

Five years later Rose King (b. 1949) – incidentally Angela Firman's cousin – was one of several women following on. By the 1970s a few score women had qualified. Worldwide, there were twice as many women radio officers (634) in merchant navies as in the armed services (306).[67] They included Barbara Keating, the UK's 'second girl radio officer' in 1972 on the tanker *Border Minstrel*;[68] the following year Sylvia Slattery on BP's *British Esk*; and Marilyn Stockwell, Ireland's first woman RO. In 1975 Rose King had no trouble finding jobs on a range of ships, including tankers, dry cargo vessels, research ships and latterly a dynamic-positioning vessel and three military corvettes.[69] By contrast, when Fazilette 'Bobby' Khan (b. 1960) qualified in 1984 she wrote to 150 shipping companies but only got one positive reply. It's likely that employers' xenophobia, as well as gender discrimination and the industry's downturn, were barriers to her getting work. When finally Stena showed slight interest Bobby carried on 'bugging them every month' as she said, and eventually accepted employment on less-than-ideal terms. Bobby saw gendered hostility as 'a bit of stupidity on the other side. If they have a problem it's for them to resolve it.'[70]

Bobby and Rose never met another woman RO apart from each other, once. But the success of rare women like them enabled their successors to be accepted too. On some ships the woman RO was the first woman officer a ship had ever

Junior Radio Officer Rose King operating her 'big Proper Radio' on the container ship *ACT5* in 1974. (Rose King)

had. Integrating her took some adjustment by men. Males nicknamed the women 'sparklettes' (Sparklets was the trade name of soda-siphon gas refills) and *sparkus delectus*, as if providing delight was part of their role. Initial reservations about women were that they might not be prepared to climb around fixing the radio mast or crawl in mucky bilges sorting out the wiring. In fact they did, but YLs remained rare. One master told off his female RO for knitting on watch, yet male ROs knitted too.

A Norwegian sparks wrote in 1971 that she was treated like a mascot, a pet. She felt that 'the manly instinct of patronising and an overprotective mentality' went too far and was a 'sometimes unbearable' burden.[71] One of my informants had a breakdown and is still very distressed, thirty years on, by the traumatising sexist hostility. She left the industry, partly because employers couldn't risk sending someone so ill to sea.[72]

As for career progression, there wasn't really a glass ceiling because the ROs had nowhere to go. ROs of any gender could only move up a little, from third or second radio officer to chief sparks (three gold stripes), and there was an over-supply of senior men qualified for such work in the 1970s. Progress was mainly made to jobs ashore, usually in sales or maintenance with companies like Marconi, who maintained the equipment they leased to ships in a well-entrenched near-monopoly. Other women ROs worked in vessel traffic control and harbour control, which fitted round their plans to have children.

By the 1980s the work had become increasingly electronics-based. Legally four ROs were no longer needed on large ships because the new Global Maritime Distress and Safety System (GMDSS) made them unnecessary. Sweden offers the best available statistical information on women ROs. The data show that in the early 1960s, there were about forty Swedish MN radio officers, of whom 25 per cent of were women and by 1991 just 18 per cent of Sweden's 121 ROs were women.[73]

'As radio work died out, older ROs, whether female or male, segued gradually into the job of electronics officer or electro-technical officer (ETO), a combined electrician and RO,' Rose King says. Jocelyn Parker, a 1970s pioneering RO, went on to become Texaco's first electronics officer. Fazilette Khan became an ETO and is still sailing today – as an environmental officer, meaning someone who ensures her ship complies with all the international rules about not polluting the sea and ship.

ETOs are still unusual because the courses only began at the start of the twenty-first century. About two out of every ten students, at most, are women, and only a handful of women ETOs are working on ships. The ETO role rarely attracts women. That makes these exceptional women sparks' determined progress all the more interesting. Radio officers had the briefest window of opportunity of any women in this book, between the late 1960s and the very early 1990s. The job has now ended.

4

FROM SAIL-SHIFTER TO CHIEF ENGINEER: PROPELLING THE SHIP

Arleen Cameron (b. 1985) has just finished her first year as a qualified officer, as a fourth engineer on Maersk container ships. In 2014 she was the only woman cadet on her course. This calm 28-year-old spoke to me just a few yards away from the Warsash Maritime Academy block named after Victoria Drummond, Britain's very first woman marine engineer:

> At school in Dunfermline no one told me that with my aptitude for maths and sciences, engineering could be a good option … I remember around age 15 a large number of boys in my year going for the mysterious 'dockyard exam'. A few years later I discovered that a lot were then taken on as Ministry of Defence apprentices at Rosyth. By their early 20s they were in interesting, high-paying jobs in engineering, while I was still trying to find my niche. For nearly ten years I worked in the care sector alongside people with physical disabilities and learning difficulties and then latterly as an administrator in a large fostering agency. The office job made me really miss working *with* people.
>
> This led me circuitously to my current career. I volunteered aboard the tall ship *Lord Nelson* (designed for people of all physical abilities). I loved everything about it. Then I found out that there were people who were actually *paid* to be there. That was it. No more mundane office job for me. I was off to sea. The *Lord Nelson*'s Chief Engineer Rachel Eunson was my big inspiration. She is awesome! She actually tried to talk me out of applying, however, with some awful stories about sailing deep sea.

But Arleen proceeded, towards what some call the 'magical mystery gardens' of a ship:

Many of the sponsoring companies said I was just too old, at 26, by the time I applied [most applicants were ten years younger]. A few others didn't even acknowledge my application. One company knocked me back after the interview stage. I got the distinct impression that I was not worth risking the investment of time and money in training; as a woman in my mid-20s obviously I would only work at sea for a few years before disappearing ashore to raise a family! Eventually I found one that would give me a chance, Meridian Marine Management. I am eternally grateful to my lovely training manager there, Sue Loftus, for giving me that start. When the company was dissolved one year into my cadetship I was genuinely sorry. Luckily I had proved myself by this point and was taken on by another company, Clyde Marine.[1]

Arleen Cameron outside the block named for her foremother, Victoria Drummond. (Warsash Maritime Academy)

Women ship's engineers are sought by some companies, and not just out of a desire to prove they are complying with equal opportunities legislation. The diligence and focus on the job in hand that women engineers have displayed make them real assets. Yet it's not unusual that Arleen was the only woman on her course. In one training company in 2011 women formed just 1 per cent of the trainees headed for ships' engine rooms.[2] This is part of a general British trend: women are rare creatures in science, technology, engineering and mathematics (STEM) careers. And retention as well as recruitment is a problem. By the 2000s STEM managers coined a term for the pattern of trained women leaving before they were 30 (either because of the desire to have children, or because of the uncongenial culture). 'Leaking pipeline syndrome' referred to women 'leaking out' of the career path pipeline in various places along its length, meaning few would finally emerge at the far end.

Only 7 per cent of the UK engineering workforce was female at the time of writing. That's poor in comparison with most European Union countries (including Latvia, with 30 per cent), as the Institute of Marine Engineering, Science and Technology (IMarEST) points out. In 2015, IMarEST tried to help by running a campaign, 'Women in Engineering: The Past, Present and Future', to boost female entry into the profession.[3]

ENGINEERS EXPLAINED

The history of women in the purple-insignia world of ship's propulsion is a sparse and recent one, which really began in the 1990s. These engineers are responsible for all the engines and systems that support every element of the ship, not only those which propel the vessel. Their work includes advising when to empty the ship's swimming pools in rough weather and sorting out the wi-fi zones. Most ships are thrust forward by a motor or engine which turns a propeller. Some engines are turbo-charged or even nuclear (on submarines), or fuelled by liquified natural gas or electricity. Anne Madsen, formerly James (b. 1970), a 1990s pioneer who now works on destroyers ashore, explains that her engines are called cathedrals because they're so huge.[4] They're as much as four decks high and weigh 1,500 tons, far more than the weight of Betsy Miller's entire ship in the early nineteenth century. Lisa Jenkins, a pioneer and now a chief engineer on a mega-yacht, tends engines where the output of every shaft is equivalent to the pulling power of 4,023 horses.[5]

All engineers are in the business of foreseeing and solving problems. The difference on a ship in the middle of the ocean is that engineers are isolated and relatively unsupported. Everyone depends on their skill to get to port. Anne explains: 'You monitor, you keep it going … trying to get in before things break. If you can't, you fix it. So a lot of your work is maintenance engineering and desperate repair engineering.' Many tasks are heavy and the job was of course traditionally seen as male. 'Actually,' says Anne, 'you're a Jack of all trades. So one day you're working with the finest screwdriver, the next with a huge jackhammer'. She always had a 10in spanner in her back pocket and some cotton waste in the leg pocket of her boilersuit because elements of the job are necessarily mucky. But today many hours are spent in the ultra-clean control room, several decks up from the engines. It's more like sitting in a cabin full of computers, which could be controlling anything. 'Swarfega Girl' can find her boilersuit and fleece sometimes remain white all day.

Engineering cadets like Arleen are the lowest levels of the hierarchy, understudying the senior officers: the junior engineers and the fourth, third, second and chief engineers. The second engineer is the hardest-working person on board. At the top, the chief engineer is the most highly respected technocratic god and, on a par with the captain, another four-striper who attends the daily executive meetings.

Slightly to one side are the electrical officer and electro-technical officer. Non-officer grade people are general purpose ratings (GPRs) or engine room ratings and motormen. Women in marine engineering very much tend to be in the officer grades. The table below shows how far women with engineering certificates of competency were outnumbered by men in 2014; in previous years the picture was similar.

Table 4.1. UK women and men with certificates of competency in engineering, early 2014.[6]

Job title	Women	Men	Total number	Women as % of total
Chief engineer	17	7,188	7,205	0.23
Second Engineer	16	2,632	2,648	0.006
OOW Engineer	44	3,336	3,380	1.3
ETO	2	40	42	4.7
TOTAL	79	13,196	13,275	0.5

Socially, 'it's quite a self-contained job and you work to your own rhythm,' says Anne. It's even lonely. And Lisa finds that 'Engineering is quite a thankless job at sea. Engineers are mainly seen as complaining whingers by most (only because we have to fix the things that other ignorant people break and this gets you down after a while)!' Vestiges remain of the traditional antagonism between the 'grease monkeys' and deck officers, who argue over which workforce is most vital to the ship.

Women engineers don't see it as a difficult job for women. They rise to the challenges and point out that they use ingenuity, figuring out that a smart, non-brawny way to handle it will have been incorporated into the design. Some don't stay in the job for long, because employers make few efforts to make it a more congenial situation. But after all that training most give it their best shot, many times over. It's a truly tough environment. In the engine room you wear ear-defenders, which means you can't have conversations. You need very strong hands. And the banter can be excluding, as even sensitive young men find. It's harder to become accepted as a woman engineer than a deck officer. Male engineers are still proud of doing 'manly' work, whereas deck work tends to be a polite, more middle-class world and one where any misogyny would be less likely to be voiced.

1750–1909: GREASE MONKEYS, HEAVY METAL AND DYNAMIC INNOVATION

When ships switched from sail to engine propulsion (from the 1830s) the role of engineer emerged, became increasingly sophisticated and then specialised. Vessels began to be illuminated by electricity rather than oil lamps. Passengers washed with heated piped water, no longer with ewers lugged down long corridors by stewards. Refrigeration enabled new cargos to be carried: for example, beef from Argentina. Steam engineering was, like the new railway industry, heavy engineering. The men who did the work learned it from other men, through apprenticeship systems. These 'rude mechanicals' were a breed unlike the 'gentleman on the bridge' and didn't achieve officer status on ship until the 1860s.

Campbell McMurray, historian of ships' engineers, found that from the 1840s engineers were highly skilled, even elite, tradesmen:

> familiar with engine building and repair ships ashore … [who were] typically appointed in the first instance on the recommendation of the engine maker. This was reasonable; these men were required to handle with skill and address, for the time, very large pieces of machinery – limping giants of doubtful efficiency and temperamental disposition – and to be responsible for their successful functioning in what would often be isolated and perilous circumstances.[7]

If you were a would-be 'lady grease monkey' in this period you'd have to have been privately educated in science (expensive and rare, but possible, as computer inventor Ada Lovelace (1815–52) proved), then tried out in a tough industrial workshop for three years. Then you'd need to be trusted by manufacturers so deeply proud of their machines that only exemplary experts would do as their 'hands and brains' at sea. It would have been impossible for an out woman to break into the proudly technocratic world of enabling iron steeds to turn into ocean greyhounds at sea. Certainly the lower job of stoking and trimming coal was open to unskilled bantamweight men who wanted to work their passage. But no disguised woman could have entered this black and brawling netherworld, so unsuited to 'the fair sex', and remained undetected, because men stripped to the waist in the heat. Wives of masters on small family-business vessels may have cleaned and reassembled the engines in a crisis – or at least held the parts – but I have not yet found evidence of that.

Privileged ladies associated with men in engineering development show that females had the *ability* to work, certainly at management level, in STEM careers if given the opportunities, as widows in early shipbuilding show. Isabella Ure Elder (1828–1905) in 1869 briefly headed the vast and innovative Elders shipyard on the Clyde (where Anne Madsen was building aircraft carriers in 2015).

Doing engineering tasks in industry and at sea was socially a step too far for gendered social ideas of the time. Katharine and Rachel Parsons were able to explore somewhat because they did it on land and were privileged as members of Sir Charles Parsons' family. As the inventor of the revolutionary steam turbine, he was acclaimed even more than the visionaries who created Apple computers 150 years later.

Katharine and Rachel Parsons: Pioneers of Women in Engineering

Witty, sharp-minded and courageous Katharine Bethell (1859–1933) married Charles Parsons in 1883 and was acclaimed as 'one of the few wives of an Inventor who could discuss the technical details of his mechanical achievements'.[8] In 1919 she became the first woman elected to membership of the North East Coast Institution of Engineers and Shipbuilders.[9]

From her very early years Katharine and Charles' daughter Rachel (1885–1956) created toys using turbines and methylated spirit, attended the science-minded Roedean School and went with her father on voyages to test ships, including on the *Mauretania* in 1909. In 1910 Rachel began studying Mechanical Sciences at Newnham College, Cambridge (a radically new subject for women). Lady Parsons later told a story: 'Three girls, daughters of engineers, who were going to Newnham, persuaded the late Professor [Bertram] Hopkinson to admit them to his course in engineering. He had broken the fact to his class, after standing in the door for a few moments, with the words, "It has come!"'[10] It had. And the sky didn't fall in.

Rachel left Newnham in 1912. She trained Tyneside women engineering workers in the First World War and in 1919 co-founded an all-female engineering firm, Atalanta Ltd. Rachel, Blanche Thornycroft of the famous shipbuilding family and Eily Keary became the first three women to join the Institution of Naval Architects, in 1921.[11]

In other words, women's abilities in engineering were becoming clear. Elite women had a role on the outer edge of engineering. They were paving the way for other women to go further and become, slowly, a little more mainstream.

1910–1945: FROM LADYLIKE STUDIES TO SWEATY ENGINE ROOMS

Rachel's time in Cambridge slightly overlapped with that of Elsie and Eily Keary, who also studied mechanical engineering. Finally, Britain had female mechanical engineers. When the war came they were joined, at a lower level, by over 4,000 happily grimy, tooled-up women in boilersuits who began earning their living coke-stoking, electrical engineering, wire-splicing and block-making as well as attending joggling machines and driving cranes and lorries in shipyards.

Rachel and Katharine Parsons tried to ensure women's sense of their potential wasn't scotched by the 1919 Restoration of Pre-War Practices Act. Their efforts led to the founding of the Women's Engineering Society (WES). WES's two main aims were to encourage women to study and practise engineering, and to enable engineering-minded women to network. It's still fighting on today.

Those two first decades of the twentieth century meant a major shift. Privileged women such as Eily Keary had proved they could work in mechanical engineering. And working-class women had shown they could build and service engine parts. Logically, women could now become engineers at sea. Eily predictably worked as an assistant, on land, but her post-war career can be seen as the biggest recorded formal step at that time in women's progress towards completing a voyage as a ship's grease monkey.

Eily Keary: Sorting out Ship Design

Eily Keary (1882–1975) went from Roedean to Newnham College in 1912 and was one of the very first women there to complete her mechanical engineering Tripos. She began work at the National Experimental Tank, set up by the innovative marine architect and engineer William Froude to study the dynamic properties of hulls. By 1925 she was addressing the Liverpool Engineering Society on 'Manoeuvring of Ships: Model Experiments of Rudder Forces under Service Conditions'. An adventurous traveller, she left work only in 1930, after marrying a ship's engineer she'd met on a Furness Withy ship. Their son Peter was born in 1936. Peter describes Eily and her sisters as 'rather dictatorial and somewhat extrovert and mannish ... yet at the same time [Eily was] ... rather shy and seldom spoke much about her past.'[12]

How long would it be before a determined – and probably elite – woman tried to tackle a ship's engines on the high seas?

Enter Victoria Drummond, surprisingly early: 1916. Twelve years younger than Eily Keary, and very practical, but it seems that Victoria never approached the

Eily Keary working with model ship in the 1920s. (Peter Smith-Keary)

WES sisterhood for support in opening ships' engine-room doors. The history of women's marine engineering in these decades is of this lone woman spending her youth being rejected for her chief engineer's ticket thirty-one times.

The Lone and Path-breaking 'Miss D': Britain's First Seagoing Marine Engineer.

Victoria Drummond (1894–1978) was an anomaly for half a century. From a Scottish aristocratic background (she was Queen Victoria's god-daughter), at 21 she decided she wanted to be a marine engineer. A year later, in 1916, she began an apprenticeship in a Perth garage, under a former seagoing chief engineer. She was tolerated as just another lady helping out during the hostilities. Good fortune continued. Her mother arranged an introduction to the Caledon shipworks in Dundee and they accepted her. In 1922 the Blue Funnel Line gave her a start, after an chance introduction of her boss and the Blue Funnel director to her parents.

'I don't think I shall ever forget the excited elation on signing my first articles.' Then in 1924 she passed her second engineer's exam. After passing, 'I wrote at once to the

Blue Funnel Line to take me back. It was a great shock to me that they would not have me. I suppose they feared a scandal. I could have told them it would not be like that but they wouldn't listen.' But the British India Steam Navigation Company dared to employ her as the fifth engineer, on the troopship *Mulbera*. She began working for her chief engineer's certificate in 1929 and kept failing. In 1936 her main mentor 'finally tackled Mr Pemberton, one of the examiners, who admitted [only privately] that it was a question of sex. They would not pass me because I was a woman.'

After years of trying to get by odd-jobbing on car repairs, selling her photographs, co-managing a small goldfish-importing business with her sister and fruitlessly retaking her chief's exam, the looming war in August 1939 made the 44-year-old decide: 'Chief's certificate or not, I felt it was time for me to get back on a ship. I was desperate. I wrote … to anyone I could think of. No one would have me. They might be short-staffed but that was no reason to employ a woman engineer.'

Finally in March 1940 her former donkeyman from the *Mulbera* gave her a tip: 'If the Red Duster won't have you, go foreign.' She did. But the ship she worked on, *Bonita,* taking china clay from Fowey to Africa, was attacked by a Focke-Wulf Condor. Victoria staunched the broken main water service pipe, from which scalding water was threatening the engineers (whom she told to get out – they did). For saving the ship and the crew in this way she won one of the five Lloyd's War Medal for Bravery at Sea awarded to women in the war.

'Miss D' carried on sailing and tried to get a British chief's certificate, on top of a Panamanian one she had already acquired. 'It was no good though … I was a woman and they would not let me pass the exam.' Eventually she managed to find work as a refrigerator engineer. At the Cape of Good Hope in July 1943 she discovered she was an international heroine. 'I dashed ashore [shopping] … went into the Chinese restaurant, the Purple Cherry, and what should I see but my photo cut from the papers and pinned to the wall.' Finally, by 1948 Miss Drummond started sailing as chief, on foreign ships. In 1951, 'I was tired of sailing on small, dirty boats with often disagreeable Chiefs. I had decided to find a shore job. I was nearly sixty.' She did so, but sailed on and off to help the family income, until 1962. In 1978, as her niece Cherry wrote, 'Victoria Drummond was finally Finished with Engines. Or perhaps … she was at last Full Away.'

Victoria Drummond working in her engine room.
(Nautilus International)

In the Second World War Victoria Drummond's valour did not bring a call for more women to join ships' engine rooms. Her success wasn't even marshalled to help recruit women to engineering work in shipyards. Instead she was – conveniently – seen as an anomaly, not an act to follow.

Yet women were working in marine engineering in dockyards, doing a greater range of skilled tasks than they had in the First World War.[13] By summer 1944 13,000 counterparts to the US's shipbuilder-heroine 'Rosie the Riveter' had been mobilised.[14] Many shipyard jobs were risky, cold, dirty and had long-term effects on health. Women's general difficulties in working with men in shipyards were predictable: a culture that was discriminatory and had stereotyped ideas about how to treat females (signs warned 'Women – No Bad Language'); what today would be called sexual harassment; and restrictive job opportunities. In other cases, men could be gallantly protective as they'd been to the young Miss Drummond, appreciative and helpful, understandably defensive about a feared dilution of their skills, sexually opportunistic, unfairly prankish, and occasionally bitterly contemptuous. This behaviour was a foretaste of what would later greet women ship's engineers at sea.

Verena Holmes, a co-founder of WES who worked with the Ministry of Labour in the Second World War, argued that 'in the long journey from the crinoline to the boiler suit … women seem to have become different beings both mentally and physically.'[15]

Over in the Royal Navy the nearest thing to a seagoing engineer was a WRNS category just 570 strong: Boat's Crew Wrens. They worked on small boats from October 1941 to late 1945. In 1943 the first six women, including Rozelle Pierrepont (later Raynes), became stokers.[16] They were proud of being able to make even the most stubborn of engines work, no matter what the weather, on their diesel-fuelled harbour motor launches, large open cutters and pinnaces.[17] Male instructors proudly praised 'their girls'. Sailors were shocked, impressed and bewildered to find themselves outsmarted by competent women trainers. Misogynistic hostility was often replaced by enduring respect and indeed professional admiration. But *peacetime* women engineers on shore, let alone at sea, were not even discussed.

1946 TO TODAY: FINALLY IN THE SHIP'S ENGINE ROOMS

When the war ended, Verena Holmes and the WES went on campaigning for women's rights to become engineers. Women's successes at the bomb-threatened workbenches surely led eventually to a climate that enabled women to consider STEM careers and be better accepted on ships. But initially there was just Victoria Drummond, who was looked upon as an elderly posh anomaly, not an accessible role model.

By the late 1950s and early 1960s an aspiring woman marine engineer wouldn't have known that she had any precedents, since Victoria Drummond was not well known enough for school career advisers to present her as a model. Colleges were reluctant to take on a girl, especially if they feared that no shipping company would sponsor her or that male students would be unwelcoming.

The breakthrough came in the early 1970s. Reasons for women's progress into engineering included WES campaigning; the law; the Women's Liberation Movement; and women's accompanying sense of entitlement to attempt to do a job they fancied, which was expressed in the 1975 founding of the supportive network Women and Manual Trades.[18]

Above all, the industry needed to deal with the shortfall in high-calibre apprentices. In summer 1974 Shell and BP were giving recruiting talks to girls in schools. BP was prominent among the companies that sponsored women, even before the 1975 Sex Discrimination Act. The women selected for sponsorship had strong science and maths skills as well as congenial personas. They were acclaimed as exceptional figures, especially by employers, who wanted to show that they supported equality. Newspapers were tickled by the contrast: someone in a boilersuit ('boilies') who normally wore pretty dresses.

Transition to this new stage of evolution was somewhat helped by engineers being among the most convivial folk on ship. Although they could be highly conservative about women, the engineering team also respected people who were skilled and who shared their devotion to ensuring the ship's smooth functioning. But progress was also hindered by that community's traditional ideas about women, and by the misplaced macho pride of those like the officer who called himself MCP (Male Chauvinist Pig). Who knows what balance of anguished hostility and cheeky irony were behind his 1977 poem, 'Women engineers':

> Employ women? … embroidered boilies, funny smell.
> What's wrong with sweat? – it beats Chanel …
> They'll be making hammers from aluminium
> So that the weak sex may them swing
> And convince themselves they're the real thing.
> Oh woe to us when it comes to pass
> That women do our jobs at last
> We'll be back on the dole, no booze at night
> Sober black gang – frightful sight.
> With this thought this tale must end
> Women will drive us round the bend.
> But they have their uses, I must declare
> They're really quite good at pouring beer.[19]

Anne James as third engineer on the P&O container ship MV *Mairangi Bay*, in August 1992. (Anne Madsen)

In the 1980s one or two women marine engineers – in non-embroidered boilersuits – were working their way up the career ladder – and politely *not* pouring beer over rude shipmates' heads. From 1984 initiatives like Women into Science and Technology (WISE), which aimed to draw women into STEM careers, made a big dint in negative perceptions of what was possible for women sea pioneers.

No one now seems to know who was the first to become a chief engineer. Anne Madsen thinks perhaps she was the second, but that someone came between Victoria Drummond and her.

Anne – Victoria's Successor

Anne Madsen's interest in travel was triggered by two Hammond Innes novels about the Antarctic, *The White South* and *The Blue Ice*. 'They filled me with a desire to get there. Going to sea was a means to an end; it would let me see these things I'd read about.' To help her decide her career, Anne's dad took her to see her old babysitter (who'd been a third mate with P&O Containers) and her cousin Susan, a children's nurse with P&O Cruises. That did it. Anne began training in 1988 when she was 18, encouraged by her mum, who'd been a QARNNS (Navy nurse) and partially backed by her dad who'd been a Royal Navy artificer in submarines. Her ignorance now astounds her. 'I went in blind. If I'd been able to Google "Merchant Navy, number of women" I'd have been put off.'

Getting in wasn't easy for her. She wrote fifty letters and got five replies. Shell Isle of Man told her they didn't employ women in the engine rooms and asked, had she considered secretarial work? 'That was stunning – men had the right to tell you to go away.' Finally, after two interviews P&O Containers took her on, saying that they already had women in the engine room. Jane and Marion (surnames now unknown) 'had left a legacy of something positive behind them', Anne realised. She was offered a cadetship at Warsash, where she was the only woman in the UK training as a marine engineer.

In engine rooms from 1988 to 2001 Anne found 'not just a laddish situation but a culture that was aggressive and bullying. It was vicious and nasty, with alpha men who played power games and a pack mentality where the weakest was torn to shreds. It's horrible.' Older men were the nicest to her.

Her many stories of hostility include one 'three-month hell trip [when] I couldn't go to the public spaces on the ship because an officer would throw a glass ashtray at me.' Nobody stopped him. She says many women endured far more than they should: insults, groping and even rapes. 'You don't speak out. There'd be no proof anyway.' Also she felt a kind of responsibility not to report such behaviour. In a climate when women were still seen as to blame for inciting men's sexual desire, for example 'inflaming lust' by wearing alluringly short skirts, it was better to withhold complaints that could give women a reputation for whingeing or tale-telling. If no gain was possible, then silence was a more productive tactic. She thinks 'it'll be there until there are more women at sea. It's better on passenger ships where there's "the cargo" for men to sexually engage with.'

Over time Anne didn't find attitudes to women changing, 'but attitudes to *me* did. People worry about the unknown.' Some had never heard of a woman engineer. When they met the reality and saw she wasn't a problem, that shifted initial scepticism. What made her accepted was 'That I'd done my job and hadn't caused anyone to do any extra work'. She came ashore after thirteen years, married a Dane, became a lecturer in marine engineering and had two children. At Glasgow Nautical College, now City of Glasgow College Faculty of Engineering, 'One of the greatest moments for me was to see two Indian girls complete their HNDs and head off for their sea time, some of the first in the Indian Merchant Navy. I was proud to be a role model. At first they were shocked to see that one of their engineering teachers was a woman. It gave them a lot of kudos and shut the boys up, who had been giving them trouble over caste as well as gender.' She found that her chief engineer's certificate brought total respect. 'No one ever commented on being taught by a woman, because they respected the licence.'

Anne left college to work with BAE Systems in Scotstoun as a warranty engineer, resolving faults in ships delivered to customers. The work included taking vessels out for shakedown trips. Her company had never had a woman doing this before, but as the only person with the requisite licence she had to sail. And she went again when the RFA *Lyme Bay* needed sea-trialling. Her great pleasure was doing so when twenty-four weeks pregnant. Her company had a rule that pregnant people couldn't be on their ships. But Anne was needed, and she insisted that it was her legal right. 'Many things go wrong in a shakedown. You're living with your heart in your mouth most of the time. I'd have thought my daughter would be a nervous wreck, but she's not.' Anne felt she was a role model for the naval women aboard, who hadn't previously had one: 'Here was a woman who *ran* that propulsion system, was in charge … they'd seen it being done!'

Today Anne works designing power and propulsion systems for ships and then sea-trialling them. She's active in the WES as well as being a STEM ambassador, someone who goes into schools and explains their job to students thinking about careers. As someone who had her kids in her late thirties she hates the assumption that only exceptional women go to sea. Nor does she like it that young women have dropped out to have children, because it gives other women a bad name, and means they're assumed to be unreliable. Her experience showed her that 'Women *can* get to the top. I did.'

There's no *technical* obstacle to a woman becoming a chief engineer. But Anne thinks, 'there needs to be cultural change and shipping lines can't be bothered. To them it makes no sense to go to all that trouble when you can just get a man to do it instead.'[20]

Sometimes men make plain objections to women, and sometimes their stated objections mask a femiphobia that is less easy for them to articulate.[21] One such objection is that women aren't strong enough, and need men to help them. Actually, strength depends on many factors: some men are physically weaker than some women; some small wiry women can handle astonishing weights. And if the team is working well it's normal for people, whatever their gender, to routinely compensate for each other's deficiencies so that co-operation and mutual support get the job done. But too often men stood by with arms folded waiting for 'That Woman' to fail and thereby prove No Woman Could Ever Ever Be an Engineer.

When Anne taught, she met female engineering cadets, which enabled her to reflect on the differences between women and men in the job. A key difference was that 'women read manuals' rather than just steaming ahead. They do so partly to figure out how to do jobs that might seem to involve heavy weight. 'Things usually take technique not huge strength,' these women engineers repeat. But timing was a problem too, thinks Anne. In the 1990s there was a mismatch: British women were entering the industry at a time when ships were no longer officered by British people. So women, feeling equal and expecting to be treated as such, found 'we were going into a situation that had just gone back twenty years, because officers were men from cultures that still found it hard to accept women as equals.'

Lisa Jenkins, who always played with Meccano as a girl, began her career a few years after Anne. She's still working at sea over two decades later. She's found very few other women in the job and thinks this is partly because girls' science education in school was poorer or non-existent. Women marine engineers of the 1990s were usually unsure how much the obstacles to promotion were due to the glass ceiling affecting women and how much to their exclusion by Freemasons. This controversial society (which today is still said to be four times as strong in Scotland – whence most marine engineers came – as in England) didn't actively recruit women then as any sort of member. Indeed, membership of any Masonic Lodges that embraced women engineers might have alienated conservative brethren.[22]

Lisa: Veteran Chief Engineer

Lisa Jenkins (b. 1973) says, 'I don't think I'm the first chief. I think there is a lady in the New Zealand Navy, and perhaps a girl I was at college with called Joanna who worked for BP shipping. She had a real passion for engineering whereas I didn't, so if anyone is going to be, she would have.' Lisa initially went to South Tyneside College in 1991 to become an engineer. She was offered sponsorship by Cunard, P&O and BP. At her college Lisa found little sexism; there were three other women on the course. 'The boys are fine 'as long as you're fine with them and don't expect any different treatment,' she told oral historian Sheila Jemima in 1991. 'I think they respect you more if you carry on just as you are.' When she was on the *QE2* all in the engineering department were male, except the chief engineer's secretary and one of storekeepers. She didn't feel lonely – because she was on a cruise ship where there was a friendlier climate and more women than on a cargo ship. Over twenty-three years later she told me, 'I remember hearing about a female chief (possibly Victoria Drummond)

Lisa Jenkins in the engine room when she was fourth engineer on the *Cunard Countess* in the 1990s. (Lisa Jenkins)

years ago. But sadly and typical for that time her name was associated with her being related to the Queen – that somewhat detracted from what was in itself an amazing achievement.' Anyway Lisa didn't feel a lack of role models. 'To be honest I'm really my own role model. I'm an only child and have an "internal feedback mechanism".'[23]

She went on to work on the *QM2* as an environmental officer, a step which Cunard required at the time. 'I never felt held back on my way up the ladder at least until becoming first engineer in 2005. And then I left Cunard when I was offered a chief's job on yachts, five years after obtaining my certificate. Five years is fairly quick to become chief.' Since then she has sailed on superyachts as chief.

'When I first went to sea I hated it, but I just never considered switching careers as an option – too proud and embarrassed to admit I may had made the wrong choice. But then I went on a work-hard/play-hard ship and started to enjoy the life as well. What's helped me stay? The money is fantastic. If that were different there's no way anyone would work away from home for months on end. Not a female, anyway.'[24]

It's hard to imagine that climbing the career ladder is as hard for modern women as it was for Victoria Drummond, deliberately being failed in her exams so many times. When Anne passed her class four licence her examiner flung her licence across the table, saying, 'I can't fail you but I never want to see you again.' Why the hostility? I asked Anne. 'He was preserving the purity of the profession, believing that it is *not* a place for a woman.' But when she got her chief's certificate, 'I really felt it was a level playing field at last. It'll work better if men have seen women in power and doing physical labour.'

As Anne discovered when she was briefly in RN vessels doing tests, RN women engineers initially found it even harder to make their way up the career ladder than did MN women. US Navy women had it a little easier. Eight women engineering officers, including Charlene Albright, made history in 1978. Hard-hatted Charlene was pictured aboard the missile test ship *Norton Sound* in Long Beach. When in 1979 a further 375 ratings and fifty-five officers were introduced, the 'Snortin Norton' was re-nicknamed 'the Love Boat'. It was a kind of test ship for women, the US equivalent of the UK's *Brilliant* ten years later.[25]

Charlene's 1970s junior counterparts in the UK were only employed ashore, in naval yards and private yards, such as on the Clyde. It seems that they weren't in high-tech jobs, but in lighter roles, for example assisting sheet-iron workers. Pat X, a senior shopfloor man who trained the women in a Govan yard, explained the way women were treated. 'They became pets. After all, they were the sisters or daughters of workmates … they had a good improving influence in the shipyards.'[26] As so many men said, women made work a nicer place to be, sweeter-smelling and with cleaner language.

Linda Pattison was one of those partly welcomed incomers in 1981. At only 17 she became the first woman electrical apprentice to work in HMS *Fife*, a County-class destroyer.[27] There may have been other women pioneers at other yards, and there's no record of what pioneers felt about being pets or pin-ups. Linda would not have been allowed at sea at that time, except on brief trips.

Naval women with engineering skills progressed at sea and beyond. In March 1990, Deputy Weapons Engineer Officer Chella Franklin became the first Wren to go to sea as a member of the ship's company on HMS *Norfolk*. Being allowed to sleep aboard was a crucial stage in getting a foot in the Navy's door. She'd studied for a BSc in mechanical engineering, just like Rachel Parsons and the Keary sisters. Her opportunities to sail began when she joined the WRNS in 1986 and did more training at Royal Navy Engineering College, Manadon. (The RN had been training 'engineers' boys' since 1863.)

Six years later in 1996 Sophie Shaughnessy became first female frigate marine engineering officer and continued to climb up the ladder. She's famously quoted as saying, 'You've got to make these guys realise you are their boss.' She did, and in 2015 was working ashore for the Navy's Maritime Commissioning and Trials Agency.[28] Jennifer Osbaldestin, a mine warfare specialist in the Navy in the 1990s, went on to become BAE's sea trials manager. Jennifer was managing HMS *Daring* when Anne was the sea trials chief engineer, and by 2015 had become the director one of BAE Systems' cutting-edge programmes.[29] In other words, these RN sailors' careers somewhat parallel those of civilian women marine engineers, but a decade later: Sophie's career pattern of going to sea was like Anne's, ten years earlier.

In the 2000s MN women at sea were qualifying with that very impressive qualification, the combined chief engineer's certificate in both motor and steam. It's thought that a Lancashire woman, Corinne Davies (later Burley), achieved it first. She was followed by Claudene Sharp (b. 1974), the first woman in Australia with a class 1 (motor) marine engineer qualification, who gained the dual certificate two years later in 2002.[30]

Women marine engineers of the last few decades have been rare, though talented, significant and successful, at least before they hit glass ceilings. In 1993 Helen Marshman became the first merchant seafarer to win Young Woman Engineer of the Year Award. IMarEST published the biography of Victoria Drummond the following year, which dramatically boosted awareness of women in marine engineering. When in the 1990s the marine officers' union (then called NUMAST) established the Victoria Drummond Award for women of outstanding achievement, the global publicity promoted the message that women could succeed, and had done so before, despite terrible odds. However, Victoria Drummond was of little more relevance to young women than Queen Victoria was a model for Victoria Beckham. In truth, the students were more helped by having women lecturers, real role models such as Anne, standing in front of them.

In 2014 IMarEST had 427 female members, making up just over 3 per cent of its membership. The majority of them are scientists, not seagoing engineers. Just over a third of marine engineers (36 per cent) were working in companies with a less than 1 per cent female workforce. But IMarEST's boosting of women's profile is providing useful models for girls and young women. Women continue to win prizes: IMarEST-sponsored Nicole Fiolet in 2007 became Engineer Cadet of the Year, and in 2011 Sara Smith, an engineer on *Queen Victoria*, also gained the title.[31]

AND ON THE SHIP'S COMPUTERS ...

Since the 1990s a new job has appeared that's slightly to the side of engineering: electro-technical officer, or ETO for short. The job came into being because of the most important technological breakthrough in maritime safety since wireless in 1899. Global Maritime Distress and Safety System (GMDSS) revolutionised shipboard communications with the outside world. It is an integrated system using terrestrial and satellite-based communications systems. It alerts rescue authorities, and other ships, if there is an emergency. Systems are fully automatic and have dispensed with manual watch-keeping. Nor do they require anyone to know Morse code.

The insignia for an ETO is two to three gold stripes and their electrical technical assistants (ETAs) bear half a gold stripe on their sleeves. In most cases ROs would, as Rose King put it, 'segue' into ETO work, as she and Fazilette Khan did in the 1980s. Unlike an RO, though, who was part of the deck crew, ETOs and ETAs are on the technical side of ship work, working under the chief engineer.

In early 1990s, briefly, women from the hotel side of ships could ease their way over into the technical side in the new job of ETA, which was a support role for the ETO. Telephone operator Jane Nilsen was on P&O's *Oriana* in 1992; the whole switchboard was pulled out as it was no longer necessary after automation. Her radio officer told Jane and her tele-op colleagues about the coming revolution: Global Maritime Distress and Safety Systems (GMDSS). He foresaw that radio officers would become deader than dodos or telephonists.

Jane, who had two daughters to feed, wanted to explore the opportunity, before it was even announced. Being science-minded, in the past she'd been invited to become an engineering cadet on her Scandinavian ship. So straight away she booked herself onto a five-day course on GMDSS and three brief courses on word processing, leading over time to a City and Guilds qualification. This was enough to get her the job, as P&O was anyway seeking ways to redeploy redundant staff. In May 1993 she embarked on her new role, and was joined by other ETAs who were ex-Women's Royal Army Corps signallers. She didn't see it as a career where there'd be progression to ETO. ETA was initially a paired job, presumably because it made berthing arrangement easier having two women sharing a cabin. The ETA job split in the late 1990s and the deck team took over the GMDSS aspect of the work and the purser's office took over the telephony aspects.[32] Relatedly, a new post, the Information Technology (IT) manager, sometimes called the 'Techspert', emerged in the ship's hotel department. It was a 'man's job' in effect. The Techspert looks after the on-board internet suites, rather like internet cafés. The job of ETO remains today, and Nicole Fiolet is one of the few women doing it in the early twenty-first century.

ETO Nicole

Nicole Fiolet is an ETO on the *Maersk Dunkerque,* one of the ferries on the Dover–Dunkerque route. She's placed her inspiring story on the internet. While deciding what to do with her future, Nicole sailed as a waitress for a few months then decided sea life – in engineering – was for her. So she started doing a cadetship in marine engineering/electro-technical engineering on a container ship to the Far East. 'Sailors were really friendly and helpful in my learning process.' She loves 'the sense of achievement that I get after a hard day's work ... The only thing about sea life that I think is a shame is that there are so few women. We can all do the job ... [but] a lot of women are still scared of going away and spending time away from their loved ones. To them, I can say that we're never really away from a telephone call or an email, and it's great to be visiting faraway places while earning a decent living. It makes the "coming home" times all the more better.'[33]

SAILING TOWARDS THE FUTURE

Anne Madsen sums up the story of women marine engineers. 'There's been a few. They've got to the top. There's not enough now. And they've proved themselves just as capable as men. They haven't been a burden. They've enhanced ships.' In the future the increased number of women engineers generally must mean that more role models exist for young women. Anne, Lisa and Nicole can be the Rachel Parsons and Victoria Drummonds of the twenty-first century. That, and schools talks and web-based publicity, may help women move into the world of making ships work as they cross the world's oceans. In developing countries it's looking even better. Roland Tan, the director of Singapore's Maritime Academy, said in 2007 that the ratio of women to men in marine engineering was thirty to seventy.[34] And it was set to rise.

PART TWO

THE HOTEL

5

FROM STEWARD'S WIFE TO CHIEF HOUSEKEEPER: DOING THE DOMESTIC TASKS

Fiona Rush (b. 1978) is one of the thousands of modern women who know all about ship's housework. When she was 16 in West Belfast in 1995 an opportunity came up to work in a hotel in the Channel Islands.

> So I packed up my Guns N' Roses posters and kissed my mummy goodbye – and worked as a chambermaid/waitress/receptionist … [and later] ran a chain of guesthouses. Although I liked my job, by twenty-four I had a yearning to meet new people and travel. My friends' back-packing days were over by the time I'd saved up enough to wander … So … why not work in a floating hotel? And I was delighted to be offered a job as housekeeping supervisor [sometimes called assistant chief housekeeper] with the *Royal Caribbean*. I will never, for the rest of my life, forget the moment that I pulled into Fort Lauderdale port and set eyes, for the first time, on the *Radiance of the Seas* … I felt overwhelmed, and a bit scared, by her vast and regal appearance. Once I was on board my anxieties melted away. I felt excited and – strangely – at home!

'From 2002 to 2003 I worked on the *Radiance of the Seas*, supervising 180 housekeeping workers from twelve different countries. My job was to ensure that all the 2,100 passengers had the highest standard of personal service in their cabin accommodation.' Fiona's heaviest day was turnaround day, when 2,100 disembarked and 2,100 new passengers arrived, all within four hours, meaning over 1,000 cabins had to be made afresh. And the work was of course inspected by the room's inhabitants, as well as officers on checking visits.

Fiona found that housekeeping staff were seen as being 'as low as the ship's cat'. In 2002 her staff didn't even earn a set salary: their income was based purely on gratuities. Now, thanks to Maritime Labour Convention 2006, they are paid. She later made a very unusual transition from hotel work to deck work. The stories that deck officers told her 'helped me know that I didn't just want to maintain the vessel's cleanliness. I wanted to sail her!' And she did.[1] But most domestic staff these days stay in the guest relations sector.

In today's floating hotels, with all these fierce social divisions, people like those that Fiona supervised are as crucial as the person who does the housework in your home. The bedroom stewards/cabin attendants/housekeepers (still called stewardesses on some ships) are to ships what chambermaids (now usually called room attendants) are to hotels – the bedrock. And more, because they are subtly and varyingly your hosts and guides, as well as room sanitisers. These ratings (of whom slightly more are male than female) make and change your bed, clean your shower, vacuum, dust, wipe, ensure you have ice and full supplies in the minibar, take away rubbish and laundry and generally act as a fairly invisible host. You won't see them much as they only do the work in your absence. And they'll most likely be from the Philippines or Eastern Europe, not the UK.

Filipina Pamela Marrero has a high profile on the internet outlining her job as a stewardess on a cruise ship. She and her assistant (who does the bathrooms while

Former housekeeping supervisor Fiona Rush in her new uniform as deck officer, 2010. (Photo: Thomas McMullan; courtesy of Fiona Rush)

she does the bedrooms, and changes the beds with her) look after a block of twenty cabins, pushing around a trolley full of detergent, towels, replacement shower caps and so on. Pamela's morning starts at 5 a.m., she has a short break at noon, then carries on. Finally around 10 p.m. she prepares her trolley for the following day, hands in her pass keys and signs off.[2]

Typical housekeeping department hierarchies are headed by the executive purser or passenger services director – titles vary with the company. Next down the chain is the hotel manager (who in the past was called the chief steward). Then there's the executive housekeeper/chief housekeeper. Often a white European woman with one or two degrees in hotel and catering, she supervises all the services, including laundry, bell service and baggage. Next down the ladder is the assistant chief housekeeper (as Fiona was called) or the floor supervisor. Then there's the cabin steward and finally the assistant steward.

In the section called 'catering/hotel/other' on the British ships surveyed in 2013 women were 36 per cent of the officers and 35 per cent of the ratings. In other words, men outnumbered women by two to one, even in this 'women's work' area. UK female stewarding staff numbered about 1,500 and their female officers 250 at most.[3]

Housekeeping is the largest department on the vessel, and the people in it work the longest hours. Different shipping lines organise matters differently but usually the housekeeping department on a passenger ship has two subsections: one that deals with cabins and the other that is responsible for cleaning public areas such as corridors, decks and pool areas. Men are more likely to be employed in the public areas because it is heavier work and doesn't need them to demonstrate emotional care for passengers.

On cargo ships and tankers the cabin stewarding work is even more likely to be done by men, particularly men from less-developed countries. There the chain of command is far less long and complex than on cruise ships because cargo ships don't attempt to emulate a luxury hotel's standard of service. Worldwide, the pattern is that about 70 per cent of the people aboard passenger vessels do hotel and catering work.

In the Royal Navy domestic jobs tend to be done by women and a few men. People in the branch are nicknamed the White Mafia. There may be over a thousand women employed, plus a smaller number in the Royal Fleet Auxiliary. Some RN stewards are called 'steward-catering services logisticians'. Multi-tasking is always expected on such ships, so as well as domestic tasks they may also work with helicopters, operate several kinds of weapons and help refuelling at sea.[4]

Stewards on cruise ships and ferries are safety professionals, like air cabin crew: as stewardess Alice Pickles says, 'the person cleaning your toilet could save your life' because she's trained to help cope with the ship's evacuation in emergency.[5] Unlike chambermaiding on land it's one of the few peacetime jobs that may require the worker to give up her own life for that of the guest. More subtly, such stewards are part of the subtle passenger control system, regulating the 'cell's' inhabitants to suit the institution's convenience. And in what sociologist Thorstein Veblen called the 'symbolic pantomime' stewards enable wealthier people to feel superior and at ease, for example by providing a perfectly ordered cabin with a corner of the lavatory paper reassuringly turned down just at the right angle.[6]

When I first began interviewing interwar stewardesses in the 1980s they strikingly described their work as 'looking after' the passengers. Indeed Edith Sowerbutts said 'one very senior White Star stewardess … always described her work as a "vocation". And she meant it.' Stewards' long-established nickname, 'po-jugglers' (chamber-pot handlers) reveals the tension between what women like to think they are offering, and what employers require. But for over a hundred years stewarding was British women's main way of travelling the world by ship, for free, at a time of very limited mobility. It could be a low-status charring trap, but it was also an oh-so-glamorous-looking opportunity.

1750–1820: WITH A MATERNAL AIR

For over a century 'going into service' on land had been one of the main ways women could find paid work away from home. Housework, especially cleaning, became of central importance: because of the increased use of dirt-producing coal; higher affluence for some, which meant there was more to clean and greater desire to be seen as part of an elite; and rising concern for hygiene and control of pests (including bed bugs).[7] Understandings of the causes of ill-health created more work – particularly in the King's Navy, as it was understood that a clean ship was a healthier ship.

As such work was low status and therefore low-paid, it might have been assumed that women's cheap labour was welcomed at sea too. Not initially. The reasons include the fact that to most people a ship was understood to be quite the opposite of a safe, patriarchally controlled, household. Seafaring men far from home ties were cast as feckless, even barbaric. Authorities worried that women of low enough status to do household drudgery would also be promiscuous and cause rivalry between heterosexual men in that powder-keg that was the shipboard community. Conversely it may have been feared that 'low' seamen would besmirch decent women, which would outrage the community at home. I think too that shipowners, who were necessarily focused on transportation from A to B, didn't initially understand the importance of passengers' emotional satisfaction. So only the most farsighted would have thought ersatz 'mothers' might be useful.

The Housework Needed at Sea c. 1800

- ◈ bed making
- ◈ emptying of slops including vomit and excreta
- ◈ delivering of ewers of washing water
- ◈ 'attending' the passengers, especially if sick or distressed
- ◈ tackling bedbugs
- ◈ sewing and mending ship's linen and clothes
- ◈ sweeping with birch or heather brooms
- ◈ scrubbing with hog's bristle brushes
- ◈ childcare and care of domestic animals
- ◈ laundering, drying and ironing clothes
- ◈ waiting at table
- ◈ wiping, dusting, polishing

By the 1750s there were several ways a woman could get a housework-type job at sea: disguised and working as a boy on naval or merchant ship; as the master's relative on a ship so small that there was no steward to do housework for 'the royal family'; as the maidservant of a seagoing captain's wife; or as the wife of an established steward on a passenger ship, acting almost as his subcontractor doing work for ladies.

And on slave ships some of the favourite women (who were usually not shackled like men) did jobs for officers, as well as performing sexual services. Historian of slave ships Marcus Rediker found that women, and some men, prepared food such as cleaning rice and pounding yam, washed the decks, scraped the slave departments, and laundered and mended crew clothes – for which they were rewarded with brandy, tobacco or extra food.[8]

Mary Lacy/William Chandler was one of the cross-dressed women on Navy ships. Many seafarers on RN vessels had servants called 'boys' or sometimes 'cabin boys' aboard to look after the 'housework' of the ship. It was what we might now call the entry-level job, seen neither as skilled nor manly. Mary (1740–95) was taken on the *Royal Sovereign* as the carpenter's servant. Here she did the domestic support work most wives would do, and which she'd already done in service on land. Mary also benefited from many opportunities to do small paid jobs on the side, 'the boatswain observing me so very tractable, by which I gained the good will of everybody.' Such tasks included laying the table and getting the key for women's visits to the round house (toilet) 'by this means I got several pence from each of them.' She also dressed fish for the boatswain's wife and parents who came on board, for which she was given 6d (2½p) for serving it up so carefully. When she fetched pints of rum for the deputy purser's wife and her guests, they said, 'Ay, he is the best boy on board.'[9]

Out women also laundered, but seemingly didn't clean, on warships. Admiral the Right Honourable the Earl of St Vincent in 1796 recorded that some lower-ranked wives (or women brought out clandestinely) were laundering for men, including for those who didn't have accompanying boys or wives.[10] (He was irascible about women's use of precious drinking water for rinsing). Very rarely women might be, effectively, stewardesses on Royal Navy ships. Mrs Davies in 1819 became the at-sea maid for the Duchess of Clarence and the two ladies Fitz-Clarence on his Majesty's yacht *Royal Sovereign*. The Admiralty required that a 'respectable woman, sufficiently used to the sea' be taken on. She was registered as an able seaman because there was no other category for her.[11] Mrs Davies was able to do this unusual job at sea partly because it was temporary (for a short trip to Antwerp), partly because it was unthinkable that an aristocratic lady would be looked after by a male sailor, and partly because being married to a Greenwich hospital pensioner made her almost 'one of us', an RN member. Not only had she been socialised into the naval ways of life. Simply by virtue of having a husband, she was perceived as deserving, respectable and unlikely to be sexually pursued by men aboard.

Women hired by captain's wives often disappointed their employers – as maids did on land too. In the 1780s Frances Barkley had to do their work for them, 'our two black girls being completely knocked up with seasickness and fright'. Probably such maids were casually picked up abroad from a very tiny pool of untrained available servants and people who'd never before sailed. Winée, Frances's earlier maid, had simply come out to their ship in the Sandwich Islands, by canoe, and indicated she wanted to join them.[12]

Like the Admiralty, merchant shipping authorities had sexual anxieties about women on ships, which is why the wives of stewards were accepted. As the bed-partner of someone already on ship, a steward's wife didn't require a separate berth. No troublesome new spatial arrangements were needed. Monogamy was presumed, meaning that this female newcomer would be under her man's protection. And she was a known quantity, not 'loose' or 'spare'.

So the best possible chance of sailing available to a woman at that time was to marry a steward. It was these 'helpers' or 'maids to one and all' who become the new nineteenth-century phenomenon, stewardess, the most common role for women on ship.

1821–1880: LIGHT WORK AND KIND LIES

Crucially, the heavy aspects of housework on British passenger ships, such as cleaning floors ('decks'), were done by men. Similarly in grand houses ashore, footmen did 'rough work' and women did the lighter, cleaner work, including the personal service that general maids, between maids, parlour maids and even ladies' maids usually gave.

Captains' wives didn't do heavy housework at sea, unless they were poor. Historian of petticoat whalers and hen frigates Joan Druett found that the captain and his wife would maintain status by being waited upon by a steward. Unusually, captain's wife Mary Dow on the 279-ton barque *Clement*, sailing in 1838 to the Baltic, regularly cleaned their quarters, 'which is something of a job I assure you'. She had to work round the cramped clutter in their box-room-sized bedroom-cum-ship's office-cum-spare-sail store.[13] Household tasks included cleaning skylights, small square windows and portholes, mending smashed ornaments after a storm, and tending the canaries.

Better-off captains' wives gave opportunities to local women to sail, though often without having much time to check them out. Jane Penelope Herring confided to her journal on the Calcutta-to-Muscat run in March 1850: 'I have neither ayah nor woman, having been obliged to dismiss the former for insolence, and in the latter I was disappointed at last, having got a Free School girl, and she turned out to have leprosy and I was obliged to send her back after a deal of trouble.'[14]

Some steam passenger ships were advanced enough to carry several stewards and offer boarding-house-level (not yet hotel-level) service. Charles Dickens implicitly recognised that the 'ship's mother' did emotional labour as well as physical tasks such as being 'actively engaged in producing clean sheets and tablecloths from the very entrails of the sofas, and from unexpected lockers, of such artful mechanism, that it made one's head ache to see them opened'. Crossing the Atlantic on the *Britannia* steam packet in 1842, he welcomed her kindness:

Housework at sea. The captain's wife sews in their cabin. Artist's impression of whaling wife by Ron Druett. (Joan and Ron Druett)

God bless that stewardess for her piously fraudulent account of January voyages! … all happiness be with her for her bright face and her pleasant Scottish tongue … and for her predictions of fair winds and fine weather (all wrong or I shouldn't be half so fond of her); and for the ten thousand small fragments of genuine womanly tact [in reassuring passengers] that what seemed to the uninitiated a serious journey was, to those who were in the secret, a mere frolic, to be sung about and whistled at![15]

Dickens doesn't mention whether she was married to a steward. But on the increasingly comfortable passenger ships, especially as steam took over from sail, 'stewardess' was no longer just the convenient label for the steward's or mate's seagoing wife, but a job in its own right. Stewardesses are listed in censuses from 1821 onwards. When passengers came to expect better service on ships, so the number of stewarding staff increased. The emigration trade and the setting up of the empire created stewardess jobs because it was axiomatic that a female passenger, particularly a lady, must be looked after by another female.

Although male stewards might clean and tidy a *cabin*, it was felt a stewardess should be available to help the cabin's *inhabitant*; for example, if a lady was so seasick she needed help looking after her children. Nevertheless, male bedroom stewards far outnumbered female. And there were jobs for at least two level of stewardess, saloon (first) and second class. Steerage passengers usually had to just help themselves and each other.

Stewardesses could only exceptionally find work on non-passenger merchant ships, as there were rarely enough women passengers aboard to justify a stewardess's wage. Margaret/William Armstrong got her job looking after ship's officers and their spaces because she seemed to be a man. It would have been unseemly for a female to go into men's cabins, especially as at that time even chief engineers were not seen as gentlemen.

Margaret/William: From Tough Steward to Stewardess

Margaret/William Armstrong (b. c. 1860) in 1873 was one of the last women in Britain recorded as being a cross-dressed sailor. Born in New Jersey, Margaret, said the newspapers, 'had a strong masculine appearance, tawny Dutch countenance, and in stature she towers above several of the crew.' She felt impelled to leave home when her mother married again. Taking her father's suit and going to New York she somehow found work in 1872 and several ships later she secured the job of engineers' steward on the *Eskdale*, a collier sailing for Italy. For three months and five days she looked after the engineers, which included making their beds and tidying their cabins, as well as waiting at their table. Before that she'd also cleaned the ship itself, 'at scrubbing the decks and scraping the masts she'd proved remarkably useful'. But the master's wife suspected Margaret because she was secretive about dressing and undressing at night. 'The truth came out at Genoa and before the English consul she signed herself as stewardess.' At Aberdeen she was 'decently attired', given a few pounds and sent back to New York.[16]

There were only three possible career steps for ships' stewardesses: from steerage (the very lowest area, where people were copped in no-frills dormitories), to second class, and then up to saloon class. In 1881 Captain T. Wilson told a government inquiry that: 'Stewardesses will not remain in the steerage, they expect to be promoted to the [higher-tipping] saloon … A stewardess who willingly remained long in steerage I should at once suspect of blackmailing.'[17] This suggests that stewardesses need to be recognised as, like most service staff on ship, capable of being canny entrepreneurs, in a situation that many say was 'dog eat dog', where women quickly learned to toughen up.

1881–1914: A HOTEL NURSE, AN ADVENTURER?

In the late nineteenth century passengers came to expect a pleasurable, civilised journey. A thousand women were working as professional stewardesses. They wore something like a nurse's uniform (which they even bought from nurses' outfitters). Women with nursing experience were preferred, and many were 'hybrids': ranked as stewardesses but expected to nurse when required. It was increasingly unusual for stewardesses to be just a passenger moonlighting.

Jobs were still few: far less than 1 per cent of the total maritime workforce was female.[18] This was despite jobs in seagoing hospitality work increasing. As maritime historian Val Burton found, in 1894 at least 43 per cent of crew were stewards, cooks and waiters, whereas by 1921, this had risen to 70 per cent.[19] A mismatch between the demand and supply was clear. Employers needed matronly sea-wise stewardesses who would mother the passengers a little, get on with their work and not be man-traps.

But on offer was a huge over-supply of adventure-seeking younger shoresiders. Empire-minded women, 'surplus women' and 'new women' were increasingly expressing desires for overseas adventure, fuelled by juvenile literature by Bessie Marchant, 'the girls' Henty'.[20] Working a passage by stewardessing, or being a 'lady's companion', could look more attractive than permanent emigration. Women journalists had to disabuse dreamers. In 1891 an expert on women's jobs, Veva Karsland, pointed out that stewardesses 'are forever at the beck and call of other ladies, and have a hundred mistresses instead of one … Therefore they need to be very amiable and willing and not easily ruffled.'[21] Stewardesses were tellingly nicknamed 'tabbies', until at least the 1960s.

As Mary Rogers's story and many magazine advice columns showed, stewardessing was not a handy opportunity for would-be young gadabouts. It was a role for older women already socialised into the sea transport business and good at social survival. Mary had been married to a seafarer, so knew the culture. And, like Mary, it was quite usual for stewardesses to be responsible for winning the bread for at least three other family members. Most, unlike Mary, couldn't return home every night.

Mary: A Stewardess of the 1890s

Mary Rogers (1855–99) was a sea widow. She got the job after her husband died when she was six months' pregnant. His employers, the London and South Western Railways, offered her a job on the Channel Islands ferries. As the sole support of her parents, Mary handed over the care of her Mary Ellen (aged twenty-two months) and new baby Frederick and sailed, though she was seasick. Presumably knowing well how to be supportive and firm, yet respectful, Mary rose to the rank of senior stewardess (that would be one rung). She came to the world's notice at Easter 1899 when their ferry, the *Stella*, sank in fog on its way from Southampton to Guernsey after hitting the Casquets Reef. Mrs Rogers made sure that all 'her ladies and children' in the ladies' cabin got safely into the lifeboat. To one she gave her own lifebelt. Witnesses reported that the sailors in the lifeboat called, 'Jump in, Mrs Rogers,' but she replied, 'No, no – if I get in, the boat will sink … Lord, have me … Good-bye, good-bye.' Monuments were built and in 1908 the Girl's Friendly Society funded her memorialisation as a heroine, along with Grace Darling, in the Lady Chapel of Liverpool's Anglican cathedral. Some wonder if the romance of the story diverted attention from her employer's culpability.[22]

Stewardess Mary Rogers is commemorated in several ways including as part of the *Stella* memorial, Southampton. (Photo: John Lawrence; courtesy of Sheila Jemima)

The best way a woman could break into business was to be visibly steady (and maybe God-fearing) like Mary. And the easiest way to get up the short ladder was probably to be the well-educated but unstuffy widow of a senior officer, so that the captain treated you as respectfully as he'd treat his wife.

1915–1950S: STEWARDESSES FLOURISH

Stewardesses were sailing at the start of the First World War, even though civilian passenger shipping was largely stopped. Violet Jessop was one of the women who initially wanted to carry on.

Violet: Intrepidly on from the *Titanic*

Violet Jessop (1887–1971), whose autobiography meant she was to become the world's best-known stewardess when *Titanic*-mania hit in the late twentieth century, worked at sea for forty-two years on and off. She turned to the work because she needed to keep her poorly mother and siblings, although really she had set her mind on becoming a governess. Her mother had been a stewardess for the Royal Mail Steam Packet Company from 1903 to 1908; that added to the knowledge Violet herself had gained sailing home from the Argentine as a girl after her father died in 1903. Usually only women over 25 were allowed to sail (and in Union Castle's case over 28). Violet was only 21 but an exception was made by Royal Mail Steamships. She sailed to and from New York for six years, including on the *Titanic* in 1912, when twenty of the 322 stewarding staff on board were stewardesses. All bar three of them survived, including Violet. She carried on sailing until a few months after the First World War began; she worked as an auxiliary Voluntary Aid Detachment (VAD) nurse then returned to sea in 1916 because 101 nursing sisters were on the hospital ship *Britannic*, and four stewardesses were required to look after them.

In the interwar years she sailed fairly constantly. When the Second World War began in 1939 Violet was one of the first to give up the sea. She went back, as about two-thirds of stewardesses did, after the war's end in 1945. In 1950, aged sixty-three, she 'swallowed the anchor' after over 200 trips on Royal Mail, White Star, P&O and Red Star Line ships. Such a lengthy career was unusual; a British India Steam Navigation Company (BISN) stewardess's average career length then was four and half years, or twelve voyages.[23] After Violet left the sea she added to her 1930s memoir and lived alone in a cottage in Great Ashfield, Suffolk. Her niece sent the manuscript to a publisher in 1996. The book succeeded, not least because best-selling maritime author John Maxtone-Graham, who'd previously met Violet, took it under his wing and edited it.[24]

Although domestic staff in the MN sailed patchily in the First World War, the new women stewards in the Royal Navy services in that war did not sail at all. A recorded 13 per cent of wartime Wrens, 955, worked as stewards on land, in effect as Violet's counterparts.[25]

After the First World War, stewardessing was still the main job for women on MN ships (for example, the *Titanic* had had twenty stewardesses but only two cashiers and one matron). On the *Duchess of York* in 1934 only six roles were open to women, primarily stewardess; 150 roles were open to men.[26] So if a woman wanted to sail she still had to do so as the housework-focused servant. Ignominy was somewhat mitigated by the proximity of famous passengers.

One of the attractions was that, remarkably, seawomen had equal pay by the First World War. This arrangement (which was true in other countries too) may be because when the unions negotiated wage rates there were not enough women for a separate case to be made for women and men. Equal pay for people doing the same job continued, despite stewards thinking women did lighter work (which was somewhat true).

Initially the pre-war veteran stewardesses continued to sail, weathering the waxing then waning of service jobs at sea during migration, fuelled by 'travel-mindedness'[27] but hit by the 1931 Depression. For the first time stewardesses were selected to create a good impression of the shipping line, and not mainly because they were deserving maritime widows. When the ultra-modern *Queen Mary* came off the stocks in 1936 the British public were as proud of it as we today might be of our first spaceship. Edith Sowerbutts, who was someone not averse to fixing her broken specs with string, wrote that her senior lady superintendent came aboard their less-prestigious ship:

Cunard Stewardess Anne Smith (centre) and colleagues, 1920s. (National Museums Liverpool, N2004.0066)

to sort us out. She took one look at me and it was enough. My cheeks were glowing and rosy at the time … I had just emerged from a wardrobe … I looked fine, was slimmer than I had ever had been in my whole adult life … it appeared that I was earmarked for the *Queen Mary* … [T]he Chief Steward … had asked for some new and younger blood; it was said that some of the senior 'girls' on that big ship were also on the big side, perhaps getting too weighty for the speed required.[28]

On larger ships a new rung on the ladder emerged: the title, leading stewardess or chief stewardess, depended on the company. Some saw the post as being almost equivalent to being the queen's lady-in-waiting, a very superior version of the deck

Stewardess looking like maid-cum-nurse in her laundry-proof apron. Advertisement in *White Star* magazine, October 1923. (Eve Tar Collection)

ratings' bo'sun. Such women were usually extremely strict, which helped protect their more naïve underlings from making social mistakes with the wrong men. Maida Nixson wrote a wonderful memoir of her time at sea in this period, the first to be published by a stewardess, which shows what a precarious career it was.[29] You never knew if you'd be asked back at the end of each trip.

In the Second World War stewardesses' progression towards higher roles or posher ships was disrupted by the requirement to leave the sea for the duration of hostilities. Stewardesses working for BISN sailed on a quarter of the company's voyages, by comparison to roughly a half in the First World War.[30] Probably fewer than 200 stewardesses in all sailed after 1939, and this dwindled to zero after 1942.

Several thousand women in the newly re-constituted WRNS worked as stewards on land. It was an even less popular job than in the First World War. But as Freda Price found, it did give Wrens skills that were wanted by at least two small cargo shipping companies after the war.

1946–1990: MORE LIKE AIR CABIN CREW

In merchant shipping, a new opportunity arose, post-war, for would-be stewardesses: a handful could, like Freda, work on tramp vessels roaming the world freely, owned by Buries Markes and its sister organisation, the Medomsley Steam Shipping Company. Elsewhere in cargo shipping, enough male stewards were available. So shipping companies didn't need to invest in the expensive installation of female crew lavatories. And as women got equal pay under the Board of Trade agreements, companies couldn't reduce costs by employing women.

Buries Markes' revolution proved that where there was a will, there was a way. Initially it may have been that the two companies simply expected women crew to use the toilet facilities meant for the twelve passengers (twelve was the pivotal number: any more passengers than this and a ship legally had to carry a doctor). First of all, ex-Wrens such as Margeretta Godefroy[31] signed on as stewardesses on *La Pampa*.

Unfortunately the National Union of Seamen feared it would be the start of shipping lines undercutting men's hard-won rights. It scuppered the attempt.[32] Then a fourteen-strong all-women team, including flamboyant Happy Valley heiress Juanita Carbery,[33] joined the *La Cordillera*. And finally, Medomsley built several new ships, including the *Langleeclyde*, with women's bathrooms. The future had come, and it worked.

Stewardesses on these exceptional cargo ships were hit when tramping ended. Stewardess Gloria Thompson continued to get work partly because she was prepared to sail on whatever ship was available.

Gloria: The Lady's on a Tramp – and Venturing

Gloria Thompson (b. 1925) was a cargo ship captain's daughter. 'He was still "on the bridge" when he came home. Very very strict. Now I think we'd have been good pals.' As soon as home circumstances allowed, wanting to 'spread my wings', she joined the WRNS as a deckhand on small boats, then as a Fleet Air Arm mechanic, from 1944 to 1949. She left because the camaraderie seemed to go out of the WRNS. In her uniform she hitchhiked up to north Scotland looking for jobs in merchant shipping. Finally, she got her first berth on *La Cordillera*, as an assistant stewardess. From 1949 to 1962 she sailed on eighteen vessels and worked for eight different shipping lines. Destinations included the Far East and Australia with the 'Ten Pound Poms' (assisted emigrants) aboard. Sometimes she was a nursery stewardess and sometimes just an ordinary stewardess. And several times she 'went trooping', meaning she was a stewardess on ships chartered to take servicemen and their families en masse to overseas postings. She married a bo'sun she'd met ashore, who insisted she stopped sailing once she became pregnant. They had two children; he carried on sailing. Now Mrs Hudson, Gloria explains she has no interest in sailing again on holidays, when we met in her well-established home in Southampton.[34]

Adventurous women with money could pay their way as working passengers on the last working sailing ships, Gustaf Erikson's wonderfully anachronistic fleet.[35] Others tried foreign shipping lines, which would actually employ them. In 1959 Lily Brown-Try on a Norwegian supertanker found: 'A glamorous and exciting life? Well, not exactly. You slept on the deck rather than be thrown out of your bunk in storm. You listened to the creaking and groaning of the ship and the boom-boom-boom of heavy seas against the ship's sides and you thought, "heaven help the sailor on a night like this" … [But] I wouldn't have missed it for anything.'[36]

You could get a job as a stewardess fairly easily in the 1960s, 1970s and early 1980s, as more and more British-based and European companies launched and developed the cruise industry. Experience as a Wren or a nurse boosted applicants' opportunities. The changing social climate meant older and motherly looking ship's stewardesses were no longer wanted, because air cabin crew were setting a new trend: 'trolley dollies', women hired on the basis of their looks.

Many stewardesses from the 'golden years' of early cruising saw this period as a terrific opportunity to go round the world, several times. But this boom ended in the 1980s when shipping companies began flagging out their ships, and bringing lower-paid foreign workers on board. Memorably, staff on the *Cunard Countess* went on strike in the Virgin Islands in October 1980, after Cunard announced it would now be registered in the Bahamas and the British ratings would have to go. Similar

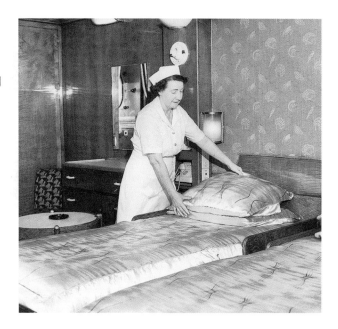

Miss M. Quirk, a Cunard stewardess, tidies up a passenger cabin in 1960. (University of Liverpool Library, D42/PR2/3/26/18/1)

changes took place in P&O in 1988 when the company tried to make such drastic cutbacks that seafarers went on a sixteen-month strike.[37] They didn't win. Catering workers left in large numbers while others agreed to be re-employed on terms that ripped the heart out of British crews. Instead it became a time of new opportunities for would-be stewardesses from the Philippines and East Europe.

At the same time there was increased access to higher education and the general acceptance that it wasn't a waste of time to educate girls. This led many more young women to do hotel and catering degrees, and thus enter the higher levels of the ships' housekeeping world. Most room stewardesses and stewards now have university-trained managers, usually white though not necessarily British. Some, like Alice Pickles, have been up then down: fortunes fluctuate in shipping and you need to be flexible to keep on sailing.

Alice: Ex-Supervisor Turned Room Steward

Alice Pickles is not her real name: Alice's details have been disguised as she fears she might be sacked for being in this book. She was born in the 1960s. Because her parents were publicans she grew up familiar with hotel life. She did two part-time courses at a catering college and then worked weekends for a catering agency – as well as tailoring in the week – before she started work in 1990 on ferries.

Her ferry company gave her a series of interviews to assess her suitability. When finally selected, she and her cohort were nicknamed 'The Untouchables', because they were better trained than her colleagues and 'got away with murder'. Initially, on ships she worked as a steward in the dining room, where she later became a supervisor. Today, because of cutbacks she's been demoted to rating level. She chose to be a room stewardess (as they're still called) rather than leave the seafaring life altogether.[38] And her job is like Pamela Marrero's, but more rushed, as on ferries new passengers come aboard twice a day, not weekly or fortnightly.

No frills for Northern Producer oil rig stewardess Jennifer Douglas, 2001. (Aberdeen Art Gallery & Museums)

The story of bedroom stewardesses today and in the future is a mixed one, with British women now in a minority in the job. Some work on superyachts, and in grand apartments on the floating year-round cities, others are on the many cruise ships. Scores of websites, unlike the early advice columns, tell would-be stewardesses that they don't need particular qualifications – but that some hotel experience helps. They are very often seeking brief, round-the-world adventures as their counterparts did a hundred years ago, but nowadays they'll have a degree behind them too.

Unlike Mary Lacy/William Chandler and Margaret/William Armstrong, stewardesses today certainly don't need to disguise themselves as men to get a job – although it might make it easier to deal with male colleagues. Certainly it would be easier to do the job in trousers or shorts (as on superyachts), not skirts. None will have been offered the work by their late husband's employers, as Mary Rogers' did; employers don't have that charitable mentality today. Stewards were the seafarers least likely to be born into traditional maritime communities and this tendency is even more marked today. Nowadays, it seems, seawomen from maritime families tend to become deck officers or join the Royal Navy. The twenty-first-century cabin stewardesses might be puzzled to be asked 'is it your vocation?' as it was for Edith's Sowerbutt's friend. It's 'time out' and they wouldn't expect it to be a lifetime career, as it was for Violet Jessop of the *Titanic*. And should their ship encounter disaster, they are now much better trained in how to deal with it. No one can get on a big ship without having passed their STCW95 Basic Safety Training course. And the loss of the *Costa Concordia* in 2012 was a salutary warning.

Stewardessing work is still as hard, despite labour-saving equipment. And it's still as lowly, as Fiona Rush pointed out. Stewardesses are seldom on cargo ships, where low-paid, non-British men are employed as stewards by agencies notorious for taking advantage of would-be seafarers. But some, like Jennifer Douglas, work on oil rigs, which can be seen as a sort of static ship, or seastead. There they service the rooms of male workers not lady holidaymakers. And women stewards are at sea in the Royal Navy now, although that is a dwindling force.

6

FROM LOBLOLLY BOY TO SURGEON: CARING FOR HEALTH

Upmarket bush medicine, A&E and intensive care on the waves: that's what health-care workers at sea have to be ready to do. It's a challenge. And the reward is that these professionals, responsible for others' health, tend to be the most cherished people on board.

As this chapter was being written, Sally Bell, a ship's doctor, became the first woman chief medical adviser at the Maritime and Coastguard Agency (MCA), the British body that aims to prevent the loss of lives at sea. Sally and her team, in effect, are Britain's main regulators of seafarer fitness. For a woman to hold this position at the MCA is major progress, because even as late as the 1970s women doctors were rarities in shipping companies.[1]

Two swallows don't make a summer, but it looks as if a new trend is beginning: women medics in top maritime jobs. In 2010 Sue Stannard (followed by Kate Bunyan) became Carnival UK and Princess Cruises' first woman medical director, apparently the first in any major international cruise company.

Sally Bell: Overseeing Maritime Health Standards

Sally Bell (b. 1958) is the granddaughter of someone born at sea, and she comes from a medical family, so her influences are clear. She qualified as a doctor at St Mary's Hospital Medical School, London, in 1982 and practised for six years in the NHS, including in emergency medicine. Then the sea called. By that time shipping lines had no problem accepting women doctors and from 1989 to 2001 she worked for P&O Cruises and Princess Cruises as a ship's doctor and senior doctor. She cruised the world on prestigious passenger vessels including the *Aurora*. Sometimes she was mistaken for a nurse – because she's a woman. Nurses and doctors now wear very similar uniforms, including pyjama-like scrubs for ease.

During her time on cruise ships, Dr Bell was twice seconded ashore as fleet medical officer. She started a new career in 2001, working as a clinical quality consultant with various shipping companies and insurers. In 2009, unusually, she did a master's degree in maritime medicine at the University of Tarragona, Spain. Specialist maritime medicine courses are rare and much precious information is gained on the job and from colleagues: ship's sick bays are mini-universities. Her new job at the MCA began in 2014.[2]

Dr Sally Bell is introduced to the Princess Royal at the naming ceremony for the *Aurora* in 2000. (Sally Bell)

So what *is* a ship's medic – a floating healer? Someone whose aim to secure the best possible health of everyone on board: crew, officers and, on cruise ships, the guests expecting to have an ideal holiday? And why is their work on ships so crucial?

Why medical care is crucial on ships

1. The ship's movement can cause injuries – or simply seasickness, for both passengers and crew.
2. Being in foreign ports means people pick up diseases to which they may have less resilience. They also get tummy bugs, cut their feet on coral, become embroiled in local fights, etc.
3. Health problems already present on land can intensify at sea. Being in confined shared spaces means epidemics can spread more readily.
4. Ships are enclosed spaces where the use of many chemicals such as cleaning fluids may be dangerous if not used sensibly. Also if refrigeration fails, ensuing cargo problems may affect health; for example, fermenting grain produces carbon dioxide.
5. On holiday voyages people tend to do things such as eat and drink to excess, get sunburned, and fail to exercise enough.[3]
6. A ship's medic will usually help distressed survivors of sea incidents or poorly crew on other ships.

Today the majority of maritime health workers are on cruise ships. Nurses and doctors, sporting scarlet insignia, have their own department in a complex that includes bedded areas and consulting areas. It's surgery and mini-hospital in one. Sick crew on cargo ships, by contrast, will just be treated by deck officers who've done some first-aid training (most of which is validated by Sally Bell's department at the MCA). They'll use *The Ship Captain's Medical Guide*,[4] which is a downloadable pdf file, not a vast battered tome. And their medical chests are no longer Stephen Maturin-style mahogany cases of fragile brown bottles, but orange Kevlar zip bags. Over in the Royal Navy just one ship functions as a Primary Casualty Receiving Ship in time of need, the Royal Fleet Auxiliary ship *Argus*.[5] Every naval ship has a leading hand or petty officer with medical training. Women doctors are rare, reflecting the RN gender imbalance of female and male officers (less than 10 per cent). However, there are more female than male nurses in the RN.

Women medical staff working on today's cruise ships carrying, say, 2,000 people, are part of a team comprising the senior doctor, doctor (nicknamed 'Baby Doc'), nurse practitioner, between two and six registered nurses, a paramedic (a role previously entitled sick berth attendant, orderly or doctor's steward), sometimes a dentist (especially on world cruises) and sometimes a physiotherapist (whom some shipping lines see as more part of the beauty team than the health-care team). The longer the trip, such as a world cruise, the greater the number of health-care staff because the greater the chances of health problems developing. In theory medics could all be women. In practice, on the thirty-two Carnival UK and Princess Cruises ships, 50–70 per cent of nurses and 40 per cent of paramedics are women. And an estimated 30 per cent of doctors are female, an increase since 2010. By the time Sally joined her first ship in the 1990s, being a woman doctor was not a problem. She's even worked in all-female teams.

What sort of people are ship's medics? Angela Devine (b. 1948), who was on P&O's *Canberra* in the 1982 Falklands Conflict, tells me that on passenger ships 'you have to be positive, confident and able to deal with your own feelings.' When Jane Yelland was recently selecting ship's nurses for Cunard and P&O she recruited those who above all had broad experience. Ideally they'd worked abroad and therefore were adaptable, as well as familiar with foreign drug names and terminology, and non-NHS nursing models – they deal with passengers from so many countries. They should be able to manage being away from home, survive life in the floating goldfish bowl that a ship environment entails, and take a joke. Jane also said that ship's medics need a can-do attitude: 'If a job needs doing, you do it … [accept that] it's all hands to the pump until the problem's solved.' Crucially they also need to be able to adjust to working seven days a week, as their foremothers did in the past.[6]

1750–1800: MEDICINE AT SEA: CAN WOMEN 'HELP'?

In temporary, wet, cramped and unsatisfactory sea-homes anyone helped who could. Rather than being wielders of the bone saw, the rare wives aboard helped treat illness and wounds. Little could be done for those with tropical fevers, dysentery and falls except feed, bandage, and wash them. Women on slave ships and convict ships assisted each other. And surgeons accepted their help as assistants, not least because high mortality rates (15–30 per cent was normal on slave ships) were unprofitable. Despite the increasing male professionalisation of health care, women practising complementary medicine (now sometimes called 'subaltern therapeutics' to make clear the power relations involved) were appreciated by sick British sailors overseas. Cubah Cornwallis (*c.* 1750–1848), a 'doctress' who ran a rest house-cum- boarding house, treated the 20-year-old Horatio Nelson for dysentery in Jamaica in 1780. The commander-in-chief of the naval forces on the island had recommended this 'kind-hearted negress', a former slave.[7] But full-time, paid seagoing 'doctresses' would have been unthinkable. It's certain that any woman wanting to work on a ship (or on land) as a surgeon would have had to be disguised as a man – though how she would have got past the Navy's physical inspection of new men, afforded any training, bought tools and survived so many physical situations where men would have noticed her body is another thing.[8]

In the King's Navy scores, if not hundreds, of nameless seagoing naval wives acted as volunteer assistants to surgeons. Part-time, intermittently recognised, they gave aid in the ambitious naval campaign against the French Republic when ship's surgeons were overwhelmed by bloody casualties. Most large warships had only one surgeon to every eighty sailors (smaller ships just had an assistant). So in the 1798 Battle of the Nile Sarah Bates, Ann Taylor, Elizabeth Moore and Mary French of HMS *Goliath* were typical of the many wives of petty officers allowed – indeed, required – to help the solo surgeon in what might be called A&E care.

As well as battle casualties, the wider problems of keeping the Navy fully staffed included scurvy and louse-born typhus. Like loblolly boys (surgeon's assistants, called after the thick porridge they served to invalids) wives were ad hoc unofficial paramedics who spoon-fed the weak, changed bedding, cleaned instruments such as saws and pestles, emptied chamber pots, held people down during surgery (as there were no anaesthetics apart from rum), and looked after any medical supplies. If allowed, they may also have brewed herbal tisanes and made poultices as they'd been taught to do by their mothers or wise women from their villages back home. Troopships may have been the healthiest ships afloat because they carried the wives of soldiers, who did the freelance laundry work that kept disease down.

Nelly and Christina: Mothers who Helped in Nelson's Navy, 1798

Nelly Giles (1770–1860) was on HMS *Bellerophon*, the worst-hit naval vessel of the Battle of the Nile. It sustained 201 casualties. Surgeon George Bellamy was said to have been 'so greatly in need of helpers that he sent a message to the Captain begging him to let some men come to his aid. The battle was at its height and the answer came back that not a man could be spared, but that if he could persuade a woman to come ... he was at liberty to do that. The appeal was sent to the handful of women, all together, panic stricken, in some cabin on the ship. At first none of them would come – then one woman dared, and all through those ghastly hours, she bravely stood by the hardworking surgeon, carrying out his orders as far as she could' under the swinging oil lamp in the cockpit.[9] This was Nelly Giles, the wife of a coxswain. It was only three days before she was to give birth (although some sources say six months).[10]

In that battle the *Majestic* was the next worst hit, with 193 casualties. Christina White, the mother of two young children who were aboard, helped the surgeon not only during the battle but for eleven weeks on the voyage home from Abukir Bay.[11] Usefully for the Admiralty, these 'incorporated wives' were not entitled to food and pay, so this nursing was free.

By contrast, women workers lower down the scale had long been *employed* to nurse naval men on hospital ships as well as in port hospitals and boarding houses. As early as 1696 women were working as laundresses and nurses on naval hospital ships, which were at sea as well as functioning at times as off-shore annexes. Historian Suzanne Stark found from Admiralty records that such women's value was controversial. Later Admiral George Byng claimed: 'they take up a great deal of room and are rather an inconvenience than otherwise.'[12] The information about them amounts to one tiny, much-repeated, story that they were wanton mutinous drunkards who helped sailors desert. So all the non-newsworthy healers' stories are lost to history. Usually sailors' widows, these 'nurses' or nurse-laundresses were awarded the job as a kind of pension, whether or not they had aptitude. Suzanne Stark found that in the early days it was recommended that nurses be over the age of 50, to avoid anyone on board being seduced by them (not vice versa).[13] Very few female nurses appear to have worked on hospital ships after the Seven Years War (1754–63).[14] But those who did so were paid at the same rate as ordinary seamen.[15]

1800–1852: ASSISTING HUMAN CARGOES IN ARRIVING HEALTHY

In the Napoleonic Wars (1803–15) women on ships continued to take the role of informal assistant. Kathleen Harland, the main expert on naval nurses, believes nursing at sea was 'performed almost solely by men' in those days.[16] In theory, there might have been up to 300 nurses and laundresses aboard the twenty-nine dedicated hospital ships,[17] if we assume that the old pattern of approximately five nurses and five laundresses per ship was still in operation. The Merchant Service had no hospital ships, of course, as it was not engaging in combat. But some carried a Navy-trained surgeon and had a rudimentary sick bay, in which women passengers might help during their voyage, tending both passengers and personnel.

How could a woman be a 'doctor' of some kind on any ships in the period between 1800 and 1850? The answer is really that she couldn't do it as a job, unless she was passing herself off as a man, as did Army surgeon Dr James Barry/ Margaret Ann Bulkley (1789–1865).[18] No women were allowed to train as surgeons at that time. Therefore any woman would have to both pose as a man and someone possessing qualifications she did not have (unless she'd been disguised during her training too, which at that time was barred to women). In addition, surgeons were *imposed* upon any merchant ships carrying a certain number of passengers – they had to withstand hostility and impose authority. It is not likely that any woman would be seen as tough enough to accomplish that.

However, women passengers could offer their services as nursing assistants on the hundreds of convict and emigrant ships. When plain cook Jane Taite, a 30-year-old convicted of burglary, was being transported on the *Emma Eugenia* to Hobart in April 1844, she was the 'chief hospital nurse'. Surgeon Wilson recorded that she was 'most attentive to Sophie Jacobs, by day and night, turning her in her bed, lifting her out of it, when necessary, giving her drinks, instantly removing the stools etc.'[19] A woman who could take notes – for example, as Jeanne Baret, the cross-dressed assistant-lover of de Bougainville's botanist, had recorded herbs' efficacy in the 1760s – not only contributed to the advancement of maritime medicine, but could add to the marketable skills she could offer on landing, as well as avoiding voyage tedium too. In other words, she could get off the ship culturally richer and of higher status.

On merchant ships, including whalers, a few hundred wives and their women servants, if they had them, did ad hoc health care at sea. Betsy Cadwaladyr, as the nanny of a sea-captain's family on the *Iris* from St Vincent, helped when the master's Creole wife was unexpectedly confined:

> I began to recollect that I had formerly seen a person in that state before. I also thought over what I had read in Dr Buchan's book, and became quite certain about the case. I gave her a Cup of green tea, which had wonderful effects, and at about two in the morning a fine boy was born – I being the sole attendant … this was my first experience in such matters.[20]

Betsy Cadwaladyr, Nursing Afloat

Betsy Cadwaladyr (c. 1789–1860) was the daughter of a Methodist preacher. Her chance to sail came about when she was working in a grand house as a laundress. A midwife she knew 'who had often heard me say I should like to go abroad, came and told me of a sudden opportunity'. Betsy began roving the Far East, the Antipodes, and the East Indies as a nanny to wealthy people who travelled, including 'Captain S'. Her assets included her toughness and her adaptability. Weathering earthquakes, rattlesnakes, and opium dens, dodging men so keen to marry her that they kidnapped her, and teasing immigration officials that she was the captain, Betsy chose her own high-principled path. She took up nursing at Guy's Hospital and for private patients. Then, reading a *Times* report of Crimean soldiers' plight, in 1854 she volunteered to go 'to see what was going on, and to take care of the wounded'. A year before the war ended she came home to her sister, with dysentery and cholera. She wrote her autobiography, then died of an internal abscess in 1860. Although buried in a pauper's grave, she's now celebrated: the Betsi Cadwaladr University Health Board in North Wales is named after her.[21]

By contrast Charles Dickens's rather demonising 1843 fictional character, Sairey Gamp, brought about the public 'Gampisation'[22] of home nurses as drunken, lying

Elizabeth Davies/Betsi Cadwaladyr: freelance nursing at sea and in the Crimean War. Engraving from an 1857 photograph. (National Library of Wales, NLW MS 12353D)

and callous sluts. Mrs Gamp was part of the third category of nurses identified by Kathleen Harland: nuns, over-feminised ladies (too spiritually minded to be of use) and rough-and-ready types. Shipping companies probably wouldn't have even considered employing nurses on ships, given these limited options. But rich passengers hired private 'nurses' and many passengers took their own medicine chests, including castor oil, laudanum, raspberry vinegar and mustard poultices.[23]

1853–1902: WOMEN BREAK THROUGH INTO THE PROFESSIONS

In the Crimean War of 1853–56, two key figures in nursing history came to prominence: nursing pioneer Florence Nightingale (1820–1910)[24] and Jamaican sutler and healer Mary Seacole (1805–81), who was a similar figure to Cubah Cornwallis.[25] Public concern about poor health care in the war led to the later professionalisation of the nursing profession and the demise of the Sairey Gamp caricature. It paralleled the advent of women doctors, led by Elizabeth Garrett Anderson (1836–1917) in 1873, who later helped found Schools of Medicine for Women in the 1880s. Changes in civilian nursing in the 1860s and 1870s had a ripple effect through military, then naval, nursing. In the 1880s both services conceded that female nurses could be useful in war – not just because of a shortage of male 'nurses' but because women's presence 'uncommonly' boosted men's morale. The Admiralty envisaged that female nurses would only 'exceptionally' work on naval hospital ships.[26] Such exceptions meant three pioneering sisters in the Naval Nursing Service (founded 1884) sailed on the first modern naval hospital ship, the *Malacca*, in the 1897–98 punitive invasion of Benin. The US Navy's decision to form the Navy Nurse Corps in 1908 must have been affected by this climate and by nurses' overseas role in the Spanish–American War of 1898. Australia was organising a similar initiative.

Hundreds of professional nurses got the chance to nurse at sea in the Second Boer War (1899–1902) on troop transports and the eleven hard-pressed hospital ships. Sister 'Mack All' explained the perennial problems of nursing at sea – cramped spaces and motion:

> It was not always easy work either, the men in the lower bunks were troublesome enough if one had a long back and was obliged to duck under the berth above to attend the patient. But it was still more awkward to stand on the lower berth, hold on with one hand to the one above, and make the patient comfortable while the ship rolled and tumbled. One felt that if one had a little spare time one could be very seasick.[27]

In 1901–02 Queen Alexandra's Royal Naval Nursing Service (QARNNS) and Queen Alexandra's Imperial Military Nursing Service (QAIMNS) began. Now women seen as terrifying tartars were in charge of flocks of women. Tellingly, the Royal Army Medical Corps initials were jokingly said to also stand for 'Run Away, Matron's Coming'. These professional single women were expected to work on ships in future wars, with all the discipline of officers, somewhat mitigated by white billowing headgear and the new idea that all nurses were angels.

Commercial shipping companies, who were competing for new custom, must have realised that civilian nurses could act as useful professional 'assistants' to ship's surgeons, if customer demand warranted the expense. New thinking about public health and the 1854 Merchant Shipping Act and the 1855 Passenger Act made free health care compulsory on most large passenger vessels.[28] With the growth in luxury consumption hospitals were being referred to as palaces of pain. New palace-hotels like The Savoy, which opened in 1889, grew to satisfy (and manufacture) elite needs for fine service. Savoy-style grand liners followed suit. The demand was there for a charming style of looking-after, as was the supply of middle-class educated nurses who could offer that service. Shipping lines advertised 'surgeon carried' and 'stewardess carried'. However, the new female doctors were not employed, perhaps as it would be thought unseemly for a *lady* doctor to be the only surgeon on board. Would the passengers trust her? Was she strong and brave enough for all the emergencies that arise in remote medicine? Wouldn't it be a scandal if she treated male crew's sexually transmitted diseases?[29] Class status as well as gendered stereotypes culturally debarred Dr Garret Anderson's scores of skilled daughters from becoming ships' surgeons.

1903–1950: NURSES WELCOME, BUT 'HYBRIDS' BETTER

At the beginning of the new century, shipping companies increasingly employed stewardesses who had been nurses, but only 'let them *help*' with nursing duties when the need arose. From 1903 to 1911 doctors and sisters argued in nursing and medical journals about these hybrid nurse-stewardesses. Some ship's surgeons thought nurses weren't necessary. Other doctors thought proper nurses were very necessary, but opposed 'half measures' – relying on busy women to do an unpaid favour on top of tending cabins.[30] Sister Kate Penn, a 1903 campaigner for the provision of trained nurses on liners, pointed out that shipping lines wouldn't combine the positions of steward and doctors. So 'Why, therefore, should trained nurses be expected to act a stewardess? Presumably because always women's work must be done on the cheap.'[31]

'X.Y.Z.', two gloriously stroppy nurse 'hybrids' on a big mail steamer, told the 1904 *British Medical Journal* about the ill-defined situation that was affronting perhaps a few score of nurses. 'Nurses should be taken as such, given the rating of a saloon officer, and badged as officers, with the status of a first class passenger, and put in the medical department. On such a footing alone will the movement be successful.'[32] This was the start of pressure to give nurses officer status on ships (doctors already had it, but it was only status, not actual rank), and the start of medical departments on ships (stewardesses, by contrast, were controlled by the purser's department).

If there was such opposition to nurses, how much more difficult was it for the 212 women doctors in England and Wales (who were less than 1 per cent of the 23,486 doctors in 1901)?[33]

Elizabeth Ross became the very first woman ship's doctor in 1913. She sailed for Yokohama and Hong Kong, in the small Glen Line *Glenlogan*. Her breakthrough was possible for three reasons. The ship 'taking emigrants to Australia was waiting at the Tail of the Bank, [Upper Clyde] but the Board of Trade official couldn't allow the ship to sail because there was no surgeon aboard'.[34] Someone had to be found, pronto. Dr Ross was available and known. Plus she was well travelled, mature and highly competent. And anyway shipping companies often took on new, or less-than-ideal medical practitioners, so this *skilled* practitioner was a definite improvement at a time when ship's doctors were stereotyped as alcoholic dunderheads who'd kill anyone unlucky enough to come under their scalpel.

Dr Ross, the First Female Ship's Surgeon

Elizabeth Ness MacBean Ross (1878–1915), later acclaimed as 'the Scottish saint of Serbia', was born in Tain, near Inverness and trained at Glasgow University. After qualifying in 1901 she lived in Persia (now Iran) assisting a prestigious Armenian physician, 'had many thrilling adventures', and become 'Chieftainness' of the powerful Bakhtiari hill tribe. In January 1913 she sailed from Madras to London on the *Nigaristan*. On this brand new Strick Line cargo ship, with space for twenty passengers, she had 'performed duties as ship's doctor', although it's not clear whether officially employed or just gaining a free passage. She joined the *Glenlogan* as ship's doctor for just one voyage. In the First World War she worked heroically at the First Military Reserve Hospital at Kragujevatz, Servia (now Serbia), but died after putting in just three weeks there on typhus wards. Today Dr Ross is still acclaimed in Serbia as a brave healer.[35]

Dr Elizabeth MacBean Ross tends a patient on the *Nigaristan* in 1913. (Ross family/Tain Museum)

In its journal, the National Sailors' and Firemen's Union picked up on the implications of Dr Ross's breakthrough:

> Whether this lady doctor's experiment will encourage others to follow her example may perhaps be doubted; more particularly in long-distance ships of the class chosen in this instance. The case is interesting, however, as showing that under the Merchant Shipping Act the male doctor has by no means an exclusive right to practice on board.[36]

They were right. It was another forty years before Elizabeth Ross had a successor, even though the huge medical needs of the First World War might have been expected to usher in women doctors on hospital ships. However, that war saw a huge and impressive initiative by scores of highly competent women doctors, such as Elsie Inglis and Alice Hutchinson of the Scottish Women's Hospital units, who sailed overseas though didn't practice on board. Dr Dorothy Hare (1876–1967), who became the WRNS medical director in 1918, had previously sailed to Malta with the RAMC and worked there on land in 1916, though not at sea.[37] Certainly their US sisters in 1918 travelled to Europe to help, including Doctors Cecile Greill and Frances Haines.

Nursing in the grand converted lounge of the luxury liner, then First World War hospital ship, *Aquitania*. (Eve Tar Collection)

At its peak in the First World War, eighty-five Queen Alexandra's Royal Naval Nursing Service nursing sisters were on thirteen hospital ships, about a third of the QARNNS total force.[38] They mixed, as in the Boer War, with civilian and military sisters and with VADs from many parts of the English-speaking world, including 10,000 US nurses who'd crossed the Atlantic. As many as 2,000 women may have nursed on Britain's seventy-seven hospital ships.[39] Mainly converted liners, they were medics' residential workplaces for weeks on end. Larger numbers sailed than ever before and they 'have more exciting times than the majority of nurses who are doing war work,' an anonymous Gallipoli hospital ship nurse exulted.[40] They worked in danger zones. Because hospital ship nurses were at risk of enemy action, the Admiralty in 1917 decided sisters would be gradually replaced by male sick-berth orderlies at sea.[41] Presumably their lordships feared public outcry if many 'angels' were on ships attacked by the enemy.[42] In fact Army sister Katy Beaufoy (1868–1918), matron of the *Glenart Castle*, was one of the few who lost her life. New Zealand nurses sustained the biggest losses, when the *Marquette* sank.[43]

First World War nurses taking part in lifeboat drill on hospital ship. (Wellcome Library, L0049038)

Former nursing sister Pat Grossart-Reid, a 'hybrid' nurse-stewardess, takes time off, c. 1930 on her Shaw Savill ship to the Antipodes. (Norah Rivers)

In the interwar period nurses on big passenger ships won their rights: they were full-time and officers, no longer hybrids. In the late 1920s stewardess Jessie Kenney noted that:

> the Sister as she is called … has officer's privileges, and on board a large liner these are many. She has a cabin to herself, not by luck but by right, and has the attendance of a steward. She has early morning tea brought to her, her cabin cleaned, dines in the salon from a First Class menu, and can join in all the ship's recreations. She generally begins work after breakfast and has finished by dinner time. She must not accept tips but she can accept presents.[44]

By this point ship's nurse was being seen as an enviable job.

Four years later when the Second World War began it offered hardly any informal opportunities for doughty independent women doctors and nurses to sail off and start up auxiliary hospitals in wild locations, as in the First World War. Early in 1939 the Admiralty decided that sisters should not be afloat on the RN's hospital ships because it would mean that what was politely called 'living spaces and sanitary annexes in these ships' (sex-segregated cabins and bathrooms) didn't have to be fitted. But shortly before war's outbreak the policy was ditched: 'female nursing staffs must be carried in the interests of patients.' Sisters improved male morale, not least because men felt obliged to appear courageous when females were around, so as not to show themselves up. Also men thought that if there was a woman (meaning member of that species usually kept far from danger) there then maybe the situation wasn't so bad.[45]

In this war personnel were far more under the control of bureaucratic regimes in each of the armed forces, not least on the sixty-odd hospital ships. Depending on the hospital ship's size, usually four to eight (but in some cases up to twenty) sisters and female nurses from the Army and RN and its reserves were aboard. Between 960 and 4,800 served over all.[46] Other women medics were on troopships going to postings overseas, where women worked closer to the front line than ever before. Such women even eventually began wearing khaki slacks for modesty (particularly when stepping over male patients lying on deck) and to enable fast action and safety. Of the 1,341 naval sisters, Kate Gribble on the *Aguila* was the only one who died *at sea* through enemy action.

Images of be-trousered women medics breaking through into war work *sounds* like progress. But that belies the truth once again: women were only being allowed in briefly and in certain safer places. Debates about how close they should be to danger waged on. Women were accepted because there weren't enough men and because nursing was seen as women's work. However, war did offer some women exceptional windows of opportunity. At least one women doctor was on a merchant ship as its MO (medical officer): Dr Nancy Miller.

Wartime Doctor at Sea: Nancy Miller

Dr A. Nancy Miller (c. 1915–88) graduated from Glasgow University in 1938. By 1941 she was MO on the *Britannia*, an armed troopship sailing to Karachi via Cape Town in convoy. It seems that a woman doctor was given such a post because she was known of and needed. As so often in shipping, somebody 'spoke for her'; and the requirement for a surgeon could not be denied. She would tend to the twelve outbound servicewomen on board (although usually a sister was seen as sufficing) as well as male patients. Dr Miller's father, Dr Thomas Miller, was also working for the same line. Her Glasgow-based employers, Anchor Line, must have assumed she could be trusted as 'almost family'.

In 1941 the German raider *Thor* fatally shelled *Britannia*, east of Freetown.[47] During the shelling 'Doctor Miller displayed calmness and bravery when caring for the wounded and dying. She continued her good work after the company had taken to the [life] boats … it was due to her bravery, skill and attention that many lives was saved.'[48] After five and half days at sea the lifeboat carrying Dr Miller was picked up by a passing small Spanish cargo steamer, *Bachi*. Serendipity struck. The *Bachi* was apprehended by the *Cilicia*, the very ship on which Nancy's father was sailing. Via his ship's wireless he'd heard about the attack on the *Britannia*. After radio contact was lost, Dr Thomas Miller had had to resign himself to his daughter's death. When the boarding party brought *Britannia* survivors on board it's said that 'Dr Miller was the first up the ladder, and able to embrace her relieved father.'[49]

She became the only British civilian seafaring woman doctor in any war to win the Lloyd's Medal and an MBE too. In 1943 Dr Miller married (becoming Dr Ambler), had two sons and worked in general practice and community medicine in the Bradford area. She was active in the Yorkshire Association of Medical Women, one of the support networks that helped women doctors where the British Medical Association had not.[50]

When war ended QARNNS and QAIMNS continued, mainly working on land. From 1949 Wrens could become sick berth attendants in the new Medical Branch of the WRNS. In the Korean War (1950–53) Ruth Stone and Barbara Nockolds were among the four QARNNS sisters and six naval VADs who served on the hospital ship *Maine*.[51] Like their Second World War counterparts, nurses' verdict was that 'Nursing on a hospital ship is exciting but difficult because it's a man's world.' Tact, sense and humour were essential. When I met Ruth Stone over forty years later she confirmed that diplomacy was crucial. Most said it was among the most rewarding and stimulating experiences of their lives.[52]

1950–TODAY: SHIP'S MEDICS AS MASS-MEDIA STARS

In this half-century women medics' presence on passenger ships became something like the situation today. It was absolutely axiomatic that a doctor needed a (female) nurse as an assistant on ships carrying many passengers. And women doctors increasingly had a greater presence in the world. In 1947 all UK medical schools finally became co-educational. Possibly the role of women medics in two world wars had now made sceptics open-minded enough to let more 'lady docs' up their gangways. In 1950 Wynne O'Mara (1925–2010) was told she was the first woman doctor in the Merchant Service and in Blue Funnel lines. According to *Gangway for the Lady Surgeon*, Wynne's novelised memoir, the Blue Funnel medical superintendent said it wasn't normally done because it was an 'awkward situation. Crew prejudiced against them. A woman treating a man for all sorts of things … one woman isolated for months with a hundred men. Could be dangerous.'[53] Wynne seemingly gained her opportunity to sail because a Blue Funnel line director's wife who was strongly committed to equal opportunities persuaded her husband to accept Wynne for the cargo ship *Perseus* bound for the Far East.

Dr Wynne O'Mara, then Proudlock, enjoys her time on land, c. 1958. (Eve Tar Collection)

Ship's surgeons had been the subject of fascinating books before, such as Tobias Smollet's *Roderick Random* (1748); Richard Gordon's *Doctor at Sea* (1953); and Patrick O'Brian's fictional physician Stephen Maturin. But Wynne wrote the first that showed what it was like for a woman. *Gangway for the Lady Surgeon* (1958) was translated into French and Dutch. Although she portrayed the job as fun, she usefully demonstrated that women could indeed become doctors at sea.

Wynne must have directly paved the way for other Blue Funnel Line women doctors, such as Joyce Watkin (1924–2015) who was employed on a Blue Funnel pilgrim vessel talking Muslims from Singapore to Jeddah, the port for Mecca. Dr Watkin was employed precisely because 'lady docs' were culturally acceptable to women passengers, many of whom were heavily pregnant because it was lucky to have a baby en route to Hajj.[54] And the advent of educational cruises for school students brought increased opportunities for other women ship's doctors in the 1950s, because of the idea that women medics should look after children.

In 1951 the sea transport industry in England and Wales had one woman doctor and fifty-seven male doctors, according to the census. That one was probably Joyce. Maritime nurses numbered twenty-four, by contrast to just five men.[55] Clinical work afloat appeared such a desirable job that some deliberately acquired midwifery skills as they waited to become the acceptable age, 27 (or 25 in some companies). Their work not only involved travel but sometimes dramatic feats such as escorting patients to foreign shores, even by seaplane or helicopter, for emergency treatment. (The Australian *Flying Doctor* series on BBC radio at that time popularised the idea of such derring-do health care.) And maybe some nurses (although I haven't met any) fancied the version of the life being peddled in nurse–at–sea romances.

Publishers Mills & Boon began the new genre with *Ship's Nurse* by Alex Stuart in 1954. It continued until the 1980s, increasingly showing a focus on career rather than on simply being swept into the arms of hunky captains or surgeons. Behind the romance was the reality: there were too many worryingly ill elderly passengers far from land. And over-amorous Greek and Italian officers who fetishised nurses' uniforms were a menace.

Over in the Royal Navy no women were routinely health-care staff at sea, not least because most ships were combat-ready and therefore deemed unsuited to women. In 1959 increasing naval staffing needs brought the founding of the QARNNS Naval Nursing Auxiliary. This meant that the service was no longer officer-only but two-tier. From 1960 ratings, including the few remaining Naval VADs left, could join the new Naval Nurse section of QARNNS and become Naval Nurse ratings. Three years later these QARNNS began training for both state-registered and state-enrolled nurse qualifications; they might be deployed at sea in emergencies. By that point the RN was starting to take on women MOs. The first commissioned surgeon is thought to be a Dr Barltrop, or Colette Green in 1963. Dr Green was certainly an early pioneer following a ten-year gap. Pamela Young, who began training at Haslar in 1966, is seemingly the second.[56]

Sister Nicci Pugh has written up the story of the forty-one naval nurses who staffed the *Uganda* hospital ship in the 1982 Falklands Conflict. The RN blocked women doctors from sailing but couldn't prevent the usual MN nurses and one woman MN doctor sailing on their cruise ships, which became troop carriers. *Canberra's* young assistant surgeon Dr Susie West carried on into possible war because: 'It seemed the obvious thing to me.' Initially Dr West was told: 'It's going to be a military operation and they won't have any women. I was absolutely outraged … I was a doctor and it didn't matter what sex I was.'[57] From the 1980s equipment on the biggest cruise ships improved and the number of women doctors increased.

In the Royal Navy medical environment, women and men were integrating. Increasingly they'd been training together. Then in 1982 the ranking system changed as a preparation for the introduction of male officers who became in effect 'sisters', members of QARNNS, in 1983. The matron-in-chief gained the rank of commodore. And in 1995 QARNNS officers began to use RN rank titles and insignia. Women naval sisters and ratings served in the hospital ship *Argus* in the Gulf War, August 1990–February 1991, and in the Second Gulf War of 2003–11.[58] Currently *c.* 300-strong, the branch includes doctors, medical assistants, medical service officers (formerly called ward masters) and medical technicians. These women and men sail on regular naval ships, not just the *Argus*. Having more women sailors on board didn't mean more women health-care staff were allocated to work with them, as in the WRNS. Female and male medics were equal and trained together, including on gynaecological problems.

Finally, QARNNS became part of the Royal Navy in April 2000. It's a very equal situation, and one where Medical Assistant Kate Nesbitt, who in 2009 became the first woman in the RN to earn a Military Cross, is spoken of with great pride. As the Navy's nursing service, QARNNS works alongside the Royal Navy Medical Branch, but is separate.

Relatedly, in the Royal Fleet Auxiliary women were accepted as seagoing doctors in the 1990s. In 1991 Victoria McMaster became the first doctor in the RFA (and its first woman officer). Her opportunity came about because the job advert omitted to stipulate that post-holders should be male. The women applicants' calibre was so high that the RFA put into action the equal opportunities principles it was just considering.[59]

Today on modern freight ships and tankers without passengers there is no doctor, but strong long-distance support and several officers with some clinical training.

The future looks reasonably bright for women medics in both navies and the RFA, although the RN is being cut back repeatedly. Cruise shipping is still growing and women are still being seen as suited to health-care work. Gender is now largely irrelevant in the selection of doctors, who all work with increasingly advanced technology and medications, as well as telecommunications. With so many female pioneers behind them, women seagoing health-care workers are progressing more straightforwardly then their sisters battling to become chief engineers and head chefs at sea.

7

FROM CONVICT MATRON TO CRUISE DIRECTOR: SUPPORTING THE PASSENGERS

When Judie Abbott recently gave talks to Women's Institutes on 'The Life of a Lady Cruise Director' she explained that her job was not really like the stars of the television series *The Love Boat*. Rather, she said, a cruise director is someone who has to think: 'I'm going to make my passengers' cruise wonderful, from dawn to dusk to dawn again.' And she certainly tried to do so.

On both sides of the Atlantic, the 1977 TV series *The Love Boat*, based on cruise director Jeraldine Saunders' book, led millions to see cruise directing as the most fun job in the world.

Judie: Cruise Director

Judie Abbott (1932–2014) had just retired as the cruise director on Silversea Cruises when we spoke in 2013. Then 72, she told me she was probably the longest-serving women's officer in the Merchant Navy. That also made her the 'merchant seaman' who'd worked in glitter and feathers longer than any other British seafarer (although in the daytime she always wore suits).

Judie's sea career began in 1964 when she was a singer, headhunted by Chandris Lines. Rather than be their leading lady, after a few years of singing on ships she thought: 'I'm going to be a cruise director.' This was highly unusual because few women at that time were masters of ceremonies or even TV presenters, just Valerie Singleton on *Blue Peter* from 1962 and Cathy McGowan on *Ready Steady Go* in 1964. Judie was encouraged by John Butt, the cruise director she assisted on the new QE2. She moved on up the ranks and then on to other companies. 'I had to work hard; you're in a man's world. I did find you had to work twice as hard to be seen as half as good.' She became deeply respected; people turned to her for advice. And she still loved the role just months before her death in 2014: 'I've been very fortunate. I found out, early on, what I wanted to do in life. And I did it.'

A cruise director is one of the four people who attend the captain's executive meeting each day, along with the hotel director, captain and chief engineer. In theory all four could be women, as nearly happened on the *Pacific Pearl* in 2011, where Zoltina J. Medwick-Daley was the cruise director (after working her way up from dancer, singer, magician, youth director and photographer).[1] People in Judie's position manage all the entertainment on a cruise. This not only involves programming all the acts but handling all the performers and support staff, such as the stage manager and stage electrician.

Cruise directors manage not only the ship's dedicated entertainment spaces (which might include several theatres), but all the social activities, including prize-giving for sports events. They also manage all the international social hostesses. As masters of ceremonies (MCs) they have to have strong 'microphone' skills. Judie believes women can be particularly good at cruise directing because 'they excel at people work' and really can multi-task. It helps to be mature too. 'You've got to really like people – because they can be so difficult.' It's more like a vocation than a job.[2] These particular staff members don't just proceed along company-approved lines doing the right thing *to* that item of cargo, the passenger. They really do genuinely care for their passengers – and they have fun along *with* them.

This chapter explores what certain women have done for passengers' hearts and minds, rather than bodies. In that complicated organisation – the shipful of displaced strangers with under-informed expectations – the ship's officers have to preserve order in acceptable ways. Necessarily iron fists are usually gloved in something that looks like velvet. Maritime safeguarding of women passengers is a peculiar spectrum, with frivolity at one end and surveillance at the other.

Women's seagoing roles in this sphere have progressed in five steps: from convict matrons, via emigrant conductresses, social hostesses, social directresses, to the top: entertainment directors (called cruise directors on some ships). Once a woman doing such work had to behave like a warder, albeit a kind and altruistic one, doing chastity patrols and regulating 'her girls', and her status among crew was problematic. Now she is, effectively, a theatre impresario, ensuring that every guest has such a good time that that they come back again to ships, which some see as upmarket holiday camps.

In this transition the convict matron's, emigrant matron's, and then conductress' role became one of increasing authority. A *woman* in a powerful shipboard position was a new phenomenon. So the complex settling-in process took at least half a century. But it set an important precedent: women could become officer-like figures on ships and then eventually real officers, with four gold stripes (the maximum) like Judie.

Oddly, Elizabeth Fry, the woman whose face until recently appeared on £5 notes,[3] was largely responsible for establishing women who were sort of ship's officers nearly two centuries ago. But how did the floating police wardress-type role die out, while the pleasure-maker became increasingly important?

1750–1800: DO-IT-YOURSELF ENTERTAINMENT – AND NO PROTECTION

Looked at in economic terms, passengers are simply items on a production line, processed by the women described in this chapter. Broadly three sorts of human freight were sailing in this period: people travelling with some choice (for example, early imperial administrators, migrants and troops); slaves; and transported felons. For all of them, though to varying degrees, the *quality* of voyages was poor and the outcome uncertain; the aim was just to reach your destination alive.

Cultural differences, including class and gender, meant tensions could easily arise, especially if there were no helpful mediators. And a supportive friend on board was a boon in managing the complex shipboard relations. In the early 1790s passenger Eliza Fay wrote in a letter home that at meals in the cuddy (elite passenger cabin),

> the gentlemen were too fond of the bottle to pay us [women] the least attention. After tea we never asked to cut in at cards … Captain Lewis swore so dreadfully … and became so rude and boisterous, that Mrs Tottingham [Eliza's shipmate] finally

withdrew entirely from the table and never left her cabin for thirteen weeks … I had no one [like Colonel Tottingham] to send me food etc and was therefore forced to venture up among them or risk starvation below.

Captain Lewis, who was cross at being beaten at piquet, admitted to her 'I cannot abide *ladies.*' Possibly he was anyway of the All Passengers Are Pests school. Her purser, Monsieur Pierot, by contrast, was 'a lively well-informed little Frenchman … the soul of the party … he sings an excellent song and has as many tricks as a monkey.'[4] Clearly on-board entertainment was needed but not officially provided. Social relations could be tricky. Eliza's story shows women, as invitees, had it harder than men (who often had the position of inviters, even if they too were passengers). And solo women had it harder still, especially without someone to liaise with the ship's authorities.

If ships' officers' wives were sailing they sometimes acted as unpaid hosts and mediators during what could be a very prolonged (and uncomfortable) 'house party'. On land, prominent early English society hostesses such as Hester Thrale (1741–1821) had proved themselves adept at conducting *conversaziones.* Anyone on ship with similar people-management skills was welcome, and this role overlapped with the oversight of others' welfare by older married women passengers (significantly, married women were called 'matrons' in that period). They exerted an informal guardianship over younger women feeling lonely or scared. Warning off dangerous sweet-talkers or attempting to control too much could be a hazard: it meant such self-appointed chaperones could be seen as nosy-pokes and spoilsports. Looking after others' welfare was a subtle art.

By contrast, in the 'odious trade' of slavery, powerful friends to protect the perhaps 4–5 million African women being transported across the Atlantic in hell ships were sorely needed, and rare.[5] On some of the four-to-six week voyages 'the common sailors are allowed to have intercourse with such of the black women whose consent they can procure … The officers … sometimes are guilty of such excesses as disgrace human nature,' said a ship's surgeon who became an abolitionist.[6] The situation varied with individual captains but women could be double victims, of both racial and gendered abuse. Occasionally, brave surgeons or interpreters might venture to mediate on women's behalf. Some of the kidnapped African women, such as the 'Amazonian Boatswain Bess' on the *Hudibras* in 1787, were appointed by the captain to keep order. But also natural leaders emerged, who organised solidarity that helped enslaved people survive, including group story-telling. At least one irritated captain had singing women flogged.[7] The most famous case was pictured by Isaac Cruikshank and used by William Wilberforce in the cause of abolition. It marshalled the idea of young enslaved women as in extra need of protection – as they were. Captain Kimber of the *Recovery* was tried but acquitted in 1792 for whipping a 15-year-old African girl captive who refused to exercise. No one intervened. She died.

A slave being made to 'dance': Isaac Cruikshank's image of Captain Kimber's alleged cruelty. (Library of Congress)

Felons being transported to penal settlements also had no formal mediator other than the (male) surgeon, who didn't necessarily have much authority to stop mistreatment. Between 1718 and 1775 about 3,000 women convicts were shipped out to what was to become Australia and Tasmania, as well as thousands of wives of felons. In 1790 John Nicol, an apparently tender-hearted steward, wrote that every man in the crew on the Port Jackson-bound *Lady Juliana*, the first convict ship primarily for women,[8] 'took a wife' from the 226 women on board. He describes a kind of sexual mayhem. John protected the 'modest reserved' Sarah Whitelam from other crew.[9] But such protection was a pot-luck matter and problem-laden for the protectees. The problem was that something needed to be done to stop the sexual abuse of women felons on voyages where debauchery and exploitation were rife.

1800–1850: A PREFECT FOR THE CONVICT INMATES

Quaker reformer Elizabeth Gurney Fry (1780–1845), who became one of the few women featured on British banknotes, proposed an answer. And unintentionally her early efforts to protect women convicts *en voyage* led to the first women

143

being established as ships' officers. In 1817 Mrs Fry began the Association for the Improvement of the Female Prisoners in Newgate in 1817. It called for women warders, matrons, to regulate women convicts in jail.[10] When the move proved effective the Association's Convict Ship Sub-Committee, led by Elizabeth Pryer, extended their scheme to establishing matrons on prison hulks (floating depots) and on vessels taking felons to the new penal colonies overseas.

Two levels of matron were created, although often the records don't spell out the distinction that I am going to make here for clarity: supervisory matrons and sub-matrons. They were the counterparts of the male constables and head constables/superintendents.[11] The sub-matrons or assistant matrons were selected from the convicts being transported; they acted as prefects but their authority was flimsy. Sub-matrons, like constables, weren't paid but were awarded a few privileges such as extra food and a good reference from the surgeon, who acted as their line manager. In 1828 William Conborough Watt, the surgeon superintendent on the *Edward* to New South Wales, seemingly had twenty sub-matrons, each of whom was 'responsible for the correct demeanour and cleanliness of the … [women's] persons and drawing all their rations' and 'also to give me information from time to time of irregularities … or any circumstances which might in the most remote degree endanger the quiet of the prison.' In other words, they had to be snitches, two-faced allies of the inmates.[12]

Policy makers worried about whether such amateur temporary matrons could really deliver the human cargo in the required virginal, meek and literate state. Seemingly it wasn't always possible. So in 1834 the first supervisory matron was sent out on a female convict ship. Elizabeth Pryer told a House of Lords Select Committee on Gaols and Houses of Correction the following year that it was desirable that 'a Lady of competent Talent and Religious Views' should go with *every* convict ship, as a paid employee (of a charity or receiving country). A supervisory matron played a kind of headmistress role. She had to impose order and propriety, over many months and – at sea – in a small wooden-sided hamlet that resisted outsiders, especially elderly spoilsports such as herself. It was a balancing act. She was the convicts' advocate and trainer yet also a kind of wardress and spy, and interloper in the merchant ship's staff team.[13] So to get that opportunity you'd need to be a lady (meaning what today might be called middle-class), Christian, over 40, single and rather tough.

Convict transportation declined,[14] but migration grew. The 'right sort' of respectable woman could get work as a supervisory matron on ships carrying emigrants, privately funded free settlers or visitors overseas. In a way matrons did for the lowly what some captains' wives were doing unpaid: acting as hosts or 'mothers' for the middle-class passengers. The best US example is Alice Howland Delano, a captain's wife, whose story Joan Druett, the expert on seagoing wives, shares.

Alice: Captain's Wife and Ship's Hostess

Alice Howland Delano (1806–34) was the daughter and granddaughter of shipowners. At 19 she married Captain Joseph Delano and for her honeymoon sailed on his Black Ball clipper *Columbia* in 1827 from New York to London and back. She said of her sixteen torpid guests, 'I know not a more idle set ... Half the time is passed in lolling on the sofa, reading a little, looking at the chart, playing cards, &c.'

Alice's hospitality duties included companionable 'promenading with the ladies, solicitously tending to the weak-stomached and the poorly that were travelling alone, tactfully evading the amorous attention of Mr Shettler'. This hostess was seemingly on duty at nine for breakfast, at noon for tiffin, at four for a four-course dinner and at ten for supper. If she was lucky some of her charges occupied themselves, cross-stitching and writing journals.[15]

Twenty years on from Mrs Fry's moves to 'civilise' convict ships, women campaigners on land began pushing for more and better shipboard matrons, and a climate of respect for them. Begun in 1849, the British Ladies' Female Emigration Society (which, tellingly, was also known as the British Matron Society) and later other well-intentioned, somewhat feminist organisations, tried to ensure voyages were safe and productive, especially for young working-class women going out to be domestic servants.[16] Supervisory matrons were the committees' on-board hands, the imperfectible extensions of that elite new category, lady emigrators who stayed in London recruiting matrons and imposing privileged values upon the thousands of shifting women economic migrants.[17]

1850–1918: HYPER-MOBILE MISSIONARIES DOING 'HOPELESS WORK'

Caroline Chisholm, the key woman campaigning for the rights of emigrants, and especially of wives and mothers, had sailed herself. She is almost certainly the writer of a detailed job specification for her seagoing supervisory matrons. The 1850 *Hints to Matrons* was one of the Society for the Promotion of Christian Knowledge's very revealing Emigrant Tract series of tiny handbooks. It makes clear the mission-like nature of supervisory matrons' jobs – at a time when mission work in slums and in the empire's 'heathen' reaches was anyway developing fast. But it recognised a matron's difficulty as the lone female authority figure: 'from her superiors [aboard], from whom she would naturally expect help, she might receive nothing but opposition ... need I say how more than cautious the matron

Matron (second left) supervising her emigrant charges. From 'Sketches Aboard an Immigrant Ship' by Samuel Calvert, engraved by Ebenezer and David Syme, 1875. (State Library of Victoria, IAN24/03/75/40)

should be in her own conduct; neither saying nor doing anything that could lessen her influence!'[18]

These should-be paragons did daily tasks very similar to those of convict matrons, but less coercively. For example, the emigrants' supervisory matron shouldn't quite *make* the hundred-odd 'potential brides' get up. But she could '*encourage* early rising'. Matron saw the women to bed at night, but did not *lock* them in. Rather than herself teaching she should '*induce* them to form classes for *mutual* improvement' (author's italics). Above all she should be a mix of Canute and Sisyphus, keeping women sexually segregated from men.[19] Certainly the emigration commissioners in 1857 recorded: 'It is rather a matter of surprise that so many should have succeeded, than that a few should have failed.' Of the forty-three reports on matrons to New Zealand, thirty-nine were said to be satisfactory.[20]

Subsequent decades in emigrant shipping brought many varying arrangements about the shipboard supervision. By the 1880s some matrons were allowed to sleep in their own cabin instead of in canvas cubicles within their charges' dormitory. They ate in first class. Some earned bonuses based on the number in their party, whether it was a repeat trip (meaning they had accrued valuable expertise), and whether their group was especially well behaved. Mary Monk was one of the sixteen permanent matrons on New Zealand-bound ships.

Mary, a Repeat Matron

Mary Monk (1839–1908) is the best-recorded supervisory matron in the world, and was probably the best-travelled. She was born in Belchalwell, Dorset, daughter of a yeoman farmer. It's not clear how she became a matron, but she may have run a dame school first (as she lived in a school house, with her sister Susan). Certainly she was so keen on the United British Women's Migration Association that she often paid a subscription to them. Miss Monk made at least forty voyages as a matron from 1883–1903, to New Zealand, Western Australia and Canada. Her passage was paid by the governments of destination countries, and she was paid a gratuity of £30 at least once, as well as 30 shillings a week (£1.50) while waiting in Western Australia.

Apparently she treated her charges with affection and respect. One wrote that: 'Miss Monk could not be kinder to us all when we were in the ship if we had all been her own children ... Everything [she did] was for the girls', one of whom even sewed her a dress en route. Mary was so interested in the fate of 'her girls' that she went to their reunion meetings when she was ashore. Her sister Susan acted as matron on several trips when Mary wasn't available. But a bad fire on the *Gulf of Siam* in 1894 left Susan suffering 'greatly from nervous tension ... completely disabled and crippled from rheumatism and unable to do anything for her own living'.[21]

Four years after Mary, Alice Dale started matroning on the same route in 1887.[22] She was to continue for forty years, in a climate of increasing hysteria about organised networks of 'white slavers' entrapping 'innocent friendless girls' in transit (even from Newcastle to Euston, let alone to Adelaide). A matron was therefore positioned as a warrior, a non-sexy defender; others' fears gave her her job and travel opportunities. (And many travellers still appreciate her successors in Travelers Aid International in the twenty-first century.)

The First World War of course meant most civilian travelling ceased. Matrons like Alice Dale were beached for five years. Volunteers sailed briefly over to Belgium to escort shattered refugees; Quaker ladies brought back women and children. That was the agonised end of the spectrum. By contrast troupes of women singers, dancers and actresses were travelling on ships, sometimes performing on moored hospital ships or warships, and being organised by a kind of forerunner of Judie Abbott, London-based actor-manager Lena Ashwell (1872–1957).

But it was becoming clear that 'New Woman' could be mobile and have agency. Maybe the necessity for shepherdesses was beginning to pass? In fact, there was still work for matrons, but with less emphasis on chaperonage. Women travellers needed support, especially if they were sailing with children. In late 1918 and 1919 matron-type volunteer temporary escorts and charity volunteers such as

Elizabeth Hel, a Canadian YWCA Secretary,[23] conveyed war brides, the new wives of overseas servicemen, particularly to Canada and Australia (37,748 and 15,400 brides respectively). Where does this woman authority figure belong on ship, if at all?

1919–1950: CONDUCTRESSES, AND THE FIRST WOMEN OFFICERS

In the eyes of some shipping lines, she didn't really belong, because any such figure was part of the annoying bureaucratic controls on the immigration process imposed by receiving countries. Canadian Pacific, Donaldson, White Star and Domino lines were among the companies who initially opposed all the argy-bargy about floating chaperones. But somehow Britain accepted the Canadian stipulation that there should be 'conductresses', with officer status.[24]

Edith Sowerbutts was one who conducted the allegedly vulnerable. In her memoirs she wrote that to the 'ship's officers experienced in emigrant shipping … the appointment of conductresses seemed unnecessary'.[25]

These marginal unwanted women had no stripes and no established uniform. Nested like cuckoos on the edges of pursers' department, they 'hot-desked'. After all, they were, like pursers, dealing with paperwork about the 'cargo'. As shipping line employees, these 'daughters' of supervisory matrons were, themselves, no longer just cargo. Their position signalled that a new female officer role might be budding.

Edith: Conducting to Canada

Edith Sowerbutts (1896–1992), one of the first conductresses in 1924, would have snorted at the idea of herself as a warder, or as a Moses leading 'Israelites' to the chosen land of the maple leaf. She was still a very down-to-earth person when I met her in the 1990s. The daughter of a pioneer 'lady typewriter', during the First World War she'd spent her spare time helping the Women's Volunteer Reserve in London. In 1919 she'd replied to an advertisement, 'Wanted: Adventurous Women'. It meant she became a one-way stewardess on a troopship bound for Sydney. She stayed in Australia for four years, where she did office work for the Commonwealth Migration and Settlement Office in Melbourne. After returning to Britain, she worked briefly at Australia House and the Society for the Overseas Settlement of British Women.

In 1924 she became a conductress, taking female emigrants bound for Canada. Her wide experience in imperial migration made her highly suitable for the role. Her Red Star Line employers told her to invent her own uniform as there wasn't one yet. She picked up some vaguely suitable components in London's Oxford Street. These conductresses were now official 'British Merchant Seamen', rather than employees of charities or colonial governments as the supervisory matrons had been.

In June 1930 White Star, Canadian Pacific and Anchor Donaldson 'decided unilaterally' to abolish the conductress role, according to Canadian immigration historian Rebecca Mancuso.[26] Seemingly the decision was on cost-cutting grounds; anxiety about women travellers' moral welfare still existed, although hysterical fears of 'white slavery' (the abduction of young white women for sexual purposes) waned. Even solo working-class female passengers started to be regarded as capable of looking after themselves. ('Accompanied women', meaning any woman travelling with an adult male relative, were not seen as morally at risk. But if they were mothers, and maid-less, it was recognised that they needed support.)

Edith was made redundant after seven very empowered years. Afterwards she did typing jobs on land and then returned to sea as a stewardess in 1934.

The Second World War again interrupted her travelling life but by summer 1940 she was working again in emigration. Her employers were the Welfare and Escorts section of the Children's Overseas Reception Board (CORB), which managed the evacuation of children to commonwealth countries. She then did welfare and typing work until 1968. In her retirement she wrote articles and an outstanding memoir of mobility and motility (meaning someone's sense that they can move about the world).[27]

Conductress Edith Sowerbutts stands on deck in the uniform she concocted for herself. (Janet Buttifont)

In the early 1920s there was no natural niche or section to which this anomalous person, the conductress, could move. Maybe, like Edith, a few moved down into stewardessing or up and across into being lady superintendents (heads of female personnel) in shipping offices, on the grounds that they were adept at human resource work with women. And remnants of her former duties were moved to the expanding purser's office (particularly its travel bureau aspects), as well as to a very newly seeded sub-department, 'entertainment'.

In 1923 Hilda James had seemingly become the first woman to be employed at the joy-giving end of the passenger-escorting spectrum. A bit like a matron who'd lightened up or a conductress without the foolscap lists, she was a social hostess. Her tools might have overlapped with those of a supervisory matron: decks of cards, sheet music, helpful travel information. At the very beginning of cruising – as opposed to liner shipping – the social hostess was a novel phenomenon. Her business was not regulating morals but ensuring mental well-being. Hilda's role was to develop a full-time officer role to enhance and perhaps replace the passengers' own sports committee, and do what a purser and sometimes a captain's wife had done: divert passengers who, unlike convicts or working-class migrants, had some choice of whether or not to be chivvied and stimulated. Hilda wouldn't have thought herself grand enough to be compared to the great Edwardian hostesses such as Alice Keppel, Ottoline Morrell and Emerald Cunard, but she was going to do, for money, the same adroit people managing. Her passengers weren't bewildered future colonial housemaids but socialites enjoying cocktail parties in their suites as they headed for exuberant, post-war Manhattan and Paris. She arranged spectacle, though she was not allowed the scope of the adroit theatre managers in London such as Lilian Baylis of the Old Vic. Male pursers with a flair for entertainment did that more strategic work.

Hilda: Cunard's First Social Hostess

Hilda James (1904–82) was a 21-year-old record-breaking Olympic swimming star feted as the British Bullet when she became Cunard's first social hostess in 1923. Her opportunity arose because of her employers' enterprise and opportunism. Percy Bates, Cunard's deputy director and chief ship designer, and her Merseyside neighbour, believed that her high profile could help publicise the new ships designed specifically for world cruising, such as the *Carinthia*. Such ships and Hilda were twin symbols of the exciting new dawn. Cunard got the publicity and Hilda got the free transatlantic trips and swam for Cunard in the grand pool at the Liverpool's Adelphi Hotel. In 1923 Hilda was invited to sail on the new *Franconia*'s three-day 'shakedown'. She was supposed to demonstrate her award-winning swimming style, then 'be visible', socialising with passengers and making the voyages pleasurable for them. No other women working on ship were allowed to mingle in this way. (Indeed the issue of who has such deck privileges is still one that defines workers' status.) Hilda's patron told her to write her own job description. She herself decided what she should wear: not a uniform but clothes that seemed to look the part.

She next went on the *Franconia*'s much-trumpeted maiden world cruise. After two years of making herself available for publicity work, in 1925 Hilda became a Cunard employee and continued to invent the role of social hostess, mainly on the *Carinthia*. In between cruising she had time off for swimming competitions. Rather torn between careers, her dilemma was resolved when she realised she was becoming too old to break records. Britain had lost an Olympic star. But Cunard, and maybe cruising in general, had gained its first social hostess. In 1929 Hilda left to marry and have children. She continued to see herself as a swimming star rather than ship's entertainment staff. Her life story was written by her grandson Ian Hugh McAllister.[28]

Social hostess Hilda James waves for the press cameras. (Ian Hugh McAllister)

It's not clear whether other social hostesses took Hilda's place, or if the job waned for a while. In the 1930s cruise operators were certainly trying to woo new customers to these path-breaking holiday-making-style ships. Purser's bureau staff (almost entirely male at that time) would have stepped up their social hosting role until the advent of the Second World War in 1939 brought the end to civilian sailing.

Although the jobs of supervisory matron and conductress had died out, women lower down the scale were still working in an assistant-matron-style role. This was particularly the case on British India Steam Navigation (BISN) troopships going out to India carrying wives and families. 'Matrons' by this point appear to have been regular stewardesses selected to play a rather lowly role on a particular voyage. They offered practical support to women, especially mothers and confused non-English speaking emigrants, rather than being a walking moral template.[29]

New conductress-type workers appeared in 1940–41. These 200-odd women and men escorted children being evacuated overseas on ships, under a protective scheme run by the Children's Overseas Reception Board (for which Edith Sowerbutts later worked on land). These escorts were volunteers, most of them taking time off from teaching, and some already worked for charities such as the Salvation Army.

Escorts had the anomalous status similar to supervisory matrons on emigrant ships nearly a century earlier: they were passengers who worked, officer-types but with no formal power. All escorts' job prospects vanished when CORB ended precipitately, after the *City of Benares*'s sinking in September 1940 proved that overseas evacuation was too risky.

Five years later, at war's end, the need for escorts appeared once more, in response to British war brides taking passage to their new lands. Elizabeth Hel's successors escorted over 100,000 British war brides, again often under the firm controls of receiving governments and the military, rather than the shipping line. American Red Cross escort Barbara Lincoln described their role as educating and orienting, as a sort of hybrid of today's cruise ship lecturer, emigrant adviser and travel agent. Barbara handled questions such as 'Do I have to cook corn the way my husband says they cook it in North Carolina?' She taught songs like 'The Star-Spangled Banner' and used the ship's map to help emigrants pinpoint rail routes to their new lives.[30]

1951–1980: CHILDREN'S MATRONS AND QUEEN BEES

After the Second World War there were still emigrant matrons helping a handful of women. In 1952 Mrs Hay did the job on the *Captain Cook*, along with her husband Jim. He was one of the shipboard liaison officers newly employed by the New Zealand Department of Labour to give passengers lectures about what to expect. BISN was seemingly one of the first shipping lines with such a liaison officer on board, but it's unclear when the role began and ended, or if a woman was ever allowed to do it.[31]

Entertainment officer and social hostess jobs were emerging, as cruising developed and shipping lines increasingly emphasised the enjoyable side of travelling. Passengers' interest in organising sports and social committees waned. Social hostesses were quite like Redcoats at Butlin's holiday camps; they entertained the holidaymakers, though they were rather more upmarket than their Butlin's counterparts.

How would you get the job, at this stage? It was handy to be an ex-beauty queen. You'd be aged 26 to 34,[32] personable, neither too posh nor too 'common', and very good at communicating, teaching tatting, bingo-calling, dressing up as Calamity Jane on Wild West night, can-canning on the Continental Evening – anything to help make the passengers' voyages happy ones.

Far from the fake grass skirts, a new sort of matron role was emerging on BISN ships. Such matrons got the new opportunity because national service (two years' compulsory military service for men) ended in 1960. Troops, in any case, began flying to postings instead of going by sea. To utilise the now-redundant troopships, in 1961 BISN began educational cruises for school children.[33] Formerly, sergeants in khaki serge marshalled dormitories full of young squaddies on the *Dunera*, *Nevasa* and *Devonia*. But now assistant matrons in blue nurse-style dresses acted as aunties to excited school girls and boys on their first foreign trips.

The schools department was a whole new department on ship. In it women could easily progress because care of children was still seen as something to which women were particularly suited. From 1961 to the 1980s[34] women could get jobs as matrons, sailing on about twenty fortnightly cruises annually, to European destinations such as Venice and Leningrad. Under the matron, usually six assistant matrons, 'ass. mats', looked after the children.[35]

One of the very first school ship matrons was ex-Wren Ena Smith, who sailed on *Devonia*. She went on to become the company's lady superintendent, and organised a promotion ladder. You could rise from ass. mat. to senior ass. mat., to deputy matron (all of whom were junior officers) and then matron. Marjorie Ellison went up that ladder. Like the other senior officers and the women assistant pursers, she had her own table in the dining room where she hosted school party leaders and other passengers.

A chief officer wrote Marjorie a poem that sums up the job's challenges:

> The matron stood at the pearly gate / her face was worn and old.
> She stood before the man of fate / for admission to the fold.
> 'What have you done,' St Peter said, 'to gain admission here?'
> 'I was on the *Nevasa*, sir, as matron / for many a long year.'
> The pearly gate did open wide / and heavenly tolled the bell,
> 'Come in, come in,' St Peter cried / 'You've had your share of hell!'[36]

Marjorie: From 'Ass. Mat.' to Social Hostess – and Back to Matron

Marjorie Ellison (b. 1934), who came from a sheltered convent background in Northumberland, became a BISN assistant matron in 1964. For her, getting the job was possible partly because she was already used to authority: her father was a policeman and her great great aunt had been a workhouse matron. 'As my mother said, I was born to be bossy.' She'd been working in management on land when she saw the advertisement in the *Daily Telegraph* and thought: 'That's interesting. That'll get me round the world a bit.' Later in 1964 she was on the *Dunera*, from where she moved to the *Nevasa* and *Uganda*. By 1965 she'd been promoted to matron, and wore a navy-blue WRNS-style uniform. The matron role had its stereotypes. In the petty officers' bar was a cartoon of her as witch on broomstick, at which she laughed. 'You have to be very tolerant on ship, and have a good sense of humour.' In 1970 P&O took over BISN. This meant that she had to leave in 1974 because of their rule that every woman (officer, not rating) must retire at 40. Instead she went to Fred Olsen as a social hostess. After a year she worked on land in jobs including bursar at Warsash School of Navigation. There she looked after the very early women deck and engineer cadets, one of whom became one of the first P&O women captains. At that time Marje was not sure that women should be going into deck officer work. 'They were certainly going into a man's world and I warned them to tread very carefully,' she told me when I was fresh from meeting those women's successors at Warsash.

After P&O lifted the age bar on women employees Miss Ellison returned as matron on the *Uganda* between 1979 and 1982. When the ship was needed for troops in the

Falklands Conflict (who certainly wouldn't have welcomed a matron's control), she left to manage three tourist information centres on land. Later she retired, because 'You reach saturation point with people – so I have some sympathy for the queen!' When we met in 2013 she was still keeping in touch with her old BISN/P&O shipmates. And now she thinks it's fine that women are making it as deck officers and captains.[37]

Matron Marjorie Ellison, on the *Nevasa*, 1965. (Marjorie Ellison)

When Miss Ellison became a social hostess, her work included playing whist and keeping company with ladies travelling alone, at a time when cruises were far less focused on organised entertainment. School cruises didn't resume after 1982. It was the end of the 1963–82 window for matrons and ass. mats. However, they had transferable skills. Matron Marie Groom (later Candlish) moved to P&O's fleet personnel office until she retired; it was a job not a million miles from lady superintendent.[38]

Marje's career typifies the linkage between the two areas of work in this chapter – welfare and entertainment. She's the bridge between Miss Monk, associated administratively with the surgeon and purser, and the new breed – social hostesses, social directresses, then cruise directors – who belonged to the entertainment world (initially handled by pursers). This was really the start of women being recognised as senior officers. It was through working in the purser's bureau, which meant doing entertainment work in the evenings, that several women flowed into becoming full-time social hostesses. But outsiders were also employed to be social hostesses. Initially, a few were proud ex-beauty queens. They were replaced by mature women who were good at organisation and genuinely interested in passengers' well-being.

Margaret Newcombe was the very first social directress (the title social director/directress seems to have been used before the title 'cruise director' and later sometimes interchangeably with it) in Cunard.[39] She came through that purser's department route, rather than via welfare work, in the early 1960s. When we met, Margaret recalled that with the competition from commercial flying, 'It was necessary that shipping lines … [put] more accent upon entertaining the passengers than they had in the past.' She thinks her job partly emerged because a person 'with sense in the office must have said "someone must take care of the ladies, the lonely hearts. Make them happy. Introduce them." So they introduced what they called the cruise director and his staff.'

She became an officer with her own cabin. 'I moved from the purser's department into the entertainment side and was the first social directress on the *Queen Mary* … For the next seventeen years that's what I was doing on the three *Queens*: *Queen Mary* until she went to Long Beach, *Queen Elizabeth* for one year, and *QE2*.' She also went cruising on *Caronia*, *Britannic* and other ships.

Margaret: Cunard's First Social Directress

Margaret Newcombe (1922–2014) was born in Hull; her father was a vicar and her great grandfather a purser, so she had roots in both pastoral care and seafaring organisation. In the Second World War she was in the women's section of the Army, the Auxilliary Territorial Service (ATS), 'looking after people'. In 1947 she managed to get work as a lady assistant purser (LAP) with Cunard, sailing to New York on the *Queen Elizabeth*. The 1950s found her working in the ship's travel bureau. Then 'things were getting a bit monotonous [so] they said would I like to be social directress. And so there I was able to change my duties and have a new interest … I've gone from pen and paper to song and dance.' Nicknamed 'Dame Margaret' (she was still genuinely gracious when I met her in 2013), she enriched thousands of passengers' voyages on many ships. 'I was enjoying myself. I like people, I'm a bit of a show-off and I like giving passengers everything they wanted. I don't put myself forward but I enjoy them.'

Miss Newcombe sailed for twenty-eight years and retired in 1977. 'I thought it was time I put my roots down.' She went to live with an aunt in Torquay, but found it very hard because 'I was so used to being amongst people.' After three years her aunt died, and she moved to Hampshire 'because I had lot of friends here.' They met regularly at reunions. And they were gathering for her funeral, and at Judie Abbot's memorial ceremony too, as I finished drafting this chapter.

Margaret Newcombe (fourth from right) dines with her purser colleagues on the *Britannic* in 1951. (Margaret Newcombe)

Miss Newcombe's description of her job as a social directress resembles a matron's or hostess's in that it entailed 'taking particular care of the ladies and those travelling alone, and then assisting in every part of the programme – children's events, the swimming events.' Her day began at 9 a.m. when she'd sort her plans for the day (initially in her cramped cabin, later she had an office), then run the daily 'hostess session every morning … A meeting of anyone who wanted to come ask questions … Then of course there was Bridge in the afternoons, and then parties in the evening.' After that there was 'mixing and mingling in the public room until about midnight … a very long day. But it was great fun, I enjoyed it.' She felt that a social directress was 'the queen of the ship', yet not the captain's lady.

Margaret's work also involved organising entertainment, including inducing ship's officers, or celebrities travelling as passengers, to give talks or recitals. Some were so glamorous that, 'We were swooning every day … I've never been the same since I fell into the arms of Kirk Douglas when the ship was rolling.' She'd support lecturers who were on board one trip to teach people crafts like how to paint china (now called part of the 'voyage-enrichment' programme), and looked after Cunard's own dance team, the Cunard Cunettes.

Such high levels of professional entertaining, involving resident performers and stars who flew in for a week or two, called for serious management skills. In the 1970s the role of cruise director (a Cunard term) emerged. Men were initially appointed to the job, which required professional skills similar to that of an impresario. In other cruise companies such a person was called the entertainment officer. He managed the social director or directress, who would have been an invaluable aid to him as a newcomer to the ship. Cruise director John Butt found Margaret, by then an experienced social directress, 'my right-hand person'.

Around the time that Margaret was leaving the sea, in 1977, attitudes to entertaining were changing. More and more professional entertainers were coming on board, women and men. Increasingly the job meant dealing with the professional entertainment of passengers; there was less mutual or amateur entertainment and intermingling as the 1970s wore on. Women were also starting to come forward as senior managers, taking Margaret's job a step further. John Butt is proud to have encouraged and mentored women such as the Cunard's first woman cruise director, Carole Critchley, Margaret's 'inheritor'.[40]

Carole: Cruise Director

Carole Critchley (b. 1957) was dancing professionally in the 1970s with famous troupes including the Tiller Girls, Bluebell Girls and the Black & White Minstrels when she decided she'd like to dance at sea. Eventually she joined Cunard's own Sweet Elegance ↓

dance troupe on a world cruise on the *QE2*. She was 18 and nervous; they were all so young that they were chaperoned.

She danced, on and off, at sea until she was 27. With world cruises most winters it felt like 'St Martin's Lane one minute, Tahiti the next'. Somehow she managed to fit it round her first marriage to a MN radio officer. She sailed on cargo ships with him 'which were great fun. I used to organise all sorts of things for the guys', and also helped with sick-bay work. It showed her the less glamorous side of seafaring. After the marriage ended, when she was 30, Carole left her aerobics business and went back to sea as a fitness instructor. Almost immediately she decided she wanted to become a cruise director. Initially she worked as a shore excursions officer, and then she was promoted to assistant cruise director. She became the cruise director on the luxury yachts *Sea Goddess 1* and *Sea Goddess 2*, and then in 1990–91 returned to Cunard's *Princess*, which in the first Gulf War was chartered by the US government as an R&R vessel for their troops. 'Quite a change, being cruise director for troops!' Until 2000 Carole worked as a cruise director/entertainment director on a number of ships, including Cunard's *Countess*. She left the sea to be with her second husband, a Concorde pilot, whom she met when he was lecturing on the *Countess*.

To be successful on that role, Carole was certainly boosted by having parents who had been Redcoats at Butlin's and then owned two holiday camps. 'From when I was little I'd watch carloads of people arriving, show them around. I was always dancing and singing on the stage, I like being in the limelight. And I thrive on being busy and challenged ... I have obsessive attention to detail with regard to passenger satisfaction. When the passengers leave happy I've done a good job.'

When Carole's 10-year-old niece recently said she was going to become a cruise director when she grew up, Carole said what she'd say to any girl: 'Go for it.'

Today Carole and her husband Richard are retired and now run the family property management business in Windsor. 'I still behave like a cruise director even when I am a passenger. Old habits die hard. Always helping passengers and advising them what to do in the ports of call. I still love people and am always organising them, much to my friends' sometime annoyance. Bossy! Me? Never!'[41]

Carole's employers didn't make a fuss of her as the first woman cruise director. On the contrary, her manager in the New York office used the lack of precedent to argue that she should be paid less than a man (in line with women's generally lower pay). 'I wouldn't stand for that. Finally I got equal pay.' Judie Abbott, who appeared at the start of this chapter, was one of Carole's successors who benefited from the increased realisation that women were equally able and deserved equal recognition.

TODAY'S CRUISE DIRECTORS

In the twenty-first century both women and men are working at all levels in the cruise director's team on major ships. A typical team involves the cruise director, deputy director, several assistant directors, disc jockey and technicians. There may be a score of British women at the top of cruise directing as I write. And if they are caring (and they are), an element of their glamorous work may still be looking after the welfare of young women away from home for the first time, as many dancers are only in their late teens.

Overtly supervisory jobs at sea, such as matrons, have come to a dead end. Passenger shipping is now about pleasure, not mothering the human cargo. Staff are needed to make guests (rather than inmates) so happy that they'll return again, to spend their money, say at on-board art auctions, blackjack tables and extra-premium bistros.

Functional travel, by emigrants and other travellers, is now done by air. Conductresses' and escorts' airborne counterparts still exist. Women and men volunteers accompany refugees, trafficked people and rescued sex slaves returning home (in 2014 the Home Office estimated there could be 10,000 to 13,000 victims of slavery in the UK).[42] Such escorting is often done as a one-off duty, co-ordinated by charities; workers for agencies such as Universal Aunts do escort work for more privileged young people travelling solo.

In looking at the two sides of the same coin – women who look after travellers' hearts and minds – I've been struck by the way welfare and entertainment work is related, for all that the former once involved policing and physical misery, and the latter looks so glamorous. The women I've met for these pages have all been astonishingly socially adept – and fun, and subtly supportive. So in a sense I've been their appreciative charge, nurtured under their wise and genuinely charming wings on my own voyage of discovery.

8

From Stenographer to Administration Director: Doing the Ship's Business Afloat

Caroline Norman is one of the many young women with at least one degree who run the hospitality side of cruise ships.[1] She was what was once called a purser. Until recently Caroline was a P&O passenger services manager (a title now changed to commercial director).

Caroline: Passenger Services Manager

Caroline Norman (b. 1978) is from Torquay, and in 2003 went to sea because: 'I wanted to travel the world and wear the famous white uniform ... I started my career with a BSc in Hotel & Catering Management at Gloucester University. After graduating I worked in two hotels, and then in 2003 joined P&O Cruises as a junior assistant purser (JAP). You wear half a gold stripe when you're that status.

'Shipping lines had stopped using W (Woman) or F (Female) in pursers' titles by then, to move with the times and bring a sense of equality to onboard departments.' As the culture was changing and the purser's department was becoming more revenue-orientated (rather than very selflessly seeing themselves as hosting and helping), the name of the department became 'the hotel department'. JAPs were renamed 'assistant managers' and managed about five receptionists.

'I worked my way up to passenger services manager (three gold stripes) in a little over five years. I went through eight different roles and four progressive ranks. The training model on board ships is very good, across all departments. Training was the key to my success. Crew really do become masters in their own field because to be promoted to the next level you have to first become completely proficient in the rank below, regardless of gender. If you work hard, abide by the ship's rules and show ambition, the world really can be your oyster.

'I was incredibly proud to hold my role at sea, to see so many exciting ports around the oceans, learn from amazing professionals and exceed passengers' expectations on a daily basis. It was a very rewarding job both professionally and personally, which I would recommend to anyone.'

Caroline left the sea in the 2010s to do a master's degree in business administration. 'My next steps are to use the organisational skills I learnt on ships and progress to management in professional sporting and leisure venues, ideally as the general manager of a racecourse or large hotel resort.'[2]

Today women graduates like Caroline are part of the executive team who could all, in theory, be women. They almost were, in a 2011 headline-grabbing article: 'Women take charge of *Pacific Pearl*'. The line-up comprised Martina Damonte, administration and revenue director; Jane Herren, hotel director (Martina's line manager); Zoltina J. Medwick-Daley, cruise director; and Captain Sarah Breton.[3] Only the chief engineer, a man, was missing from this executive line-up. Formerly, Martina and Jane's job titles would have been the purser (note that in this book any mention of a Purser, with a capital P, refers to a sole person: the manager of the purser's department. All lesser mortals had a qualifying title, such as assistant purser.

Caroline Norman, proud to be passenger services manager with P&O Cruises. (Caroline Norman)

On a passenger ship pursers are, above all, dealing with a floating hotel. They're as vital as the captain and the chief engineer. They decide on the ship's logistics, from what food to carry to how to handle officials in foreign ports. And they work at what is arguably the very heart of the ship: now usually named 'hotel reception', but once called the 'purser's bureau'.

Browse the internet for a job description of a purser in the Royal Navy, by contrast, and you'll find what this person – now called a logistics officer – does. It's both essentially the same and very different to the job on cruise ships – supplying, and making things work, but without the Savoy-level frills:

> you'll be responsible for making sure your ship has everything it needs, when it needs it, to stay effective on operations. Leading a team of highly-trained specialists, you'll apply your organisational skills to stock your ship with up to six months' worth of supplies and equipment before leaving port, as well as drawing up plans for re-supplying at sea and on shore during the deployment. You'll also be advising your Commanding Officer on personnel policy and legal and accountancy matters ... It's a challenging but essential role that puts you at the very heart of everything we do.[4]

For centuries, on all sorts of ships, the purser, sometimes called the bursar or pusser, was the captain's right-hand person. He was a tough-minded, middle-aged gent with a bent for accountancy. Managing the purse strings, he decided what went onto the ship and how it was run. A significant figure who expected deference, in both MN and RN ships, the purser was valued if he was honest in money matters.

The ideal purser could manage a tricky balancing act. He met both the shipowner's desire to be economical (and preferably very profitable) and the inhabitants' need for adequate conditions. And he even made a bit on the side for himself. A good purser insisted that ships' victualling companies on land, who had the contracts to supply, sent decent quality food aboard. A bad purser cheese-pared for his own ends. Though he'd have been offended at the idea, he was as good a household manager as an excellent housewife can be.

A 1920s Cunard cartoon summed up the essence of the purser's job on a passenger ship. In his smart business suit he sits atop a safe the size of a two-drawer filing cabinet, in a tiny shipboard office where he's surrounded by piles of papers fluttering around him. And he's frazzled; there's so much to sort out. Humourist A.P. Herbert quipped that the man in this unenviable job is effectively 'the captain of trouble'. The purser was 'to blame for whatever annoys you at sea', but he loved to remedy it too, and 'for a quite modest fee'.[5]

Nowadays, as ships have become such vast hotels, pursers have modern job titles such as administration and revenue director, or executive purser. They manage large teams. Tasks are now both complicated and large-scale. And the communications revolution means their business is done with constant contact with the office ashore, whose staff were once regarded as interfering nuisances who knew nothing about sea life.

Elite heads of this biggest department of the passenger ship attend the daily executive meeting with the captain, at which the key decisions are made. They sport four gold stripes on their sleeve, like the captain, but with white stripes in between. Their offices are suites, not cubby holes; most of the money will be in virtual form. And the other sort is certainly not accessible by one big brass key stuffed in a senior chap's breast pocket. Heaps of paper don't fly around because most information is produced, circulated and tucked invisibly away inside computers and in internet cloud storage space.

For over 150 years, since large-scale passenger shipping began, pursers' department staff have done everything from fix future arrangements in ports, order supplies, allocate rooms, sort out crew wages, deal with banking in a multitude of currencies, manage the lists of whom the captain should invite to his table, arrange onward travel, and handle guest queries. (The favourite is: 'Say, what time is the midnight buffet?')

If conductresses were the strict mothers of the ships then pursers' department staff were the diplomatic corps standing by to sort out problems – with panache and what sometimes looked like wizardry. What's more, they were often the agony aunts of the ship, because they seemed to know how to sort anything out. Now pursering has developed into one of the biggest equal-opportunities areas for women on cruise ships.

1750–1800: WITH ABACUS, QUILL AND DRAWSTRING PURSE

Eighteenth-century male forerunners of women like Caroline were doing a much smaller job because ships were smaller, passengers fewer and the standard of service relatively rudimentary. On RN vessels their job was to oversee the provisioning of ships with clothes, food, candles and so on. Usually there was just one purser on ship, without an assistant. Some pursers travelling with wives may have utilised their partners as ledger clerks and backroom scribes. Artists' representations of historical pursers in this period show an upright, well-dressed man in tricorne hat, sometimes wearing spectacles.[6]

He lords it on the edge of a dock or by a ship's rail, holding quill pen and purse, supervising the barrels that a minion will later load. In this vision pursers are clearly people of the interface between land and sea, and authoritative managers whom only a fool would try to cheat.

There was no intrinsic reason why a shrewd, literate and numerate woman could not have been a purser. But the job's other components included managing resources and facing down angry crew who didn't like the way you operated,

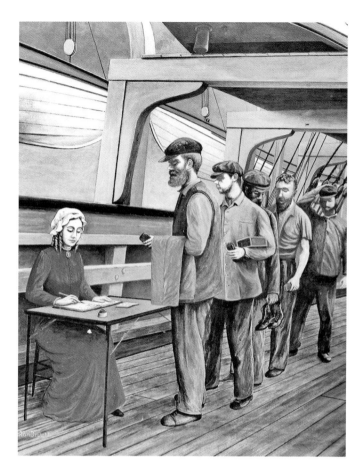

A captain's wife on board sorting out wages and deductions, which later became the crew purser's job. Artist's impression by Ron Druett. (Joan Druett)

negotiating with suppliers, and using financial acumen, indeed even putting up your own money as surety in deals. These were imagined not to be women's strong suits. (Actually, eighteenth-century women, particularly widows or wives of absentee husbands, *did* do business. Sarah Child and Sarah Sophia Fane, for example, were active partners in RBS's predecessor, the Child & Co. Bank.)[7]

Other cultural blocks to women becoming pursers may have included the assumptions that women hadn't had sufficient seagoing experience to learn how to do the tasks; that the merchants ashore from whom she ordered goods might not readily respect a woman's authority (and so palm her off with, say, overpriced adulterated flour); that the crew would be uneasy about accepting a woman's authority; and that a woman could not face down shipmates angry if rations were short.

Class, too, was an explanation. If a woman had the requisite education to be a purser, her parents would probably have bought her elite schooling – like that of the Keary girls at Roedean and Newnham much later – so she would have been too elevated to work at sea.[8] And large shipowners would have felt it totally unseemly to allow a lady of the same class as their wife to go to sea as a money-handler, at a time when ships were potentially lethal places and sailors seen as uncouth.

None of the known disguised women seafarers was recorded as even assisting pursers. But, especially on small ships, officers' wives and passengers who wanted to pass the time sometimes did paperwork, unofficially and unpaid. Effectively the purser's ad hoc secretary, their work would have included making fair copies of documents such as crew rosters, ship's manifests or bills of lading, and calculating with a slide rule. Certainly some captain's wives wrote the ship's log, not least because they were seen as possessing a fair hand, having time to spare, and being fitted to the role of helper.

1800–1900: CAN A LADY REALLY SORT THAT OUT?

This pattern must have continued in similar vein through the nineteenth century, not least because bureaucracy increased. Pursers got assistants, deputies and then teams. These male staff had no formal qualifications or training in shipboard office work, but it's likely that most had been clerks in shipping line headquarters.

Revolutionary change began with the advent of typewriting in the 1870s. Like embroidery and piano playing, it was seen as suited to the sub-species with dainty fingers. Women clerical workers increased ten-fold, to 177,000, between 1891 and 1911.[9] And men were becoming used to being 'assisted' by decorative, lower-paid 'girl typists' in a two-tier world.

Women working in shipping line offices, operating heavy typewriter carriages three-feet long to accommodate ship's manifests, implicitly learned about the pursering business, including passenger relations. So why shouldn't they do that useful 'support work' at sea, too, especially in one of the more genteel areas of the ships, surrounded by polite clerks in white shirts, not grimy stokers?

1901–1946: INVASION OR LIBERATION?

Catherine Leith was one of the earliest 'secretaries' on board a ship, in 1908. She was sailing on Cunard's *Carmania* across the Atlantic. Already aboard in some other capacity, and seemingly British, she was promoted to assistant purser – or at least that's what newspapers termed the job. Catherine's much-publicised advent was seen as a portent. 'Another pleasant opening for charming girls is foreshadowed, and it is expected that before long a trim woman purser, with every detail at her finger tips, will be no uncommon sight.'[10]

Two years later the *New York Times* was wary, in a tongue-in-cheek way, of a possible 'invasion' looming. Women in control, not just typing under orders!

We assume the female purser will be a nice woman. As such, she will find some of the traditional duties of the purser objectionable. She will not cut much of a figure in the smoking room. Doubtless, on English ships, she will not care to conduct the morning prayers on Sunday … But if she invades the profession of purser, hitherto inaccessible to her, woman will have taken another step towards freedom.[11]

While a lowly 'girl' might 'help' in the purser's office, it was seen as unlikely that she could become *the* Purser, the male grandee with the capital P.

It's remarkable that Catherine got her job at all, because it meant 'hazardous' mixing with men. Generally at that time employers of women on land provided segregated workrooms and entrances to avoid 'embarrassing rubbing shoulders'.[12] But cramped ships couldn't possibly give women typists separate gangways, offices and toilets. So shipping lines such as Cunard must have decided either that their pursers' staff were honourable gentlemen who could be trusted to behave well, or that ships had to be accepted as situations where women and men mixed – and survived it.

The First World War brought a major increase in women office workers, including in shipping offices, when men went off to war. And in the Royal Navy 2,000-plus WRNS writers and clerks stepped into men's shoes – but not sea boots.[13]

Clerical Wren Jane Rossiter (b. 1893), working on the moored HMS *Powerful* at Plymouth wrote: '… although we were not really welcomed, as women, … everyone … treated us as ladies … The captain … definitely was not in favour of having women but he was most gracious and he roped off part of his own deck … for us to use at lunchtime.'[14] This was a very typical pattern: men disapproved, but were chivalrous. Gentlemen ostensibly lay down their cudgels, even if their teeth were gritted. Then the great pay-off came: women were discovered to really be worth employing, and were highly enjoyable colleagues too.

After the First World War, selected Cunard ships began carrying first one female typist then more (Cunard's seagoing women were called 'typists', not 'assistant pursers' as Miss Leith had been). Women typists were on only a seventieth of all Cunard voyages in 1924, but a sixth by 1927. They worked 'surrounded by log books, discharge books, articles, insurance cards, passports, tickets, timetables, passenger returns, cargo and passenger manifest, aliens lists, deck chair, rug, library and bar returns, bulletins, Marconigrams, cable returns, landing cards, baggage declarations, passengers valuables, surplus stores, wages sheets, gold, silver, copper, notes, greenbacks, nickels, dimes and dollars.'[15]

In 1931 'women typists' were replaced by 'seafaring clerks', a job for men. It seems no women office workers sailed for Cunard again until after the Second World War. Indeed, one shipping line said as late as 1939 (according to a newspaper report), 'clerical work is done on the boats by male staff and we carry as few women as possible.'[16]

In the Second World War about 20 per cent of Wrens, say 15,000, were in Royal Navy office jobs such as writer, charts corrector, book corrector and shorthand-typist.[17] A few may have occasionally worked on moored RN ships. Most would have worked in 'stone frigates'. This is the navy name for RN shore establishments in which everyone acted as if they were on real ships – for example, floors were 'decks' and lavatories 'heads'. You went 'ashore', not 'home', after work and the bus that took you there was the 'liberty boat'.

1947–2000: 'DEAR SIR, WE DON'T EMPLOY LADIES'

War's end brought major opportunities for ex-Wrens, who became part of the revolution in MN on-board pursers' bureaux. Shipping lines were almost as avid for well-disciplined efficient servicewomen as the former 'Jenny Wrens' were avid for adventure at sea. Elizabeth Sayers (b. 1912), a WRNS officer with Mountbatten in the Second World War, joined Cunard in 1948 as a lady assistant purser. When her story appeared in the newspapers, shipping companies were deluged with applications.

The advent of these ladies meant passenger ships now had two types of women officer on ship: nursing officers in white uniforms and very smart women assistant pursers in WRNS-style uniforms. Now typing was done with half or even one stripe on your sleeve (white, unlike the Wrens' blue bands) not in a comfy cardigan and floral frock. Depending on the shipping line, the new post-war category of women office workers were variously 'junior assistant pursers (F)' or 'female assistant pursers' or 'woman APs' or A/P(F)s: hence they were called FAPs, WAPs and LAPs (lady assistant pursers), rhyming with 'caps', or sometimes jokingly 'lady apes', referring phonetically to the initials AP (ay-pee).

One such woman who helped with this book insisted that in her company the term was 'lady asst. pursers'. She thought any other term undignified and very offensive indeed. On Union Castle ships they were called purserettes – literally, small (but rather glamorous) pursers, a sub-variety. They were but never purseresses.

These LAPs (which is what they'll be called in this chapter, for simplicity) had made a breakthrough into men's jobs. But they were to do a feminised version of that work, and be treated as the captain's honorary daughter. Although officers, they were a separate species of officer. A chivalrous – therefore discriminatory – fuss was made about their gender. And yet young male pursers dealt with some ex-WRNS officers' disconcerting confidence by seeing them as 'really one of the chaps'.

LAPs could break into this new field partly because so many passengers were women, and male crew were uneasy about handling women's emotions. Therefore, female WRNS officers who'd had wartime experience of organising other women away from home were ideal. They could chair a table in the dining room, just like men, whereas a chief stewardess taking such a role might be seen as *infra dig*. They could type and do shorthand (at 120 and 45 words per minute respectively).[18] But above all these disciplined, flexible workers had a thirst for action, were at ease with male colleagues, and had knowledge of sea life. Mature, disciplined and used to authority, they could act decisively and appropriately.

LAP Margaret Newcombe was precisely this sort of ex-services person, but very good at not being too breezy. As a wartime Army officer she'd done welfare work with women. When we met in 2014 she told me how much she'd longed to go to sea, as a purser, in 1947. Cunard responded to her application with 'Dear Sir, We don't employ ladies.' But then a year later she saw a newspaper picture of Elizabeth Sayers (who became *the* beacon) and three other women doing pursering work. 'So I wrote back to Cunard and said, "Dear Sir, you *do*."'[19] She got her job.

Gender distinctions meant women were promoted less and paid less.[20] They didn't usually handle money. And they did extra tasks: companies hired out their services as 'lady stenographers' to businessmen passengers. They did shorthand typing, copy-typing and typing from a Dictaphone (voice recorder). 'A flurry of steno. appointments really stretched us … to keep abreast of the workload we would often go back to the office after dinner and just crack on, often into the early hours,' said Muriel Arnold of her time a little later.[21] Passengers importuned them, which

MISS K. E. SAYERS, ASSISTANT PURSER, *"QUEEN ELIZABETH"*

Ex-Wren Elizabeth Sayers' publicised success as a purser inspired many applicants who wanted an officer's job at sea. Picture from Cunard poster, 'Women, too, Play a Vital Part in Cunard Service at Sea', *c.* 1950. (University of Liverpool Library, D42/PR3/20/20)

Cunard lady stenographer taking dictation in passenger cabin. (University of Liverpool Library, D42/PR2/6/2/55)

was a nuisance. But they also dictated fascinating letters and offered LAPs interesting job opportunities ashore.

The 1951 census shows the degree to which higher-level clerical work in shipping offices ashore was still men's province. Out of the 7,671 clerks in the sea transport industry, only 831 (12 per cent) were women. This was reflected at sea, probably to an even greater extent. 'Both men and women worked the counter position. Only women fulfilled the secretarial role behind the scenes during my time at sea,' said Linda Brown of her time at P&O in the early 1970s.[22] Different lines had different divisions of labour, and women were always in the minority, and in lower-status jobs. For example, P&O then had fifty-two LAPs[23] but several hundred male pursering staff. In group photographs women were outnumbered by about two to one.

These pioneers on ships came up against conventional ideas about the way females should be treated. Senior officers gave LAPs perks, which caused male resentment and envy. Maurice Onslow, then a JAP, found women were allowed to finish early on port days, didn't have to work the 6 p.m. to midnight shift, and could wear civvies, not uniform, at social events. Because women officers were rare, the captain invited women pursering staff to mingle in his cabin with famous passengers.[24]

Men, by comparison, were sent on training courses that would enhance their entire future.[25] The idea was that men were in careers for life and women were not.

Most LAPs of the 1960s and 1970s have told me they didn't even think about the difference at the time, let alone consider the idea of unfairness.

Employers' belief that women were convivial socialisers rather than simply logistics staff also gave LAPs a way to progress up the career ladder and out of uniform, into social hostess work. Maureen Ryan moved from being telephonist to a lady assistant purser on the Cunard *Queens* for five years, and then on to becoming a social directress on the *Clyde* in 1968. Some LAPs were promoted – one rung only – if they worked on the new schools cruises, where women were seen as 'naturally good with children'. Frances Milroy, who became the doyenne of pursers, went up the ladder that had, until her advent, been seen as men-only.

Frances Milroy, Cunard's First 'Lady Purser'

Born in 1929 and trained at Liverpool's College of Commerce, at 24 Frances was working as a secretary for shipping agents LEP Transport and felt: 'I was going nowhere.' A friend who knew a board member at Cunard arranged an interview. She was accepted, and after waiting six months became a LAP. 'This was in the mid-1950s when most girls worked in an office until they got married and then stayed at home ... My mother was horrified. But then being on the *Queen Mary* did impress the neighbours.' The work was 'interesting and challenging', especially as this was a time when 'the concept of cruising was changing [forever] with the start of air travel'. On trips to Canada and some cruises on the *Mauretania*, *Britannic* and *Caronia* Frances mainly worked in the ship's travel bureau. In 1961 she was a LAP on the *Queen Elizabeth* with an extra half stripe, but she didn't get promoted until 1969, when she became senior lady purser on the *QE2*, and later in the same year relief chief purser. Frances was the first woman Purser in Cunard and possibly in the entire Merchant Navy.

Frances got to the top, she says, because of seniority, length of service and after being based on other ships of the company. Unlike the men, she was not trained up for the job, apart from a two-week course at Cornell University.

It was a varied career: in 1982 she was sailing to the Falklands, in charge of 'room service' for 3,000 troops, but at other times she was working as relief hostess. Frances remembers, 'I loved it all, the different people, different places. When I was on leave I'd look forward to going back on the ship.' But, feeling that she was holding younger people back from promotion, she retired at 60. At that time a young woman graduate from the Middle East was making her way up from stewardess to hotel manager; times were changing.

Today Frances still lives on Merseyside. When we met she told me she keeps in touch with shipmates and was a Friend of Merseyside Maritime Museum. 'The most wonderful thing about being a seafarer is the friendships I made. They have lasted a lifetime.'[26]

Pioneering purser Frances Milroy and colleagues on a bus on their way to the Cunard ship. (Frances Milroy)

It was in the 1970s that a major upheaval in attitudes to hotel work at sea began. The balance tipped from running ships as something like a gentleman's Pall Mall club, when possible, to instead setting up each voyage as a collection of profit-maximising consumption-focused opportunities. Pursering staff felt 'gentlemanliness' and a 'family atmosphere' had gone out of the window. This was particularly true for BISN staff after P&O took over. In other companies, too, women's duties in the ship's offices were being transformed, just as the whole enterprise was evolving sharply into something quite different from the previous quasi-naval regime. A world was being created, with new 'hospitality-services' language and job titles, almost as if the maritime aspect was being displaced by hotel culture. The starkest symbols of this were the changes in the women pursering staff's situation. They were clad as hotel-reception staff not WRNS-types. And newcomers were entering at a new, lower-graded level that focused on hotel-reception style service. In the early 1970s these new female 'bureau assistants' on short-term contracts did much the same work as LAPs. But they weren't officers, just petty officers with one silver, not gold, stripe. When some on the *QE2* realised they were victims of this two-tier situation they created what one of them called 'a hoo-hah' with the hotel manager. Why shouldn't they have the same privileges, pay and respect as the LAPs, as they were doing the same work?

After the *QE2* protest the formal situation remained, but quietly women bureau assistants were promoted if they were in the right place at right time. It was, though, much harder for women to go up the promotion ladder. Despite some having greater hotel experience than men, they had to jump from petty officer to officer status. Men, by contrast, were already on the officer track.[27]

Legal changes in women's rights slowly changed LAPs' culture. LAP Celia Cowan said that when equal opportunities legislation came in on '29 December 1975 – the day the law changed and we were entitled to equal pay for equal work – hmmmmm, yeah right – has that ever happened!!', she and the women assistant pursers on her ship celebrated very vividly at an on-board party. 'Officially the WAPs became APs and so we [six] thought we would put on the boys' uniforms for the day. It didn't go down too well with the Purser!!' says Celia, who later posted a photo of the event on the internet.[28]

Part of the problem was that women were still seen as workers who 'had to' leave on marriage. Romy Green (b. 1947) was told that the average career duration of women purser staff was twenty-eight months, before they left to marry.[29] But by the mid-1970s married women were able to continue. Most career-focused purser's bureau women at sea chose to stay single. Judy Smyth, Frances's counterpart in P&O, knew that the company allowed no woman to rise higher than senior assistant purser or continue over the age of 40. Fortunately, the 1975 Sex Discrimination Act changed the situation and instead of having to leave in 1978 she continued up the career ladder.

Judy talks about a time when she was regarded as a phenomenon. 'Nowadays of course, petticoat rule is quite the norm, but it was fun to be there at the beginning!'[30] In January 1989 Judy's captain reported: 'an almost entirely female Purser's Office … works, provided the Leader actually leads, which Judith Smyth does admirably … If she is unsure of which route to take, she either gets the map out or asks a local … There are, in fact, occasions when I feel it is a pity she hasn't got a Master's Certificate.'[31]

Judy: P&O's First Woman Hotel Manager Aboard

Judy Campbell Smyth (1938–2009) was one of the legendary first women to become an S/WAP (senior woman assistant purser) in the Merchant Navy and finally P&O's first woman hotel manager: a four-stripe coup. The only child of a naval lieutenant who was lost at sea when Judy was 2, she became a Wren in 1958. Three years later Judy joined P&O as an AP(F) in 1962, working on the *Oronsay, Himalaya* and *Canberra*. In 1977 she became P&O's first ever woman bureau manager with four AP(F)s working under her. The following year she was awarded a catering qualification at Ealing Technical College.

Eighteen career-focused years after her start, in 1990 P&O's magazine *Wavelength* was able to trumpet: 'Proudly, we introduce you to P&O's first fully-fledged female Purser. Judith, through her perseverance and determination, has paved the way for other women to achieve their career goals.' She began work as a hotel manager on the *Sun Princess*. After thirty-three years with P&O she retired to Hove in 2005. Judy later got cancer and was looked after by Alison Ross, the nursing sister from her ship, with whom she's ventured on many intrepid holidays. She is remembered with huge esteem and affection by seafarers: no mean feat for an executive. Jeremy Chandler Browne, her godson and executor, said: 'Judith was a lady of the sea, who followed in her father's naval footsteps. She loved the sea, and we took part of her ashes to Malta and they were scattered by us off Valetta at sea, 35°54'26"N – 14°31'18"W, according to her wishes.'[32]

Judy Smyth in her sea office. (Browne family)

Frances Milroy and Judy Smyth were beacons for other women but also it was becoming normal for women graduates like Caroline Norman to become hotel managers. The old purser's department is no longer a world of white ex-Wrens but is very racially mixed. In P&O in about 2003 white British female and male JAPs (now called assistant managers) were managing lower-ranked, non-British people called 'receptionists' (people who could be paid less). Then very quickly, around 2005, in P&O, non-British people became assistant managers and managers too.

Both gender *and* race were no longer such determining factors in the shipboard hotel-management world. You got your job on merit (although having a face that fitted still mattered in this still-elitist hierarchy). And of course the less you could be paid the better. One of the struggles is to make sure jobs are spread among every nationality, so there can be no accusations that there is, say, a group of one nationality offering insiders preferential career jumps.

A veteran seafarer, Jacqui Hodgson, in 2008 famously became the hotel manager of several Cunard ships, including *Queen Victoria*. She was at sea for thirty-six years, a teacher who worked her way up from stewardess, including during *QE2*'s voyage in the 1982 Falklands Conflict. She followed her dream and took an honours degree in economics and business as a mature student, then made it to hotel manager in the early twenty-first century. Ms Hodgson said that on board:

> our aim is to consistently exceed our guests' expectations. So we are always reviewing where we are, where we are going to be and what methods we have to talk about, discuss and monitor in order to get there. That is, sort of always challenging yourself, or at least I am, in my role of heading up the hotel.[33]

She was still very unusual as a woman at this level, when she retired in 2014. Not all women want to wait so long for promotion.

The future hotel managers are graduates, often non-British, women and men. Caroline Norman is impressed that on ships you really can progress from rank to rank, after putting in a certain amount of time. In fact, she found it can be quite hard to work on land, because people don't have stripes that indicate clearly what they've done and the next stage they're headed for. Shore women have to feel their way and blow their own trumpets more. So in that sense the sea is an easier place for women in hotel-style work to progress to high places.

9

FROM CANDY GIRL TO RETAIL EXPERT: WORKING IN SHOPS AND HAIRDRESSING SALONS

Sarah Bracegirdle was, until very recently, the most visible ship's shop assistant in the world, on a major website about how to obtain cruise ship jobs. Her story is that after backpacking round the Antipodes she soon felt bored and wanted to go travelling again.

Friends inspired her to think about on-board shops, those palaces of consumption aboard the mega-palaces of consumption. And so she became a gift-shop assistant on cruise ships, including the *Aurora* and *Arcadia*. Like many British seawomen she works for Harding Retail, the Bristol-based company that runs nearly 200 shops on fifty-seven cruise ships.[1]

If you only read Facebook you'd imagine it was heaven. Shoppies (shipboard slang for shop staff) and hairies (hairdressers) from the 1980s and 1990s share pictures and tell stories of the very hard work – but high-jinks off duty. However, those retailing veterans who now cruise as passengers find when they chat with modern women on the floating shopping malls and in the ultra-chic complexes of salons, spas and medi-spas that there's far less fun available now.

On some ships retail staff are no longer allowed to mix with passengers. In most cases they have to focus on sales targets. Today's highly regulated retail staff put in an average ten-hour day and are not allowed ashore in every port. Customs controls mean that in port the ship's shops are closed to the public. Staff take it in turns to go ashore because the rest have to stay on board to deal with emergencies. Concessionaire personnel normally act as stairway or lounge guides, meaning they direct guests to their allocated lifeboat assembly stations for evacuating ship.

One of the employers, Starboard Cruise Services, has the slogan: 'We believe shopping is about entertainment, discovery and creating memories of a dream vacation.'[2] Shop and salon workers are therefore acting as official dream-weavers. 'Go on, treat yourself! You're on holiday,' staff encourage passengers. They're trained in strategies to target customers who will allay on-board boredom with retail therapy. How does their vision of a dream job sit with employers' vision of the passenger vehicle as a revenue-maximisation opportunity? Apparently workers grab what pleasure they can, in the margins, and sometimes help themselves stay alert with uppers like Red Bull and a lot of coffee.

Sarah tells potential shoppies that they can succeed if they can tolerate sharing a small cabin, handle being away from home on a six-month contract and deal well with people (which she learned doing casual jobs in Australia). It is important 'that you're physically able to lift up to 20kgs [44lb] ... and that you'll be able to adapt to ship life quickly'. She thinks it's crucial that young women understand they're not going on holiday and shouldn't expect to leave after just one cruise.[3] Immaculately uniformed, ideally multilingual, often graduates, they need to know the price they'll pay for 'free' cruises.

Women never really had to break into shop and beauty-care work on ships: it was and is still largely deemed 'women's work'. This is not least because women are so good at the communications involved in the complex network of activities included in a purchase, and women are the main consumers too. At sea, as on land, women, not men, are the majority doing shop and beauty work. Women outnumber men at the highest management level these days – for example, in Starboard shops on Holland America ships. It can be a lifetime career for women now.

Such seawomen are not directly employed by shipping lines. Instead if you're a hairy (hairdresser) or body-basher (masseur) working at sea today then you'll probably be employed by the multinational empire Steiner, which dominates on-board salons and spas. Shoppies on eighteen of the major cruise lines work for Hardings, like Sarah; Hardings also have salons. Over 1,500 other shoppies worldwide are employed by Starboard Cruise Services, who operate on another eight cruise lines. Such retail workers can rise to managerial level on ships and receive a higher commission on the takings. Companies vary, but some managers get 10 per cent of sales, whereas assistants might earn 3 per cent. They can also progress to higher-level jobs within the companies if they work ashore instead of at sea.

Women such as Sarah Bracegirdle don't, of course, work on cargo ships and tankers, which have no shops or spas. No-frills ships just have a bonded store, a storage space which someone will open up if you need to buy toothpaste or a phone card.

And on the RN's ships the very basic shops are run by the Naval Canteen Service (NCS). It's part of the NAAFI (in rhyming slang called 'Colonel Gaddafi'), which does what sutlers once did on battlefields: provide sweet comforts and refreshments. Smaller ships have only managers, like Sarah Hearn; bigger ships also have assistants. No high-pressure sales talk is needed in 'the Colonel's', which provide the kind of homely bits you'd nip out to get at the corner shop. 'Jack [a generic term for sailors] likes a bar of chocolate and a fag in the morning,' comments a canteen assistant.

Sarah Serves in 'the Colonel's'

Sarah Hearn (b. 1965) is one of the four female 'canteen managers', as naval shop workers are called in the Naval Control Service (NCS). A civilian, she got the job in 2009 because she was experienced, having worked in P&O Ferries' shops, she told me. In the RN such positions had historically been men-only; NAAFI shop work first opened to women in the early 1990s, when Wrens became seagoing. Suddenly 'the Colonel's' started selling fragranced shampoo and women's, as well as girlie, magazines. Sarah's deployments (periods at sea) are for about seven months at a time. They're unpredictable, which make it an impossible job for some, especially mothers of young children.

The future for anyone in naval ship's shops is probably not good. The Navy is being repeatedly cut back. Sarah thinks 'more women may come in, as old hands leave', that's all. Basically she doesn't seem to see any difference between women and men in the role. Gender's not as issue, she holds. Equal opportunities exist on those of the twenty-six ships that have shops, and which are not stag (all-men) ships.[4]

If Navy women sailed then NAAFIs carried what women customers wanted: Miles's cartoon shows loading stock on ship, and the kinds of goods that weren't wanted when seven RN seven ships went back to male manning. (*Navy News*, April 1994/Charles and David Miles)

Scrupulously equal-opportunities-minded, the NAAFI's website offers a very similar carrot to that waved at potential cruise-ship shoppies: extrinsic pleasure. 'You'll get to travel the world – going wherever the Royal Navy goes, seeing places you've only ever dreamed of … the sense of community is amazing. Each ship is like a self-contained town, and you'll be right at the heart of life on board. You'll really feel like you're part of the team.' But it adds, 'In fact, you could even find yourself playing a non-combatant role in exercises.'[5] In wars these civilian workers on ships come under the Naval Discipline Act. They have to double up. Women like Sarah have to be ready to 'man' the guns, as well as be expert in the retailing arts.

1750–1850: NOT A LOGO IN SIGHT

No early ship had the luxury of carrying a woman (or man) paid to sell consumer goods or to devote herself full-time to all women passengers' appearances. An on-board beautician would have been as anomalous as a live pianist working on a space flight today. Passenger ships in this period expected passengers to bring their own necessities. Hygiene, not beauty, was the preoccupation for the relatively few women sailing from 1750. Voyages were periods of privation and make-do, not least because of the lack of fresh water to wash; tresses might be cleansed with Fuller's earth or oats, with maids or stewardesses enlisted to help. Sometimes hair-cutting was done by the (male) surgeon. It was a way to control vermin – or punish unruly female felons.

Shore-based women vendors from ports went out to moored ships, selling souvenirs and sex. By contrast the ship's resident stewards – and maybe their wives – from the mid-nineteenth century made extra personal money en route by selling small items to their captive consumers. Passengers and crew bought bootlaces, matches and combs. Wholesale supplies were sometimes bought from poor vendors in foreign ports, then marked up and sold on, often at inflated prices. Shop 'premises' meant perhaps a locker or a basket hung round a steward's neck. At some point later the ship's shop became a cupboard with a plank laid across it for a counter, open at pre-arranged times; behind the board presided the steward or his wife.

The plainer the ship – say an emigrant vessel – the fewer the selling opportunities. However, crew sought opportunities to augment their pay privately by selling passengers the scrimshawed whales' teeth and ships-in-bottles they'd created at sea.

As for the crew, trapped far from land for weeks or months, a sort of shop existed on most naval and merchant ships. Ships had slop chests, later a slop room. Stores of clothing, candles, needles, knives and 'baccy' were provided by shipowners or the Navy, managed by the purser (who was traditionally criticised for profiteering), and quickly served out by a petty officer with no sales patter. Hair care was self-provided or mutual. Seafarers applied high-quality tar to avoid head lice and keep their pony

CATTLE not INSURABLE.

'Cattle Not Insurable': Thomas Rowlandson's 1809 cartoon shows women being taken out to have their sexual services sold as a commodity.

tails from getting in the way as they worked: a kind of very hard-hold waterproof hair spray. (Jack Tars' large collars were designed to stop the tar brushing against uniform jackets.) But mainly it seems Navy personnel had a hair-mate who helped him, a male barber or a Marine who traditionally did the shaving and hair-cutting on naval ships.

1850–1914: BARBERETTES AND THE 'CORNER SHOP'

Floating masters of the cut-throat razor proliferated when passenger shipping became more luxurious. Proud seafarers from the old days of sail scorned these new steam vessels as awful 'poodle parlours'. So a cabin devoted to titivating, operated by a 'shoresider', must have seemed like proof of the decline. But the many male passengers travelling had become used to civilised amenities and needed a barber to shave them, not least because long exposure to sea air made men's own blades dull very quickly, despite the usual daily stropping. Self-employed male barbers left their Liverpool, London, Glasgow and Southampton salons and began renting small cabins low down in the ship. There they even imported a swivel chair instead of tilting back a dining chair, and gave male passengers (and officers) daily or even twice-daily shaves. Other could-be customers simply grew beards as long as Old Testament prophets or had their valets or wives shave them. Early barbers travelled as 'shilling passengers' (as every worker who paid a nominal shilling 'fare', such as musicians or headquarters staff, were called). By the 1890s these aides in men's maintenance of a respectable appearance sold treatments for baldness, and after-shave balms such

Women traders rowed out in bum boats to sell souvenirs.
(R.F. Zogbaum, *Harper's Weekly*, 3 December 1892)

as witch hazel. Compressed air dryers and scalp stimulators were offered after ships were wired for electricity. It was the very start of today's profitable shipboard spas.

Women found openings at sea if they were among the few 'barberenes', 'barbarettes' or 'lady barbers' already in the business ashore. So did manicurists who groomed a man's nails while the upmarket barber shaved him. Some of the more glamorous transatlantic ships probably offered manicures, which gave job opportunities to barbers' wives. Such women would have shared his cabin, and worked as deputies with limited duties. Hairstyling historian Caroline Cox points out that women were thought 'too "little" and thus too delicate to enter such a masculine preserve [as the barber's macho black leather and smoke–filled salon] … If they *could* shave they must be suffragettes!'[6] (My formidable great-grandmother, acclaimed the first lady barber in Lancashire *c.* 1900, certainly could shave, and run her own business too, while her husband drove trains. We don't know if she supported the right to vote.)

Women might have moved more into shipboard barbering had not the invention of safety razors in 1900 brought its end, as the self-shaving revolution displaced it. Safety razors were the beginning of the end for ship's barbers, both men and women, on trips too short to justify haircuts (for example, the six–day crossing to New York).

But barbers couldn't easily turn to that emerging field, ladies' hairdressing, because it was seen as such a separate field.[7] The situation didn't bring stalemate at sea. As they had premises, barbers could move into displaying and selling a range of goods, so that they were in fact the ship's tiny and only shop in many vessels.

By the turn of the century a barber who had seen the writing on the wall and needed to expand his clientele might have had the sense to take along a wife with ladies' hairdressing, manicure and retailing skills and ensconce her in his salon. Shipowners were oddly slow to see that lady customers required their own space on the luxurious new floating palaces. The *Titanic* in 1911 had no hairdressing salon for women, just August Weikman's first- and second-class barbers' shops. But by 1914 the *Britannic*, then the largest British ocean liner, was built with both a hairdressing salon and a manicurist's room for first-class passengers. Steerage women would still have handled their own hair care.

1920–1950: PERMANENT WAVE ON THE OCEAN WAVE, MADAME?

When war came in 1914 all shipboard women hairdressers, and the male lady's hairdressers, must have gone home, since civilians were barred from travelling. Barbers who did not join the armed forces themselves may have continued, on liners-turned-troopships.[8] Ten per cent of British hairdressing professionals were women by then. On land 'barber's maids' or 'barberettes' worked as assistants and cashiers, not stylists. Some must have taken over salons ashore while their barber husbands were away fighting. This surely generated women's confidence in their ability to run – indeed *own* – salons, including the new ladies' hairdressing salons that were just starting in cities, as movie-loving women clients sought self-transformation, glamour – and liberating bobs.

At some point in the 1920s shipping companies realised that ladies' hairdressing (and even a little beauty care) could profitably be offered. Probably husband-and-wife teams were envisaged, offering twin, gendered, services. Their shared sleeping quarters would have obviated the need to sort out extra berths for female staff. I suspect it's at this point that wives started getting on-board hair-care jobs.

But so too did at least one pair of unattached women freelancers such as Ann Runcie, the mother of the late Archbishop of Canterbury. Born in the 1890s, Ann and her friend Peggy Levy initially sailed on a Cunard world cruise in 1923, leaving Robert (age 2) to be looked after by his great aunt. Ann managed to combine the Cunard deep-sea job on and off, possibly as a relief ship's hairdresser, with family duties and home hairdressing as Madame Edna.[9] If seagoing hair workers were employees of the shipping line then they were on an equal pay scale. Women got the same as assistant barbers, rather than being on the unequal pay rates typical ashore.[10] Self-employed hair workers' pay was presumably a matter for individual negotiation.

Hedonistic socialites setting off on their first world trip, or to Paris, that capital of the glamorous *haute couture* world, might even want facials. So mobile women workers with beauty skills gained new opportunities to work at sea. Female Turkish Bath attendants, some of whom branched out into offering freelance massage, also cashed in on this new feminine luxury market. For propriety's sake the Turkish Baths were segregated, and women's sessions were of course staffed by women. However, male hairdressers could tend women's *heads*, especially if the men were elite Mayfair stylists. It was an opportunity for men who deliberately acted camp.

Shopping for pleasure developed with the late Victorian boom in department stores on land, staffed by workers trained to encourage consumption. Not for nothing did French novelist Emile Zola refer to these as the 'ladies' paradise'.[11] Toilers in these heady temples of delight tended to be women, not least because women were paid half men's rate and seemed more biddable and socially skilled.[12] Obviously no-frills ships did not carry enough customers to justify devoting much space to shop premises. Then early twentieth-century passenger ships began converting one or two cabins into a small corner shop-cum-souvenir kiosk, and the barber-shopkeepers started losing their profitable little monopolies to the new businesses.

'Fortunately, on every well-found liner there is always a ship's shop where one can purchase almost anything one is likely to need,' said a 1924 brochure.[13] Fortunately, that meant another opportunity for a woman employee. If you'd got the job at that time you'd be selling functional British items such as Pears soap and 'smokers' requisites', dolls dressed in regional costumes and Mason Pearson hairbrushes, and, according to a Royal Mail ship's catalogue of the 1920s, thimbles, padlocks for soiled linen bags, tiepin protectors, ebony shoe horns and needle-cases. For fancy-dress parties, staff sold domino masks, crepe hair and greasepaint.

'Hairdressers' sundries' included imperial moustache trainers, fringe nets, brilliantine brushes and vulcanite hair combs. The shop was staffed by one dedicated employee during normal shop hours. After the First World War an additional 'kiosk attendant' or 'bookstall attendant' worked on deep-sea ships. 'Candy girls' selected for their prettiness worked in a small wooden hut on the promenade deck, dispensing chocolates, cigars, magazines and film.

Employed directly by the shipping company, shop assistants were part of the regular female personnel. They were line-managed by the purser. The chief stewardess was usually their moral supervisor, and remained so until the 1960s on some ships. Shop attendants berthed in the stewardesses' area and sometimes shared cabins with stewardesses. Women-only areas were nicknamed Virgin's Alley.

Women shop staff (and restaurant cashiers by at least 1912), of course, handled money. However, women were not allowed to do so in that other on-board commercial business, the bank, which had previously been the purser's business. Banking on ships seemingly began when the Midland Bank first won the contract for the Cunard *Berengaria* in 1920. On land large numbers of women were allowed

This shop on a Royal Mail vessel in 1924 shows a male assistant but actually the job by this point had largely become 'women's work'. (Eve Tar Collection)

into banking from 1916, in limited roles. They weren't in a seagoing capacity until after the Second World War, not least because the job included discussing business matters, which was regarded as something only men could do.[14]

By the late 1920s women retail staff's opportunities were burgeoning. Shipping companies had realised that their ships, particularly if cruising, were places where captive passengers might profitably be induced to buy goods they didn't actually need: say, fancy decanters rather than hairnets. And shopping had become a recognised pastime for women, and an excuse for them to travel, as railway posters were starting to show.[15] Ships such as the *Queen Mary* in 1934, began to be designed with a 'shopping street' including a haberdasher's, a gift shop and a tailor's, meaning that a shop assistant now had a neighbour to relieve her for toilet breaks. She was no longer so isolated: shops had windows facing onto the vessel's high-traffic thoroughfares. Think Oxford Street, not quite Mayfair. The lower class the deck, the less luxurious the goods on sale. It was a short step from stocking quintessentially English goods from say Fortnum and Mason, to such stores opening up their own seaborne 'branches', such as Austin Reed's first on the *Aquitania* in 1929. Retail staff now found another way to go to sea. Rather than being recommended to a shipping company by another seafarer you worked in the land-based shop of, say, Richard Shops, and built up, first doing holiday relief work at sea then sailing full-time.

Ladies' hairdressing was enough of a novelty in the early 1930s for many jokes to run, along the lines of 'the hairdresser … attends to the permanent waves while the ship's officers attend to the transient wave.'[16] It was becoming a sophisticated job that included manicures. In 1936 at least three women hairdressers were able to sail on the most modern ship of the period: the *Queen Mary*. Records of voyages show that at times ships carried both 'lady hairdressers' (meaning women who mainly did women's hair) and 'ladies' hairdressers' (meaning males who did women's hair).

By 1935 at least one company, Royal Mail, was stipulating that hairdressers were to be uniformed: 'Black dress to Company's pattern trimmed with Company's silver buttons. White overalls to be worn over when in attendance in shop.'[17] But these women were not softies. Mrs E. Lingard, a manicurist on White Star's *Majestic*, was the third UK woman to qualify to lead the launching of a lifeboat, in 1930.[18]

The Second World War made women temporarily redundant in hairdressing (as civilian passengers were deterred from making unnecessary journeys) but not entirely in retailing. The redoubtable Mrs Marjorie Runciman carried on as shop attendant on the *Georgic*, which became a troopship.[19]

After 1945 it was now accepted as normal to carry women hairdressers for the women passengers, as well as still some barbers. Marjorie Court was one such ladies' hairdresser. When Cunard's *Samaria* was refitted in late 1946 for those emigrating

Ladies' hairdressing, 1930s-style, *White Star Magazine*, May 1933. (University of Liverpool Library, D42/PR6/3)

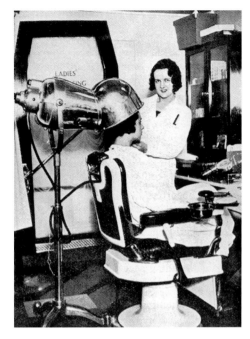

Cunard shop assistant serves the browsing King and Queen, late 1940s. (Eve Tar Collection)

to Canada, the facilities were upgraded to such an extent that the previous staff of three barbers was augmented by another male, and by four women working in the 'Beauty Parlour'.[20]

Marjorie: 'Head Girl' of Cunard Hairdressing

In the late 1940s a famous 'character', Marjorie Court (b. 1906), the 'head girl' of Cunard hairdressing, began sailing. Seemingly born in Bootle and living in Great Crosby, Liverpool, she was the lady hairdresser on the *Aquitania*, one of the most prestigious ships of its time. Although independent one-woman businesses were rare on ships, her presence was surely accepted because she was from a Merseyside and Southampton seafaring family. Her brother Archie Court was the chief engineer on the *Queen Mary* and two other brothers were Cunard marine engineers.[21] When she was only 7 she sailed on the *Sagamore*; often early voyages like this triggered a girl's determination to work at sea one day. The *Aquitania* was scrapped in 1950 and the rest of Marjorie's story is lost.

1950S–1970S: FRILL AND FRANCHISES

Independent hairdressers on ships, like Marjorie Court, found their days were coming to an end as hair-care staff increasingly started sailing as employees of hairdressing chains. Diversity continued for another decade or two. Companies paid the directly employed hairdressers different levels of pay. This was partly possible because as late as 1958, some hairdressers belonged to the Hairdressers' Guild, not the National Union of Seamen. Divided, they had less bargaining power.[22]

In the mid-1960s, there were four ways of being a hairdresser at sea: as a sole trader like Miss Court; work on one of the seaborne 'branches' of big city hairdressers, such as Prides in Liverpool; as an employee of a shipping company which was still employing staff direct; or join one of the hairdressing empires which were buying shipboard franchises. Hairdressers were prepared to wait up to a year, working in these chain's salons on land, for a job at sea. Some felt that it was the very best hairdressers who were given the chance to go to sea as a kind of prize.

In this field of shipboard salons, Steiner became the leader. First it acquired the hairdressing concession on P&O, then Orient Line in 1960, Cunard and Royal Mail in 1964, Shaw Savill in 1967 and later Union Castle Line. As a 1968 Steiner employee said: 'You were a Steiner because you had to be, not out of loyalty.' It was your only option, just as in the early days of ship's wireless you were 'the Marconi man' because Marconi provided the machinery and the service. The new regime that Steiner ushered in was so visible that seafarers referred to the Steinerising of ships. One or two of the previous hairdressers stayed on and became Steiners, but found their conditions were substantially worsened.

Every introduction of concessionaires' staff meant a lessening of the family atmosphere. And for some seafarers the incursion of modern *standardised* concessionary businesses was experienced as a blow to the uniqueness of your *special* ship and your prized, somewhat freewheeling, old world. It paralleled some men's sense a few years later that women deck and engineering personnel were a sign that a treasured way of life had ended. Steinerisation also brought an odd side-effect. Steiner allowed its staff to sail at 19, not 25, the previous minimum age. That brought women with troublingly little social experience aboard. It was perhaps the start of hairdressers being seen as the posse of glamorous, single party girls on ships.

If you didn't work for Steiner than you might be employed by some of the other hairdressing companies on the scene, particularly Ocean Trading, Freddy French (with Union Castle) or an ambitious solo entrepreneur, Tony Kaye. He put glamorous women on the small and very elderly Italian- and Greek-run cruise ships that were reviled as cowboy ventures. In 1963 his firm was renamed Coiffeur Transocean, and became Steiner's biggest rival for the next thirty years, employing as many as 3,000 people at any one time: mostly women, mostly beautiful and mostly slim. Trust Houses Forte (from 1979 simplified to Trusthouse Forte) was another employer both of ships' hairies and shoppies, from the late 1960s to the late 1970s, hairdresser Lesley Cox explained.[23]

The main differences between hairdressing ashore and at sea at that time were that spaces were smaller and clients' hair was wrecked by the sea and sun. Demand came in marked surges: everyone wanted their hair elaborately coiffed (sometimes with a tiara) for Formal Nights. Working days were longer. Hairdressers' jobs were made harder because they had no girl apprentice to act as sweeper-up, shampooer and receptionist; only fully trained women were carried. Lesley Cox affirms that: 'days off were only in port and strictly controlled/scheduled by the Salon manager. Lunchtime involved a quick run to the Lido or the crew mess room which was open only at certain hours.' There were no food outlets available twenty-four hours a day, as today. 'If you had the work during your lunch break then the next opportunity was dinner time. Room service did not extend to the concessions.'[24]

However, on some ships hungry hairies did deals with stewards, including free haircuts in return for a plate of sandwiches. (In most areas on ships staff could covertly get food or help by tipping colleagues or informally exchanging services and goods – for example, the plentiful free tester bottles of perfumes – until at least the late 1970s when bureaucratic controls increased.)

Just a few years later Julia Francis was working as a hairdresser for Ocean Trading, which ran both salons and shops. She found she'd joined a very lively culture where after-work fun was frantic and wild. This was mainly because hairies and shoppies had more time off 'to play' than the stewards and all the watchkeepers looking after the vessel. Retail people were free to party in the evenings.

Julia: Hairdressing and Partying

Julia Francis (b. 1952) found that her hairdressing skills were useful in getting her a sea job, from which she could move to another job: seafaring croupier. At 14 she'd taken to the scissors in her native Wales, became Miss Cardiff, then worked as a Bunny Girl and a croupier in London. In 1972 she met a woman who recommended getting a job at sea. Julia contacted Ocean Trading and was accepted, then began working first on Sitmar ships *Fair Sea* and *Fair Wind*, then on the *Britannis*. Sailing to Rio she was both barber and hairdresser, disliking the daytime work and all that was involved. Her boss revealed that the 'hideous' blue uniform was deliberately chosen by the company 'so that we would not be appealing to men'. By day Julia – sometimes with two other hairies, depending on the ship's size – coped with the havoc that sun and sea spray caused to their clients' hair; it compacted the heavy hair lacquer used at the time and made gluey 'bird's nests'. They did five clients an hour, 'down in the bowels of the ship: hair had low priority then'. (The barber, by contrast, if there was one aboard, was never busy.) Usually their manager was a man, who also managed the shop staff. Sometimes Julia was, she says 'the only hairdresser/barber on board ... There was no career ladder unless you wanted to work in Ocean Trading ashore.'

However, she found life at sea 'far more glamorous and exciting than the Bunny Club' because off duty was so sociable. 'We were *far* from convent girls.' So wildly did they party on cheap vodka that somehow her friend's knickers were hoisted up the flag pole. 'The captain went berserk. Caroline [Bryant, the Ocean Trading manager of hairies and shoppies] had to be flown out specially.'

However, after five years she noticed that the croupiers seemed 'more free'. So she became a croupier for the next three years. Julia left the sea in 1982, married and did a range of jobs. Now living in the Midlands, she keeps in touch with other Ocean Trading friends.

When Julia goes cruising now, as a passenger, she thinks the hairdressers' lives look 'very restricted'.[25] The boozy culture waned around 2000, when crew drinking was drastically cut back and some cargo ships and tankers, such as Maersk's, became dry. This controversial step was taken, in the main, after the 1987 *Herald of Free Enterprise* disaster, which was popularly attributed in part to over-use of alcohol, even though this was not actually true.

Women hairdressers in the 1970s were starting to find a few opportunities to do beauty work at sea because of the dawning realisation that whole-body well-being and beauty could be profitably ministered unto. Tony Kaye moved the hairdressing salon up to embarkation deck on the Chandris Line's *Regina*. It started a trend, he said, of 'taking salons and spas out of the lower deck areas and into the prime locations on liners, making them part of the overall cruise experience.'[26] The revolution led increasingly to all sorts of beauty workers being hired, to work in chic, light premises aboard ships. It was the start of today's spas.

Just as direct employment by shipping companies was ending for hair-care staff, so it was for women working in ships' increasing number of shops. Instead they were concessionaires working for one of two retail companies who rented space on ships: Ocean Trading (later Allders) from the 1930s and Harding Retail from the 1980s. Such companies were part of the new wider world of selling goods to people in transit, just as airports started offering shopping opportunities.[27] Shop work on ship had increased so much that, by 1963, on a *Queen Elizabeth* cruise there were six shop attendants out of a total female crew of eighty-four.[28]

Shop assistants on ships identified their employing company, say, the Ocean Trading empire, rather than with seafarers on the ship and the shipping company. However, most had a preferred shipping company, or even a preferred ship. And the longer their trips, the closer they felt to the non-concessionaires aboard.

In the early days, when there were no such things as sales targets, 1960s deep-sea shop assistant Edwina Parcell thought staffs were proud of their shops. 'You felt you owned your bit of the ship.' She found the main differences to working in shops ashore were that on the ship you were much more confined, spatially; the customers tended to have more impulsive buying patterns (and nationally distinct ones); and sales were far more weather-dependent than on land (when the sun was out customers flocked in for sun-screen).[29]

Staff in ferry shops and deep-sea shops were differently placed. Short journeys meant ferry workers were usually on a regular rotation of one or two weeks on, and one or two weeks off (although they had a continuous contract with their employer). Many saw it as just a way to earn money rather than a way of life. They were sometimes married with children. On some ferries you worked two weeks on, two weeks off; on others you did two weeks on, and one week off. Ocean Trading/Allders manager Brian White found on ferries that women with children were harder to manage than men, because they came aboard so sleep-deprived from

Edwina Parcell, later Cooke, looks after her wares on the *QE2* in the 1950s. (Edwina Parcell)

Robina Herrington is joined by Santa in the Allders shop on the *Rotterdam*, 1985. (Robina Herrington)

parenting that they could be snappy or tearful, especially if they'd had to work a week of nights. Some ferry shops were open round-the-clock by then, others just from 5 a.m. to 11 p.m., or less, with breaks.[30]

By contrast deep-sea shop staff were committed to working at sea for months on end. In some cases it was a career. Sales work was two-tier, just as it was in the purser's bureau. Men at the top had careers, women below them did two- or three-year stints. Initially married woman weren't allowed, which effectively meant young mothers couldn't sail. In 1975 it became illegal to operate a marriage bar. By contrast deep-sea shoppies were almost always single and childless. Or they had older children, and mums or husbands who could take over the parenting. Women found it was a job you could take up and then leave again, when the kids grew or life changed, as the doyenne of them all, Robina Herrington, pointed out to me.

Robina: From Hairie to Shoppie, Married

Robina Herrington (b. 1930) worked in both salons and shops at sea. In 1946 she'd begun her career as an apprentice to a very superior hairdresser. By 1958 Robina managed to get work at sea, for which she'd been previously rejected, as she'd been under 25. She was aged 28 when, at her interview in a wood-panelled Cunard office, the rather 'daunting' lady superintendent 'suddenly said, "but you are married … we do not employ married girls … their husbands kick up too much of a fuss." My face must have hit the floor … then after some thought, she said, "would you be interested in … filling in occasionally?" Clutching at straws, I readily agreed.' Two years later Robina got a job at sea, where her bosses were barbers and the ship's shop assistant was a Second World War veteran, Marjorie Runciman.

Mrs Herrington was on the last of the transatlantic crossings of Cunard's *Media*, *Carinthia* and *Caronia*, as commercial flying came in and liners went quickly out. Ordered to offer facials, she had to use her own creams and makeup on customers, as the barber hadn't got the necessary supplies. Post-war shortages still existed in 1958.

She left the sea, had two children and ran a mobile hairdressing business ashore until 1976 when, after thirty years, 'I felt I was out of date … [in this now] young person's trade. I moved on to a new career in duty-free sales at Allders at Heathrow airport and loved it.' She became a supervisor and in 1980 her husband said, 'Why don't you go on the ferries?' And she did, as an Allders International employee, in their shops on the Irish ferries and those from Southampton to Le Havre. In 1985 Allders lost their ferry contract. Instead of a golden handshake Allders offered Robina and the other ferry shoppies jobs on their deep-sea ships. 'I was shocked at the difference when I went back. It's much more ruthless now. It was just amateurish before.' She began working in Harrods on the *QE2* and other prestigious ships, sometimes doing world cruises. In particular, Robina enjoyed working in the jewellery shop, where she found she was very good at thinking up solutions – like how to mend passengers' spectacles. After three years she stopped going deep sea because of difficulties in her personal life. She then worked briefly in the Hull ferries' shops, before becoming a temporary office worker. Now retired, she still leads a very active life near the Humber estuary and keeps in daily touch with her many younger shoppie friends on their Facebook site.[31]

On ferries in the 1980s Robina found it possible to be married and/or a mother at sea; her colleagues were often middle-aged. Many sales staff came from big store backgrounds – for example, as Elizabeth Arden or Lancôme consultants – according to shop manageress Louise Merrill.[32] Women then moved on to working in other shops on board. As Robina found, compared with the 1960s, retailing became more professional, with merchandise carefully displayed and actively promoted. Cunard's buyer Pat Rickard was someone from the fragrance world who had an major role in teaching ships' shops staff about merchandising. From the 1960s onwards, she was part of the new professionalisation of retailing, organised from shore.[33]

More changes came in the 1990s, with electronic stock control and the new habit of direct billing to passengers' cabins. Before that some enterprising staff, particularly men, had taken advantage of the grey areas and possibilities to make additional informal personal profits on the side and subtly avenge unfair employers too.

In the 1980s it seems that some shoppies overestimated the extent to which they'd be allowed to join in the passengers' social life. They too, like hairies, were interested in having a good time. At least one shoppie says she was sacked for asking too persistently for deck privileges (the pivotal right to mix, off duty).[34] Louise found on some Greek ships women staff were forbidden to wear trousers off duty. When she challenged her captain on this she was told to go below and change, or be put off the ship. She changed.

Concessionaires and entertainers were seen as totty by some Greek and Italian shipmates, whereas in actuality some women never even dated anyone. And most were highly dedicated workers with integrity and courage. When the boat she was working on, *Prinsendam*, caught fire in 1980, shop manager Mary O'Hagan is said to have wisely opened the shop and told people to help themselves to warm clothing before it sank.[35]

One Ocean Trading woman shoppie sailed into the heart of the Falklands Conflict in 1982. Sue Woods was assistant manager on her usual ship, the *Canberra*, and sold souvenirs to the battle-dressed troops aboard, who were delighted to acquire the logoed sweatshirts and snowflake paperweights that proved they had not only been to war but had voyaged on one of P&O's greatest floating palaces too.[36]

1980S: BEAUTIFUL BEAUTICIANS NEEDED

As the two rival hair and beauty empires, Steiner and Coiffeur Transocean grew and innovated throughout the 1970s and 1980s they employed more and more women in a wider range of jobs. Now 'body-bashers' (masseuses) began to operate in the first purpose-built, on-board spas, on the *Norway* and on the *QE2*. Golden Door, the prestigious Southern California-based spa company, brought in the first major spa programme at sea, and liaised with Coiffeur Transocean to offer fitness classes on several vessels. In the 1980s spa visionary Elaine Fenard, later to become senior vice president of operations for Coiffeur Transocean, was involved in developing the first purpose-built spa at sea. Her advice affected future trends in cruise ship spa construction.[37]

Beauty therapists on such ships felt they had to be extra-competent to be allowed to go to sea. Hairdressers usually had been trained for five years: three years training for a City and Guilds qualification got them a licence, then they had a further two years working as an improver. Like women air cabin crew, they also had to *look* right, according to their employers' standards, as Tina Wignall found.

Tina Cruises to the Top

Tina Wignall (b. 1958) from Ormskirk qualified as a hairdresser and worked initially on the Royal Caribbean's *Sun Viking* in 1979. The Coiffeur Transocean company motto was: 'If you don't fit the uniform you don't get the job.' She was slender enough to be acceptable although she was told her hair was too short. So she grew it – she wanted that job. When Royal Caribbean's *Song of America* was launched in 1981 it was, said Tina, 'amazing, with five hairdressers, six massage girls and a spa area. This was the start of new ways: fake nails, body wraps, slimming treatments. Beauty had taken off.'

In the 1980s, promotion became possible for Coiffeur Transocean beauty therapists: to manager and then to floating supervisor, visiting spas on other ships, as Tina did. She was a rare high-status woman at that time. And she belonged to a part of the on-board world that men treated as frivolous and irrelevant. Yet beauty care was one of the most rapidly changing departments of the ship. It was difficult to be a woman in a man's world she found. 'As a floating supervisor I had to sit in meetings with heads of department. The salon was not important to them at all, so it was tough to get things done.' In 1989 Tina became a cruise consultant in Canada and has now been doing the job for twenty-five years. She still cruises.[38]

Changes like this meant people were now working in a coalesced version of two shipboard departments that had never been much linked in the past: physical fitness (almost a sport) and beauty. On the physical training side, ships as early as the *Titanic* in 1912 had gyms, saunas and steam rooms, which were looked after by the directly employed swimming pool staff.

Women and men on interwar ships had made extra money by unofficially offering massage (often Swedish, often improvised) sometimes in passengers' own rooms. Once, women 'lifeguards' helped women and children dry their costumes. Now the modern equivalent of gymnasium instructors are working for concessionaires. Usually men, they're employed by the contracted company to help passengers use the jogging track, do yoga and follow personal training programmes. They are much more a part of shipboard operations that help enhance appearance, with all its holistic links to general well-being, not sports or entertainment workers.

By 2011 nearly three-quarters of shipboard hairdressers and beauticians were Steiner; 155 of the company's 264 premises were on ships.[39] 'If it's on a ship it must be Steiner's,' contended cruise expert Kevin Griffin, announcing that 2,000 new Steiner employers climb the gangplank every year, ready to do the much-complained-of hard sell of Elemis products. But it's a bit more complicated than that, he added. Fred Olsen began running their own salons. Hardings set up the Onboard Spa company, which Steiner then bought into. And Canyon Ranch are competitors too.[40]

So powerful is the bonding on ships that hairies and shoppies from Allders and Ocean Trading use Facebook to exchange happy reminiscences about their time at sea. Female and male alike refer to themselves lightly as Ocean Trading Tarts. It's not a reference to sexuality, but to the fun of being 'OTT' (over the top) exuberant party people. They celebrate the extrinsic pleasures of that working life, more than the intrinsic aspects of the job, swapping photos of parties old and new.[41]

As for the Royal Navy, for crew working on British warships and freighters today, by contrast there is still no hairdresser, or barber. Charlotte Stansfield and Alison Sehar were the first two women to work in NAAFI shops on naval ships. These civilians joined the *Invincible* in 1996. Charlotte had already put in seven years in shore-based NAAFIs and said: 'I volunteered to go to sea because it will be a great challenge and I'll get a chance to see the world.' Their extra job, in emergencies, was message runner. By 2000 Bev Parkinson had become the first ever naval canteen manager, on HMS *Liverpool*. She said 'I am delighted to be a "first" in the NAAFI and I hope this will encourage more women to aim for management positions.'[42] It did.

Now at the start of the twenty-first century women have been delivering hair care for over a hundred years. It's changed from being a plain and useful job to being a role where you can be involved in a passenger's complete physical transformation, which is what some cruises offer. Nits are now as rare as tar. Most of today's credit card-laden voyagers have never even heard the words 'barberette' or 'candy girl'.

If current trends continue women on cruise ships will offer more high-tech beauty services on bigger and bigger vessels, including cosmetic surgery. Shoppies will work on ships with increasing high-tech ways of controlling stock and processing customer payments. It's likely that women from less-developed countries, who will accept lower wages, will take on more of the roles now occupied by European women. As many of them save so hard for their families back home, they don't party as hard as the 1970s and 1980s British women.

10

WOMEN IN MANY ROLES

Women have done so much on ships since the 1970s that there is not space to do justice to it all in just one book. So the next pages can only summarise briefly the many other jobs women have done on ships. But they all deserve attention.

STEAM QUEENS CLEAN UP

Next to stewardessing, full-time laundry work provided the largest number of jobs available to seafaring women in the early twentieth century. It was the lowest-status job of all for women in ships. In this sense the laundry could be seen as the female equivalent of the male stokehold, especially as applicants were allowed in without prior experience. They needed no Board of Trade certificate either. It was less a job that women broke *into* than *out of*, if they could. Heat and damp made it unendurable; high-speed labour was required, and the weight of wet items made it a heavy and tiring job. Early cleansing agents were hard on your skin. And at the lowest levels it was boring. But the pay worked out better than on land.

In the eighteenth and nineteenth centuries laundering, ashore and at sea, was seen as something that would demean a man. Additional problems facing launderers at sea were the uncertain supplies of fresh water, the difficulty of making seawater lather, even with special soap, and the way that the ship's extreme movements made large containers of water spill over. Even as late as the 1960s laundry workers such as Val Lawson might be sloshing around all day in ankle-deep water.

Most seafaring men I've known who visited their ship's laundry have rolled their eyes and declared: '*I* couldn't have stood it. No way.' And some have said: 'Hats off to those steam queens. The stamina!' They've also gossiped about the endless relay of trays of beer arriving to quash the women's thirst. This gave laundry workers a rough proletarian image, rather like women abbatoir workers, which was actually at odds with the variety of women involved, including those prepared to 'slum it' to travel. For example, Annie Kayes (1886–1948), a fancy ironer and mother of ten, was an early complementary healer for her street and also acclaimed as 'the Flower of Everton' for her yodelling performances.[1]

In the early days it seems that the high command of the RN fluctuated in its approval of paid women (rather than the sailors themselves) laundering ship's linen and sometimes clothes. But hygiene gradually was placed higher on the agenda. By 1731 the Admiralty was officially, but briefly, in favour of having four washerwomen on each of its six hospital ships. Low-ranking wives did the job on a freelance ad hoc basis if they were aboard other sorts of Navy ships. But generally it was a job done by sailors. Some could, of course, have been the cross-dressed 'boys'.

On early passenger ships laundering was avoided. Soiled clothes were jettisoned overboard or people tolerated grubbiness. Any passenger laundering was done by the stewards, and later by stewardesses as an extra to their regular wage. They used just a bathroom basin. Low-ranking women passengers laundered for one-off payments from each customer, or possibly from desperate pursers unable to rely on shore laundries (where merchant ships' linen was generally washed).

Nineteenth-century whalers and 'hen frigates', as Joan Druett discovered, were situations where 'surprisingly enough, the captain-husbands were usually ready to help their wives with the awful job.' For example, in 1860 Elizabeth and Captain John Marble on the New Bedford barque *Kathleen*, found at the end of washing day 'our hands are sower [sore] enough, I can assure you.'[2] One captain solved the nappy problem by towing a line of soiled diapers. And there was some picturesque pegging of items to the rigging, not least because the volume was small.

Miss Joan Burke, laundress on Cunard's *Caronia*, c. 1950. (University of Liverpool Library, D42/PR2/3/ 26/4/1)

Laundries capable of high throughput were established later on MN ships than on RN vessels. Initially they were only on liners doing long trips. From before the First World War increasing numbers of women got work in the newish steam laundries on land (called liner laundries and hotel laundries, because they processed institutions', not just households', linen). Such experience qualified them for similar jobs at sea too. During the interwar years and beyond, British women and boys, or Chinese men, provided the bulk of the ship's laundry labour. In some cases staff shortages meant lowly women were fairly forcibly recruited into it. Merry Black, a laundress herself, in the 1930s saw some manacled 'fallen women' from a kind of Borstal being brought aboard her ship to do the laundering.[3] It's similar to the way young unmarried mothers were used in convent-operated laundries.

Laundries offered opportunities for many different skill levels. Junior laundresses particularly operated the calendar presses, which is a bit like feeding sheets onto a conveyor belt. Women would be switched between tasks, partly to alleviate boredom. After the Second World War on-board launderettes were introduced, meaning passengers mainly did their own laundering. Professional laundresses focused more on ship's linen such as serviettes and uniforms. Work became less interesting and less skilled. Synthetic fabrics and greater informality of passengers' clothing further reduced and changed their workload. Nevertheless, a laundry had become as essential to most ships as a galley and engine room.

From the early twentieth century, educated women, particularly independent spinsters from the suffrage movement, sought management roles in laundries on land and even became proprietors, as did engineering-minded Dorothée Pullinger of the Galloway Engineering company, a pioneering women-only company in the First World War. With her husband, who had been a purser with the P&O, Dorothée set up the White Service Steam Laundry in Croydon. Georgine Clarsen, the historian of this remarkable venture, points out that such a laundry was an engineering enterprise in disguise as 'woman's work'.[4]

In some ways Joan Phelps (b. 1922) was part of this pattern of women in a kind of masked engineering job, thirty years on. On Cunard ships such as the *Mauretania* and *Caronia* from 1957 to the 1960s, Miss Phelps led an all-white British team comprising several women, a laundry boy, and from two to four men in higher roles.

She didn't see herself as having to struggle to get such an authoritative role, not least because she'd already done the job in Armley. Presumably Cunard had seen her as the best applicant for the job, with her knowledge of chemistry and her dedication to the smooth circulation of laundry.[5]

But advanced machine complexity and new cleansing agents, especially in dry cleaning, meant laundry management was increasingly seen as a science and technology job as well as a business operation: that is, more 'man's work'. And by the 1980s laundry work had become unpopular in general with white British women and men; instead, non-British people were recruited. Hong Kong men were briefly replaced during the 1982 Falklands Conflict (when anxiety about non-nationals' loyalty to the Crown was a concern), by Cunard's retired Liverpool laundry 'girls'. They left their children with grannies for the duration. After the conflict the status quo was re-established.

Today it's a high-tech pressurised job done by men, mainly Filipinos. By contrast in the Royal Navy there are what the sailors call 'Dhobi Wallahs' – like 'Tap-Taps' (shoe menders) and 'Sew-Sews' (tailors). These are Asian males employed by Hong Kong Chinese contractors. RN sailors' laundry has been in their no-nonsense hands since at least the 1920s.

SWIMMING INSTRUCTRESS

In the late nineteenth century women finally began being allowed to swim and do sports, as the advent of the *Ladies Field* magazine in 1898 showed. Their aquatic activities initially had inferior status to those of men.[6] But by the 1920s swimming was becoming a popular female sport. Synchronised or 'artistic' swimming (previously known as water ballet) took off.

Women swimmers were competing successfully, as the Hilda James story shows (pp. 150–1). Like tennis, it was now a chic way for ladies to exercise and to prove their equality as athletes as well as full citizens, after some gained the vote in 1918.

In the interwar years swimming was still very gendered, with prohibitions on mixed bathing, which called for segregated spaces and staffing. Women swimming pool attendants on ships were expected to look after female passengers and children.

Nevertheless, the job attracted some of the most active women to work at sea at that time, including Hilda Dand, who in 1925 won the ladies' long plunge record, and Mrs N. Palmer, the second White Star Line woman to qualify to lead lifeboat evacuations (in 1930). Mrs Palmer reckoned that in her six and a half years on the *Majestic* she'd spent nearly 6,000 hours in the ship's pool: 'During a very busy trip in the height of the season ... I once spent two whole days in the water except for time for meals.'[7]

Schools began giving swimming lessons, post-war, so the shipboard instructresses' work became slightly less challenging. By the 1970s these 'attendants' had to not only be ready to save women and children's lives but also 'to take charge of ladies' and children's bathing costumes; to be responsible with the male attendant for the cleanliness of the changing cabins and pool; and to teach or demonstrate swimming if requested'.[8] Today it appears to be a job open to women and men. But in practice women aquatic specialists on the ship's sports team sometimes end up with the smaller children. Males teach advanced strokes to focused adults.

Miss Edna Meech, senior telephonist on Cunard's *Caronia*, in the 1950s. (University of Liverpool Library, D42/PR2/3/26/14/1)

CALLING 'YOO-HOO!' AT SEA

Improved technology meant the ship's laundress job emerged in the 1910s. Similarly the development of telephony in 1877 meant that passenger ships started employing telephonists in the late 1920s. Liverpool-based Mrs R. Heywood Claxton (*c*. 1840s–1925), the wife of the north west provincial superintendent of the National Telephone Company, is recognised as the first telephonist, and (voluntary) trainer. Her pupils would have trained the first seagoing operators.[9] On land telephone operators (TOs or 'tele-ops') increased from 656 in 1931 to 97,480 in 1966.[10] It's likely that on passenger ships the numbers grew substantially too between the 1930s (when ships were first built with this new facility) and the 1980s. During this fifty-year window there may have been 200 seagoing TOs at the peak.

Usually two or three telephonists worked together in a small centrally located room, often near the purser's bureau. It was also a place where ship's staff dropped in for gossip. Shipboard phone work was a highly sought-after job after the Second World War. Your best chance of becoming a seagoing 'Switch Miss' was to be trained by the General Post Office, have experience on a prestigious hotel's switchboard, and know somebody who could tip you off about shipboard vacancies and recommend you.

Jo Lock (b. 1939) followed that route and worked for P&O in 1960, including on the *Arcadia* to Australia. She found that the telephonists had a complex and contradictory place in the hierarchical situation, 'very much like the armed forces really'. Jo used to play poker with the night-watchman, help out shampooing for the ship's hairdresser for a tip, and attend parties thrown by officers as well as by ratings. Hers was, informally, a freewheeling and intermediate position.[11]

Shipping companies varied in how they saw telephonists' status and title. In Cunard 'telephonists' wore uniform, but without insignia until the Falklands Conflict, after which they had a silver stripe. In P&O you were a 'telephone operator' and wore a uniform dress similar to stewardesses.

In the 1970s Jane Nilsen (b. 1946) joined the telephonists on Cunard ships. Her mates at the switchboard were women who'd been in the WRNS or WAAC (Women's Army Auxiliary Corps), possibly learning their telephonist skills there. Previously one had been an elite nanny, and one a first-class stewardess who switched jobs when that role went down market, as she saw it. Jane's father had been the *QE2*'s night telephonist.

On ships women tele-ops seemingly didn't have to fight to break into the job, not least because women were seen as especially civil and patient, crucial when speaking to customers. And there was a short career ladder, up to chief telephonist. The key sign of gendered thinking was that in the early days women were not allowed on night duty, which on land was widely seen as men's work. On ships the protective concern was even greater. It was not thought proper for a lone woman to be in an isolated job in the small hours, since ships then were relatively quiet at night with only essential crew and a few night stewards on duty.

Opportunities to become ship's telephonists disappeared when switchboards were automated in the late 1980s; people on board then had the means to dial each other direct. From the 1990s many passenger ships had satphone terminals in every cabin, so guests and staff could also call ashore without assistance. (Previously the radio officer had had to connect them to shore, expensively). On cargo ships there was never any need for a telephonist for internal calls (it was not a hotel-style setup). And in port there was just one line, connected from the ship's office. In early 1990s, telephone operators were made redundant and switchboards were dismantled.[12]

In the Royal Navy the situation was different. Wrens in both wars were telephonists on land. Civilian women telephonists worked for the RN too. It was a petty-officer-rank job. In the Second World War these telephonists very occasionally enjoyed a few hours' visit to a moored ship to see its switchboard but seemingly never sailed.

In 1997 the WRNS telephonist branch closed down entirely, indicating how much times had changed. It seems that by the time women in the RN became seagoing in 1990 telephony was not one of the seagoing jobs. The entire branch was declared obsolete in 1992. Today the RN careers website does not list such a role.

On cruise ships jobs for telephone operators still exist. Generally this work is done by the junior guest relations officer as one of her/his jobs. They handle incoming satphone calls (because a ship can have more than one satphone number on the same line, and the person being rung may have to be tannoyed). If they have technical problems they ask the ETO's help.[13]

IN THE UNMENTIONABLE

Much further down the ship, women did a job akin to laundry in that it was low-status and involved with cleaning: bath attendant. Women were seen as essential in the job because it was to do with the bodily functions of women passengers (male bath stewards attended men's facilities) and was therefore a gendered and private matter.

Between *c*. 1900 and 1950, when ship's bathrooms were seldom en suite, bath attendants' duties were not only to run baths for passengers and ensure they had sea-lathering soap. The job title was really a face-saver for people employed also to look after and clean the ladies' public lavatories, including the vestibule or washroom. At that time most public toilets in hotels and department stores had an attendant. On ship it was the job given to older stewardesses because it was relatively easy; they could sit down at times, with a tip-inviting saucer on display. In 1927 Doris Jee, a niece of Lord Milltown (as she pointed out), wrote that, as a Cunard bath attendant, 'I had to scrub floors and do a thousand other menial duties that I carried out with a lump in my throat … [but] I stifled all my social aspirations and endeavoured to do my utmost to please the passengers and reflect credit upon the [Cunard] Company.'[14]

There's apparently no such job today. The public area team clean the public toilets just as the cabin team clean passengers' ensuite bathrooms – perhaps with a similar sense of ignominy and Mrs Jee's knowledge that needs must when the devil drives: the need for an income forced her to swallow the humiliation.

TENDING THE MINI-PASSENGERS

In the nineteenth century passengers either left their children behind, looked after them themselves, or, if wealthy, took the nanny or ayah too. Childcare workers could sometimes secure jobs on small ships where captain's families were sailing. In 1857 in South East Asia, 'Fanny' was a maid taken on board the clipper *Revely*. Sarah Todd, the wife of the master, specifically employed her to look after the baby. Unfortunately, Fanny was found in 'compromising circumstances' with a man and 'we have found [her] guilty of so many things that I dare not trust my little one with her.'[15] She was sacked. Like maids, such casual employees couldn't be tried out before a voyage. Mismatches seemed to be common.

Typically the only evidence about women doing childcare work at sea emerges when things went wrong, such as when in June 1885 ayah Abbott went mad in mid-ocean, en route from Colombo to Plymouth, and threw the baby and herself into the sea.[16]

Over the decades the bigger picture must have been one of dedicated caring by the travelling family's female retainers. Other passengers, particularly missionaries or parents missing their own children, supported mothers. On convict and emigrant ships mothers helped each other. This would undoubtedly have included wet nursing when nursing mothers were too dehydrated from seasickness to suckle their own babies.

By the mid-1920s new work for seagoing women childcare workers emerged because ships were being designed with nurseries, partly to woo passengers with children. According to the number of passengers aboard and the class, the nursery in each class was staffed by one to three regular stewardesses who happened to be 'good with children'. Some young women, such as Marie Smith (b. 1906), were so keen to sail that they, as she told me, deliberately did childcare jobs on land to prepare for the time when they were 25, the right age for a job at sea.[17] (The age requirement dropped to 22 by the 1960s, then rose again to 25.)

Initially the only childcare workers were nursery stewardesses. Alone, they dealt with up to a hundred children for the entire day. By contrast, on the Cunard *Queens* in the 1960s the ratio in first class was one woman to every four-to-eight children. Isobel Wilson, a 1950s nursery stewardess, said, 'They had awful trouble getting nursery stewardesses and … having done it I can see why, because you were thrown into the Tourist nursery with about eighty children of all ages and on a rough voyage … they were sick, I was sick, it was terrible.'[18]

In the 1960s the work became two-tier, a bit akin to ass. mats and supervisory matrons. A new breed called children's hostesses ('chilly hos') were installed, at officer level, certainly in P&O, Union Castle and Orient Line. They were put in charge of the nursery stewardesses, who were usually much more experienced than them and at least ten years older.[19]

They wore no uniform and were called 'aunty' by the children. Chilly ho Barbara Symonds (b. 1928), 'Aunty Ba', said shipmates expected they'd do the job for two years, then be so exhausted they'd have to leave.[20] Another Orient Line chilly ho, Penny Osborn (b. *c.* 1920) on the *Oronsay*, stuck it out for six years from 1952 to 1958, then left the sea and became the lady superintendent for the company.[21] By the 1970s the British Shipping Federation had decided chilly hos should retire at 40. So it was a job that could be done for fifteen years at most, as the starting age was at least 25.[22] The women selected for the job were those with teaching or occupational therapy qualifications, and experience with handling many children of all ages.

Children's Hostess Barbara Symonds looks after her charges on the Orient Line's *Orsova*, 1956. (Barbara and David Wells)

By the early 1970s all childcare workers at sea had to have Nursery Nurses Examination Board (NNEB) certificates and experience of being in charge of large numbers of children under 5 years of age. In practice, if there were shortages any stewardess would be drafted in to the job for one or two trips, especially if she was seen as young enough to have energy. It seems that nursery stewardesses seldom climbed up the officer ladder to chilly ho, even though their skills would then have been better respected and financially rewarded.

Like laundry work, childcare work at every shipboard level was not something women had to break into. Men were not competing for the role. (Many ships officers, however, popped in to play, particularly if they were fathers missing their own children.) Youth activities became increasingly available and sophisticated on cruise ships from the 1970s. And some nursery stewardesses and chilly hos gave up the work because they felt modern children had become intolerably disobedient.

Childcare jobs continue, not least because shipping companies are targeting families, and some passengers are attracted by the possibility of free late-night childcare for their little ones. In 2012 Carnival catered for 710,000 children on its twenty-four ships and that number was set to increase. Childcare workers of any gender offer twenty-four-hour activity programmes that include water-sport facilities, ice-skating rinks, ziplines and merry-go-rounds. On the *Carnival Breeze* children can be dangled 150 feet above sea level on the SkyCourse ropes.

It's a far cry from the sewing cards and plaster modelling of the 1960s that stewardess Gloria Thompson supervised, and from the bouncy castles of the 1970s. Film characters from *Shrek* and *Kung Fu Panda* do guest appearances. And, reports one website, 'complementary Barbie activities, including movies and storytelling, will tickle some little girls pink.'[23]

Childcare workers now have a range of jobs: teen counsellors, youth activities programme managers, early years co-ordinators (nursery nurse) or play leaders. Some jobs are at officer level. Men particularly work as sports coaches, teaching football and cricket to boys. A very cheery, high-energy, attitude is required. Realities behind the happy personas emerged in 2011 when youth activities worker Rebecca Coriam disappeared from the *Disney Wonder*. Murder or suicide is suspected. She's not been found.[24]

Joan Roberts, ship's photographer, takes time out at Luxor in the 1980s. (Joan Roberts)

SMILE FOR THE FLOATOGRAPHERS

At the same time as qualified chilly hos were entering 'women's work' in the 1970s, so women photographers such as Hilary Beedham (b. 1954), who sailed between 1974 and 1977, were entering shipboard work that had previously been 'men's': photography. Hilary gained her opportunity because she had been a keen amateur and was married to a ship's 'floatographer' (as they were then nicknamed).

Two pioneering companies began: Marine Photo Service (MPS) in 1920[25] and Ocean Pictures in the mid-1930s. In the interwar years MPS had one (male) photographer apiece on fifty ships at any one time.

Engineer Rachel Parson's pioneering grandmother Mary Rosse, Madame Yevonde and Julia Margaret Cameron had long ago proved that women and photography were not mutually opposed. And the WRNS had employed at least two women in 'photography work' in the First World War, and 180 in the Second World War. But not at sea. It was only in the 1970s that women in any numbers began to get opportunities in photography generally on land and at sea.

Merchant Navy women began to be ship's photographers – a version of strolling photographers – as part of husband-and-wife teams. Rachel Savage was the first in MPS in the early 1970s. She and her husband Paul had worked as a team at Butlin's, where the work was similarly about offering holiday-makers professional images of a happy vacation. Women photographers were aboard as individuals in their own right, too. In 1972 Jane Hunter Cox, who'd studied graphic design and photography, became the first woman ship's photographer with Ocean Pictures. Jane sailed on the *QE2* maiden world cruise in 1975. Later she married Ocean Picture's owner and produced an anthology of voyage photographs.[26] Hilary Beedham, who was one of the very first women 'floatographers' in Ocean's competitor, MPS, thinks:

> I didn't really consider myself as a pioneer … but on reflection, I suspect that by just getting on and doing a good job, I was perceived by others as … setting a precedent for future women. Being one of the first (and the first on a Russian ship), my success was a positive argument for … [companies] that might want … encouragement that women photographers could do as well as men. Maybe it influenced MPS to reduce the training times for some of my successors![27]

Around the late 1970s photographic companies also began to employ some women as photographic assistants in the on-board team. They didn't necessarily have photographic skills when appointed. Personable women went aboard and were quickly given basic training in taking photographs by the male photographers. Some went on to photographic careers ashore. Others married the men and worked as a husband-and-wife team on smaller vessels. Women had to learn how to take authority and marshal groups without inciting antagonism against 'pushy women':

the job involved a lot of tactfully saying: 'Can you move a bit closer to the captain, please? Taller ones on the back row. Smile. Now.'

Joan Roberts (b. 1951) was in a two-woman team in the 1980s. She'd learned her skills as a Wren photographer in 1974, and became a Kodak adviser to the public. In the early 1980s she joined MPS, doing a brief spell at Butlin's. On her *Leonid Brezhnev* cruises to the Canaries in 1985 she found no obstacles to her as a woman but did recognise she was 'a woman in a man's world'. She reckons 50 per cent of her job was talking. But 'it was a lovely way to see the world (as it's presented to tourists).'[28]

By 1990 when fine arts graduate Carol Peacock (b. 1969) went to sea on the Scandinavian MC *Kronprins Harald*, 'I had no feeling it wasn't a woman's job.' In fact she'd taken over from a woman. Carol found generally that men hustled more than women, and that women's interpersonal skills were better. But apart from that, 'you were just one of the guys. [The other] photographers didn't see you as a woman.'

There was no sense of a glass ceiling. Women rose fairly easily to managerial level. Shipboard photography was and is presumed to be just a short-term job and so women (who may leave to have families) can be more readily allowed in because there's no expectation that any employee at all will treat it as a permanent career.[29]

Flagging out changed the composition of the photography team, which is now very young and multinational. Today cruise ship photographers are extremely energetic people in their twenties, often in large teams, who are skilled at selling. They work for two big agencies, Image Group and Ocean Images. Asian and Filipino men dominate.[30]

Sarah Craig (b. 1983), who's just stopped working at sea, found:

> from the beginning my being female posed no limitations in the job and it was stressed that everyone is equally expected to do the heavy work, of which there is much. And promotions are open to all … Technical jobs certainly were favoured by the men but if you had an interest you wouldn't be turned down and then in order to progress you have to learn that stuff.[31]

There's even, regrettably, a reason to discriminate in favour of women: the increased fear of paedophilia means parents can prefer women photographers, not men. Today ship's photography is arguably a dying business, because so many passengers have their own cameras, as well as cameras within their smartphones and tablets. But photographers are also highly skilled in the field of digital manipulation. So a woman photographer in search of opportunities in this dwindling field would not only have to have the strength to lift the display boards, good lens skills and a great selling style. But she should also be able to use Final Cut Pro to make DVDs into which people's own images can be edited, and Photoshop to enhance images. And you can't do it without having a crowd management certificate. This is a job that gives women undisputed rights to roam the entire ship, which is a major privilege.

TERPSICHOREANS AND CHANTEUSES HIT THE HIGH NOTES

Today, on cruise ships, entertainment is so high-tech and comprehensive that being aboard is like living in a funfair, theme park, cabaret club, sound-and-light show and West End theatre combined. It's official that both entertainers and the backstage staff can be of any gender (and it's joked that men sometimes are both, as this is now the most camp department of a cruise ship). In practice, men tend to be the techies and women the glamorous show stars. Entertainment department staff are necessarily lively night-time people in a large and varied team, ultimately managed by the cruise director, whose job partly grew from that of the social hostesses such as Maureen Ryan, described earlier.

Once there were no professional entertainers. In the earliest days passengers entertained other passengers and crew entertained other crew. Sometimes the twain met, for example when crew put on shows and formed fou-fou bands (comically cross-dressed men playing harmonicas and tea-chest double basses.) Even as late as the 1950s you'd make wigs with borrowed mop heads, and costumes from crepe paper and brown gummed tape bought from the ship's shop. Since sailing began,

The Ladies' Orchestra on the *Andania*, *Cunard* magazine, April 1924. (University of Liverpool Library, D42/PR5/8)

any passenger or crew member who could sing, recite, play an instrument, conjure or otherwise dispel the monotony was popular.

In the eighteenth and nineteenth century dancing and singing were common amusements on both naval and merchant vessels, officially encouraged as healthy social exercise. By the mid-1850s it had become the custom on passenger ships for the purser (male) to organise entertainment, and to support the ad hoc passenger sports and social committee set up on each voyage (usually chaired by males) in first class. Until at least the mid-twentieth century, as on land, class and gender determined the performances. Faded printed programmes for ship's concerts reveal that women were more likely to perform arias than make comic recitations. Budding thespianettes might deliver a Shakespearian speech as Juliet or even Portia. In crossing-the-equator rituals Neptune was always a patriarchal bloke.

On passenger ships individual self-entertainment such as reading, sewing, gambling and playing games were important pastimes.[32] Even small late-nineteenth-century passenger vessels had an upright piano or a harmonium, not least for church services. People performed to and with each other in a relatively homespun way. Times changed and from the 1920s passengers were increasingly performed *at*, rather than performing themselves. Ship operators wooed punters with the very latest Broadway and West End performers, blockbusters movies and the newest craze; it was building up to the era of bouncy castles and slot-machine arcades.

INSTRUMENTALISTS AND VOCALISTS

By the early twentieth century, naval and cargo-only ships continued to enjoy a fiddler, or small bands of men sporting pinafores and false bosoms as they strummed on skiffle-style washboards. But passenger vessels were now carrying professional entertainers as staff. Initially these were primarily musicians. Cunard introduced orchestras in 1905; the *Caronia* was the first Cunarder to carry a seven-piece orchestra.[33] Instrumentalists travelled as second-class passengers, not crew. However, it had earlier been common for musicians to travel as 'shilling passengers', supernumeraries, which meant they had an anomalous status: passenger *and* crew. They were usually all-male, but lady passengers who were opera singers, such as Madame Louise Kirkby-Lunn (1873–1930) on Cunard's *Saxonia* in 1907, sometimes sang a few numbers with them.

It seems that a few women may have occasionally *trickled* rather than broken through into playing instruments on ships. This was thanks to the proliferation of ladies orchestras.[34] Such orchestras had become a European-wide seaside and hotel phenomena from the 1870s, and so would have been acceptable to first-class passengers at a time when women in entertainment were imagined to be morally loose. In 1924 Cunard's *Andania* carried a three-piece ladies orchestra. They would have been travelling as passengers, not merchant seafarers. The Musicians' Union existed by then so the women were probably paid properly, not just given food and board in return for the trip.

However, at sea as on land, the music business generally excluded women, so it seems that relatively few women found opportunities to play at sea. Mid-century singing wives of band leaders sometimes accompanied them on voyages, sharing a cabin with their husband. Certainly, looking personable and knowing someone influential in the shipping company helped enterprising women. But even as late as 1975 only 8 per cent of British musicians were women.

'Nancy Foxley', an experienced bassist and bass guitarist in her early thirties, was on ships in the 1990s and 2000s. Her many pleasures included not having to cook and not having to drive her double bass around, she told me. Nancy was very unusual in two ways: as a woman instrumentalist in a show band; and because she platonically shared a cabin with the elderly bandleader. No other accommodation was available: 'it was a case of share or stay home.' Racism, not sexism, struck her as the dividing factor on board. However, she recalls that her band ganged up on their female musical director and eventually secured her dismissal. Other band members neither backed her nor challenged the bullying ringleader.[35]

Today the gender balance of ships' musicians is still almost as uneven as that of marine engineers, simply because there are fewer female applicants. Musicians nowadays tend to be from less-developed countries, because they will accept lower pay and the company's imposed repertoire.

It's much more usual for women on ships to be singers than to play instruments. Jane McDonald (b. 1963) became one of the most famous shipboard singers after she starred in the TV documentary *The Cruise*. In the 1980s, after touring northern clubs, she got her first job at sea on the Fred Olsen *Black Prince*. Versatility, mobility and the ability to satisfy a range of audiences are useful traits for women seeking work in this field. Stickability kept Jane at sea despite gruelling work conditions, including performing during storms. She changed. 'I'd long gone through that giddy phase, that crazy sense of freedom that everyone experienced when they first go to sea. I was now den mother … homely.'[36]

HOOFERS WITH VOICES

Today many women who sing on ships are primarily employed as dancers: hoofers who sing too. It's the main entertainment job for beautiful women aged 18 to 26. From the 1890s troupes of women trained in 'tap-and-kick' (now called 'precision

The Tiller Girls arrive in New York c. 1925 and hoof it in their coats on the chilly deck. (George G. Bain's agency)

dance') were putting on shows on land. The Tiller Girls were the most famous in Britain, and by 1920 they were popular enough to tour the US in the days before the iconic Rockettes existed.

Press photographs show that such troupes *posed* on ships, to secure advance publicity for their shows on land. However it's hard to know whether a large chorus line could actually dance on ships at that time, given the lack of dedicated performance space. (Ships' dining saloons often doubled as churches, cinemas and theatres until the 1950s or later.)

Ratings and officers on Royal Navy ships still put on 'SODS Operas', a tradition that appears to have been in existence for over a century ('SODS' stands for Ship's Operatic and Dramatic Society). These revue shows are equivalent to crew shows on merchant ships. On HMS *Brilliant*, in 1994, RN women then newly allowed to sail expressed their problems with male hostility most overtly via the SODS Opera. Defiantly they sang a alternative version of Gloria Gaynor's feminist anthem, 'I Will Survive', which includes the lines:

Hey look at us / we're people too,
We're not just some little girls / who should bow down to all of you …
Well, we're sick of all this sea time / you can sod your life at sea.
So here we go, out the door…
We will survive.[37]

Dancers' job opportunities increased because big performance spaces began to appear in the 1950s on a few prestigious merchant vessels. Women show dancers attracted audiences so shipping companies adjusted provision accordingly. Cunard formed its own dance company, the Cunettes (the name incited many wordplay jokes) in the late 1960s. Dancers also doubled as social hostesses. From then on, dancers, usually supplied by independent production companies, could find work on the increasingly grand passenger ships.

Today the stars of the ships are dancers who can sing too. Debbie Snashall, the director of the Dance Afloat Agency, explains that currently there are three sorts of dancer on the shipping lines she works with, mainly Fred Olsen, Cunard and Voyages of Discovery. Firstly, there are the entertainers who are members of production companies ashore such as Peel, Mirage, Explosive and others such as Qdos, who in 2014 provided performers to the three Cunard *Queens*, and Headliners, who worked on the seven P&O cruise ships. Secondly, there are dance host couples. Unpaid, they teach classes and have to be available to dance, separately, with passengers in need of partners at tea dances and in the evenings.

Traditionally they're a married couple although, Debbie says, in theory a woman could do it with a male friend. Those who get the job are often ex-competition dancers. And thirdly, there are gentlemen dance hosts, usually around four per ship. The 'job' (actually unpaid, you just get the trip free) began in at least the 1970s. It involves partnering any solo woman passengers wanting to dance (and tactfully fending off the many sexual propositions).[38] There aren't enough solo male customers to warrant a *lady* dance host. But as lesbian and gay charter cruises are now available it may be that this role appears in the future.

ACROBATETTES AND COMEDIENNES

Initially space and decorum meant that the only possible acts were those where women were fully clad and upright in every way, taking up little space. Because today's cruise ships are floating holiday camps they allow huge scope for other sorts of entertainers, some requiring large performance areas. Acrobats and speciality acts include juggling, German wheel or Cyr wheel acts, and diabolo. Costumes are flimsy and flashy.

Performers win more contracts if they can offer several skills, so that employers get more for their money. Gender isn't an overt issue for this work or in the other roles, but obviously a certain kind of performer is more acceptable: an outspoken comedian like Jo Brand might be perceived as worrying to conservative audiences. Other entertainers include guest/headline entertainers, comedy variety entertainers, magicians/illusionists, hypnotists, mentalists, impressionists and ventriloquists. They perform in big theatres on ship as well as in lounges and bars.

The most famous are flown out for a night or a week: others endure six-to-eight-month contracts.

In the First World War professional women entertainers of many kinds, including actresses performing parts of plays, occasionally performed on moored ships overseas (often floating hospitals or makeshift theatre spaces for service personnel). Women were recruited in wartime both to replace enlisted male entertainers, and because they were known to raise troop morale. They were placed on any 'stage' available, including moored battleships.

The Second World War brought far more women into entertainment for the troops. They travelled further too. Amateurs and semi-professionals, as well as professionals, performed on troopships and at foreign bases, such as those in North Africa. Members of ENSA (Entertainment National Service Association, the state-sponsored entertainment service), mainly women, gave a total of 2.5 million performances. They travelled millions of sea miles to do so.

After the war the influx of women personnel into passenger ships, particularly ex-WRNS assistant pursers, meant more women amateurs than ever before were available to take part in the evening entertainment organised by the entertainments manager or any theatrically inclined purser. By the late 1960s some LAPs were even allowed to be masters of ceremonies, usually just for 'the ladies' activities'.

Glitzy show styles, developed in British and US societies, brought much more flamboyance. Just as holiday-camp fun orchestrated by Butlin's Redcoats shaped tastes, so too did television variety shows such as *Sunday Night at the London Palladium*, and BBC Radio's Light Programme. Canned laughter, low-brow innuendo and the sparkly costumes worn by singers such as Kathy Kirby and Eartha Kitt may have been derided by some toffee-nosed audiences. But shipping lines in the 1960s and 1970s really brought the start of professional entertainers to cruise ships; it was becoming less and less home-made and more like Broadway-on-Sea. And the only way was up, and showier.

SILVER SCREENS ON SILVERY SEAS

On land the first British cinematograph show had been in 1896. Women were involved in the industry from the start, but the importance of their roles was diminishing from around 1910. They were principally involved as actors, writers and administrative staff. Ships began showing (worryingly inflammable) film in the 1920s in their dining saloons. Purpose-built cinemas began appearing on ships in the 1950s. Today ships have multiplexes, and in 2015 Carnival announced the first on-board IMAX cinema.

In the early days the Marconi man was the usual ship's projectionist. Women workers were not involved, even in serving refreshments (the job then of male public room stewards).When women such as Dallas Bradshaw became ROs in the 1970s, they screened some shows if required, even if only with home projectors and bedsheet-screens rigged up on cargo vessels.

As late as 1980, Lucy Wallace appears to have been the first to attempt to break into ship's projecting as a full-time job. Lucy had to fight for the right to such a job with P&O. Her case was backed by the Equal Opportunities Commission. Even today it is still the most significant anti-discrimination at sea legal battle fought by a British woman. P&O refused Lucy's application for the temporary job on the grounds that a 'genuine occupational qualification' existed: the two cabins which were usually allocated to projectionists were in an all-male part of the ship. P&O didn't have appropriate accommodation for women (meaning a women-only cabin and access to a single-sex bathroom).

The London Central Industrial Tribunal rejected the claim that the ship was a single-sex establishment (for example, like a gentleman's tailoring firm) and told P&O to provide, 'on a phased basis, accommodation suitable for both male and female crew'.[39] Although Lucy had won, she didn't take up the job. Today technical jobs on ship – including DJ, lighting technician and servicing passengers' in-cabin computers/TVs – still tend to be done by men.

FROM SERVING COLLOPS TO MANAGING CAVIAR MOUNTAINS

Women cooking and serving food on ships were almost rare as women engineers. In the 1760s the disguised Mary Lacy/William Chandler (1740–1801) was in effect a private waiter and plain cook. 'Boys, third class' each fed their own master. Some out women were in the job. Mary's counterpart in 1847, Mrs X of Newport, Monmouthshire, was a cook and steward whose strength was seen as unusual for a woman. A newspaper marvelled that she 'carried between the vessel and the shore, in a day, no less than 70 sacks of flour; while at the winch her courage never flagged and her strength never failed'.[40]

In the early nineteenth century three very different trends in women's food work at sea existed. Disguised women such as the be-trousered Mary were in the galley. Some women involved in owner's or master's families sailed in a domestic capacity. And out women were becoming seafarers whose daily work included serving food. Writer Charles Dickens described this new sort of person, the stewardess, who served his food in January 1842 on the *Britannia* steam packet: 'At one a bell rings and the stewardess comes down with a steaming dish of baked potatoes … [and] collops [slices of meat]. We fall upon these dainties … at five another bell rings and the stewardess reappears with another dish of potatoes … we sat down at table again.'[41]

Sea cooking began to change forever when the 1852 Passenger Act laid down standards. Proto-feminist middle-class women with scientific knowledge and easy authority were moving into domestic science teaching and inspecting ashore too. In the 1890s Ellen E. Mann co-wrote the main book on sea cookery, *Cookery for Seamen*.[42] Nautical cookery essentially meant mass cooking in cramped conditions, having meals available round the clock for watch-keepers, and being innovative with sparse ingredients in the days before refrigeration and canned foods.[43]

By contrast, on the US's Great Lakes women were sailing as sea cooks. At least fifty women had signed on for grain ships from Chicago by 1883. It was controversial, especially if the cooks weren't relatives of anyone aboard, because it was feared these women would have sex with crew. Indeed, some did, or were badgered to do so. It was safer to be disguised as a man like 'Ben', the cook on a lumber barge in 1878. And 'it is not unlikely that there was always a small complement of

Chief restaurant cashier Blanche Tucker leads her lifeboat crew on the *Majestic*. *White Star Magazine*, March 1929. (University of Liverpool Library, D42/PR6/10)

[camouflaged] women secretly working on Great Lakes vessels,' believes Michigan historian Theodore J. Karamanski.[44]

After the First World War Scandinavian and Russian ships were employing women cooks and stewards, who were often officers' wives. British ships did not follow this pattern, although by the 1930s a small change was happening in food service. Restaurants on White Star ships had women cashiers. Blanche Tucker, the chief restaurant cashier on the *Majestic*, came to prominence when she became one of the very first women to gain a certificate of competency in lifeboat skills.

However, in the 1930s, despite traditionalists' fears that Britain would follow the example of the US's Grace Line and employ women as waitresses, as it did on its *Santa* ships,[45] British victualling at sea remained a male world, even in the Second World War. But cooking and waiting training were given to servicewomen such as Wren steward Freda Price (1921–2014) during the war.[46] They looked after RN men ashore. And this allowed them to enter the Merchant Navy when an extraordinary door opened. With a mix of luck and determination Freda and ex-WRNS cooks such as Wynn Henderson, Betty Bloomfield and Betty Fitch were among the very first certified women sea cooks to benefit when a small cargo shipping company, Buries Markes, and its sister company, Medomsley Steam Shipping Company, controversially decided to employ all-women catering teams.[47]

Catering crew on the *Langleeclyde* gathering stores. Left to right: Chief Cook Betty Fitch, Head Stewardess Wicky Wickenden and Second Cook Freda Price, *c*. 1950. (Maud McKibbin)

Much praised for their cleanliness and skills, these teams sailed the world for several years. Seemingly the phenomenon stopped because the company sold its ships.

Buries Markes' revolutionary move didn't lead to more women pressing to be cooks at sea. The 1950s and 1960s records of the main nautical cookery school, in east London, show that no women applied. Indeed, only a few enquired. Ironically, women were established examiners there.[48] Indeed, educated ladies on land had been pioneers in setting up domestic science and maritime cookery training for the previous seventy years.

However, the change must have played a part in Union Castle's breakthrough decision in the 1960s to employ waitresses, the first British women to wait at tables on deep-sea ships. Sha Wylie (b. 1945) was one such stewardette – the new word coined for female ship's waiter.[49]

In 1976 Stephanie Rivers (b. 1955) broke through into maritime chef's work. Shaw Savill Lines acclaimed their employee as 'the first lady cook in the Merchant Navy'. Her predecessors, such as Maud McKibbin and Freda Price had been forgotten. The Sex Discrimination Act had been passed the previous year. So legally Stephanie, a former stewardess, now a certified ship's cook, had the right to fill the post on the *Limpsfield*, a small cargo ship. But the National Union of Seamen (NUS) argued that the job should have been given to one of the 800 men who'd just been dismissed.

Stephanie told the newspapers that she 'could do the job as well as any man. I am sorry for the men made redundant, but in today's world women are equal. Although I am a paid-up NUS member myself I think they are behind the times. I will be bitterly disappointed if I cannot sail.'[50] There's no record of whether she did so.

In the Royal Navy women didn't *sail* as cooks and catering workers until the 1990s. Women in the armed forces were restricted because they weren't supposed to work in combat situations. Army cook Mrs Angela Sirdar took her case to the European Justice Court in 1999. Although she lost, her brave struggle for justice helped contribute to the subsequent global change in thinking about women's right to work in potential combat situations.[51]

On passenger ships women were also excluded from bar work. From at least 1907 new ships had a multitude of public rooms, where male stewards served drinks. Prohibition from 1920 to 1933 in the US gave shipping companies a new market: booze cruises in off-shore waters, mainly Bermuda. Perhaps because it was such a romping atmosphere there seems to have been no role for 'pretty bargirls' here; men would have been needed to keep order. It's probable that women were not bar staff on pre-1970s ships for two main reasons: to avoid sexual trouble when inebriated men assumed a barmaid was sexually available; and because the job involved heavy work changing kegs, which the company would see as unsuitable for women. In addition, male bar staff probably were trying to exclude women 'competitors' from the most unofficially lucrative work on the ship. (Tips were good and extra money could be made by short-changing drunken customers and by watering down drinks.) In the

1970s some shipping lines made a decision to let women in, as public room stewards. Possibly they were initially allowed to do daytime serving of teas in ship's lounge areas and then their role extended and they continued into evening work involving alcohol.

It was only in the late 1980s on Cunard that women began dispensing drinks or managing bars. In late 1987 Sabine Machado-Rettau became Cunard's first female bartender. The public room services manager (PRSM) gave her her first chance, despite male bartenders' threat to walk out. 'Later on, I realised that the PRSM most likely had got me promoted to show the others who the boss was.' Her rise was only temporary but a second chance came later when one of the bartenders didn't re-join the ship; she was put in his place. Cunard's *Team Update* feted her: 'Women's Liberation arrives on *QE2*.' It said, 'Since the Cunard line was formed in 1840, traditionally bartenders have always been male. No one can remember why this should have been the case … I wonder when we will see the first *QE2* lady Captain?!?!'[52]

Sabine found that in the late 1980s a lot of other ships too started employing female bartenders. 'One difficulty was the Crew Chief Steward, who assigned beds on the ship. I heard something along the lines of "If there are no cabins for female bartenders, there cannot be female bartenders."' Somehow it must have been realised that women bartenders were good for the company and therefore it was worth re-making accommodation arrangements. Sabine thinks 'once that first hurdle was overcome there was no way back for the companies.'

After shipping lines recognised that women food and beverage (F&B) workers were worth letting in, on equal pay, the process was a quick one. Certainly in Cunard some women progressed, such as Karen Rogers who became the restaurant manager of the Caronia restaurant on the *QE2* in the 1990s. Increasingly women with relevant university degrees became involved as the tourism hospitality industry took off. Now women are in senior roles as F&B directors on merchant ships.

Among the 3,000-odd UK women hotel and catering workers on merchant ships there may be at most around a hundred women helping prepare food, and the same number serving and clearing food. Few British women work in lower roles such as dining-room stewards: this tends to be a job for men from less-developed countries. There may be a dozen women chefs and maîtres d'hôtel (the maritime statistics aren't broken down by gender). Sally Townsend is a ferry cook and told me she'd like to become a head chef on her ship one day, but thinks it unlikely. 'My face doesn't fit. It isn't a man's face and I'm not a yes person.' The very quality she needs in the galley, toughness, may work against her in the promotion stakes.

Sally knows only one other woman chef at sea and fulminates at the irony: 'Women on land are the ones who are *supposed* to cook, right? It's what women do at home. But are we allowed to cook in catering? No, that's a different story.' She thinks the reason is that cheffing is not just about cooking. It's about controlling a team, usually of men, and strategically managing resources. Authority and experience are required, especially in the intense social cauldron of a ship.[53]

LADY LUCK'S GLAMOROUS AIDES

Card games have been pastimes for travellers for hundreds of years. But increasingly games on ship were associated with the casinos that ships provided. Jobs for women in shipboard gambling developed because ships at sea were used to evade early twentieth-century US prohibitions on gambling. Off-shore facilities, including river-boats, were seized as opportunities to bypass laws, formally and informally.

Passengers played for money in the boozy atmosphere of the smoke room, a largely male enclave. The few women involved were vamps paid to inveigle innocents into fateful games with professional card sharps, at least according to cruise novels of the 1930s. Then, in reality, professional female croupiers were installed, probably to sweeten the atmosphere and add the kind of allure to gambling that glamorous women also lent to car advertising.

Croupier Julia Francis (second left) and casino on Costa Lines *Carla C* in 1979. (Julia Ashton)

On British-operated cruise ships formal on-board gambling opportunities began in the early 1970s. Profitable shipboard casinos were set up, followed by slot-machine arcades. Sometimes they operated as concessions. Women staff were taken on in customer interface jobs and soon predominated in ships' casinos, as croupiers, cashiers and managers. Females didn't have to break into the job at sea: *it* needed women who seemed heterosexual.

Women seagoing croupiers segued from London's West End to the cruise ships, where they found a less high-pressure world. I was surprised and touched to hear from Julia Francis, a 1970s croupier, about ships' croupiers' job satisfaction back then. She acted as a friendly teacher, enabling rookies who wouldn't normally venture inside a casino to enjoy a bit of discovery and fun on their ocean holidays.

Croupiers were – and are – usually not direct employees but employed by the casino which is a concessionaire of the shipping line. Most female croupiers from the 1970s and 1980s tended to be single women in their twenties. They'd got their jobs because they were conventionally attractive, well-spoken, numerate, socially adept and already skilled in casino work ashore. Today work opportunities are increasing because cruise operators are now running entire casino ships or casino cruises. Women are 66 per cent of the croupiers working in Britain[54] and that proportion is likely to be matched on ships.

DEFENCE AND SECURITY WORK

One of the tasks wives did on eighteenth- and nineteenth-century warships was pass the gunpowder from store to gun during naval battles. Wrens in the First World War and the Second World War handled weapons, but didn't fire them at sea. In the first World War thirty-four Wrens were gun cleaners, twenty were armament workers and twenty-four were depth-charge workers on land.[55]

The Second World War meant many more Wrens were in the gunnery branch, where they assembled guns, carried small arms, serviced shipboard Oerlikon anti-aircraft guns, taught submarine attack principles and learned how to shoot rifles. Others used .33 revolvers. In 1945 six Wrens were taught anti-aircraft target operators (they were allowed to aim but not fire). But the idea of women with deadly weapons was controversial, let alone the idea of women shooting from ships. Photographs show Wrens cheerily loading torpedoes, but they were far from firing them. They assembled mines but didn't lay them. Their branch never sailed.

After the Second World War, if you were a very science-minded Wren you could become a weapons analyst in Royal Navy services, on land. The opportunity to do that job at sea came up in 1990. One of the seagoing pioneers, Deputy Weapons Engineering Officer Chella Franklin, was the focus of discussion, not about her

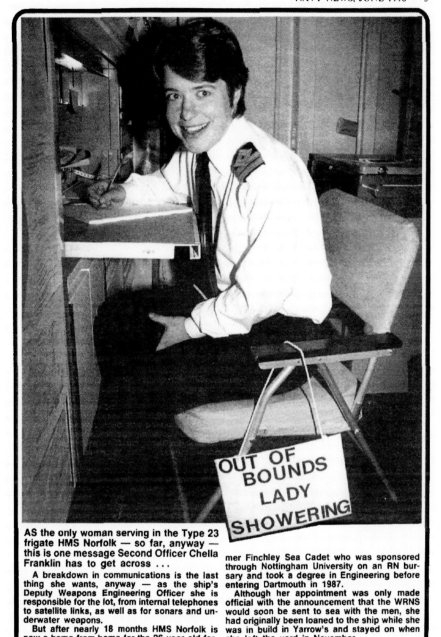

AS the only woman serving in the Type 23 frigate HMS Norfolk — so far, anyway — this is one message Second Officer Chella Franklin has to get across ...

A breakdown in communications is the last thing she wants, anyway — as the ship's Deputy Weapons Engineering Officer she is responsible for the lot, from internal telephones to satellite links, as well as for sonars and underwater weapons.

But after nearly 18 months HMS Norfolk is now a home from home for the 26-year-old for-

mer Finchley Sea Cadet who was sponsored through Nottingham University on an RN bursary and took a degree in Engineering before entering Dartmouth in 1987.

Although her appointment was only made official with the announcement that the WRNS would soon be sent to sea with the men, she had originally been loaned to the ship while she was in build in Yarrow's and stayed on when she left the yard in November.

Second Officer WRNS Chella Franklin on HMS *Norfolk* sensibly made a sign to cope with the lack of women-only facilities in 1990. (*Navy News*) work but about how she dealt with that perennial alleged obstacle, the lack of separate bathroom facilities for women. She simply put a sign on the door – 'Out of Bounds. Lady Showering.'

Among other recent achievements, in 2010 Lieutenant Catherine Ker became the first Royal Navy mine warfare and clearance diving officer, after the dissolution of fears that women divers were more likely to suffer decompression sickness than men. And in 2014 Lieutenants Maxine Styles, Alexandra Olsson and Penny Thackray became the first qualified women members of the submarine service, 113 years after its start in 1901. Women had earlier not only visited, but submerged in, submarines. The first was said to be suffragist nurse Clare Barton (1821–1912), the founder of the American Red Cross, over 120 years ago.

No such defence-related jobs on merchant vessels existed. However, in theory any women crew on 'ships taken up from trade' (STUFT) in the 1982 Falklands Conflict could have been trained, like other civilians, on the Bofors guns and Oerlikon cannons as well as smaller weapons that were installed on a few vessels.

Martin Reed, then first officer on the *Canberra*, said: 'I … set up a training programme for any of the Ship's Company who wished to join in … several of the ladies squeezed off a few rounds into the southern ocean, although we were never attacked … I cannot remember any feelings from the chaps as regards ladies and weapons, beyond the fact that we were all in it together and the … [gender] difference … did not matter.'[56]

In the last few decades the growth in piracy keeps bringing up the question of whether merchant crews should be armed and trained in combat techniques. Legally this would have to include women too unless loopholes could be found.

Once ships had a master at arms, who tended to be an avuncular ex-policemen. They were the sole person in that policing role on interwar passenger ships. Cargo ships didn't have any such job. The WRNS had regulating officers who were essentially police. Of course they worked only on land, because their job was to police Wrens, who were at that point only land-based. Today women are in the Navy Police branch (the new name for regulators).

In the MN, now women are part of the large security departments on cruise ships. P&O's *Oceana* in 2014 employed fourteen people in such work, of whom six were 'lady security patrolmen'. In at least one cruise ship the officer in charge of security is a woman. Women tend to get the positions after doing airport security work. They're needed because of the long-established convention, in customs work too, that female suspects must be frisked by another woman.

Riding shotgun against piracy is a new job for freelance workers on ships, mainly on slow-moving tankers. Today private maritime security companies provide armed teams on-board to repel pirates. Operatives must have 'recent combat experience' (e.g. front-line experience in Iraq or Afghanistan). Few women have yet done so. This restriction is down to national rules about whether women can be front-line combat troops, rather than deliberate discrimination against women specifically in anti-piracy operations.[57]

However, by the 2020s women professionals will have broken through into this booming new field. In 2014 the Ministry of Defence decided that, from 2016, UK women could go into close combat. Defence journalist Ewen MacAskill reported that:

> the main reason cited for delay is physiological … [However] the main reason for resistance, one not fully addressed in the [2014 Defence] review, is cultural and psychological, a resistance in society to the idea of women being engaged in close combat with a male enemy. Firing a shot is one thing, being engaged in a knife fight is another. Former British officers argue that women simply do not share the aggression and killer instinct that is more common in men.[58]

However, Australia, Canada, Denmark, France, Israel and other countries have for years, even decades, allowed women in close combat.

11

Conclusion: Progress and Prognosis

At the start of writing this book in 2013 I went to Warsash, Britain's main maritime training academy, to see what things were like today for a young woman who fancied becoming a deck or engineering officer. My friend Sue Diamond, a Warsash cadet in 1979 who'd become a second mate, came too. We looked at the small sea-facing window of the red-brick block where she'd lived as a 16-year-old, one of the only two women. Campus scents were the same: Solent seaweed and mud. Smartly uniformed young people moved around quietly. *Now* they wear discreet headphones; *then* 'Video Killed the Radio Star' blared out over the lawn. Google hadn't been invented then, nor the morning-after pill, nor mobile phones.

Then, if she'd even thought about it, Sue would have taken it for granted that graduates, including women, would move smoothly towards command of their ships, almost as if there was a conveyor belt that everyone could access. Sue had imagined she was the start of, if not a deluge, at least a steadily increasing stream that was become a wide river. But, thirty-four years on, she was shocked that the intake of women was no greater than in her day.

I was pulled up short too. It's happened repeatedly as I've been writing this book, because I kept expecting to be writing a history of women's progress at sea. My findings have shown an odd and patchy lack of it, worldwide. There *has* been improvement in seawomen's status and in the variety of jobs they do, as well as in their numbers and percentage. Once there were no women captains, now there are at least 132 with master's certificates. Once no woman was employed to run a ship's hotel operations. Now there are hundreds, and more are on the way up.

Once there were a handful of women, such as Sarah Jane Rees, teaching navigation skills. But by 2013 at South Shields Marine College 16 per cent of the permanent teaching staff were female, as were the CEO and deputy CEO.[1] Once seawomen were confined to stewardessing jobs. But increasingly their roles have expanded and they've switched between different jobs and even different departments too. Maureen

Ryan moved from P&O telephonist on the *Chusan* in the 1950s, to Cunard lady assistant purser, to becoming a doyenne of social hostesses, and finally in the 2000s to the glorious heights of the *madrina*, a sort of godmother to a ship – one who's feted at the launching or pre-launch. Fiona Rush crossed the great gulf from housekeeping to deck officer to now working in vessel management ashore.

Opportunities become available and are taken up, often with immense determination and usually with shipmates' generous support. Early captain's wives like Eliza Underwood and crossed-dressed cabin 'boys' like Anne Jane Thornton would not have recognised seawomen's conditions today, although they might think that seafaring men's attitudes towards women have not shifted much.

Seawomen's opportunities have come slowly, spasmodically and in piecemeal fashion. Ratios of women to men vary hugely, in different countries' maritime workforces. In 2005 Finland had the highest percentage of women, with 42 per cent. Japan had only 3 per cent.[2] In the UK the 3,000-odd seafaring women in 2014 were about 10 per cent of the country's maritime workforce. That's not the 51 per cent that would reflect the general population – but it's high. So UK seawomen could be said to be doing comparatively well, in numerical terms, even though their working conditions wouldn't be tolerated were it not for all that exciting travel that sweetens a sometimes-dire pill, and high wages for some.

THE OBSTACLES IN WOMEN'S PATHS

In the great graph of life the curve of women seafarers' progress has not rocketed splendidly upwards. Old attitudes still prevent the creation of a climate where scores of women deck officers reach the stage when they can pull out their iPads and triumphantly place a £28 e-order, finally, for master's gold lace epaulettes in the electronic shopping cart on Miller Rayner's website. The 'wo' is still not being put in sea-men, and certainly it is not put in so firmly that everyone automatically says, and means, sea*farers* not sea*men*. More profoundly, as being on the sea and exploring the world can bring metaphysical pleasures, as well as light ones. But seafaring is not often fulfilling enough for these seafarers who turn from land in the hope of something special, perhaps a dream of self-actualisation.

Women's struggle over the past 250 years makes so much sense when you look at it through the lens of today's concerned maritime experts. Implicitly these lens show that the key problems facing seafaring women today aren't so different from the past.

But nowadays they are recognised and named: gender discrimination, sexual harassment, glass ceilings, poor career expectations, lack of role models, a need for better work–life balance including maternity rights provision. Today, too, support organisations and good policies exist. No longer does a lone woman on a ship have to imagine that the problems are somehow her fault, or a fluke of that particular ship.

For at least 250 years the energy-sapping restrictions on women working at sea were caused by custom and cultural attitudes. Powerful people – usually men – be they captains or bo'suns, employers or parents, had ideas about what was appropriate for women. At the core of them is prejudice, meaning what people *think*, which leads to discrimination, meaning what people are then allowed to *do*.

Discrimination comes in two forms: overt and covert. Overt (direct) discrimination is, for example, throwing an ashtray at a woman when she walks into the officer's mess, as happened to engineer Anne James. It's organising a mass protest to oppose a woman student's entry, as deck cadet Myrna Galang Daite's male peers did at the Philippines Maritime Academy as late as the 1990s.[3]

Covert (indirect) discrimination is much harder to challenge, and may even be unconscious. A shipping company manager may assume that a woman will only be doing the job until she leaves to have a baby, and that therefore she is not worth employing in a professional-level job in the first place. It includes men imagining that women are aboard their ship for men's sexual gratification, and that those women's sexual attitudes are the same as men's, such as welcoming one-night stands.

Discrimination is often complex to tackle. For example, it was with genuine kindness that one woman engineer's shipmates gave her a 'beefcake' poster so she wouldn't feel out of place with all their girlie calendars up on the bulkheads. They didn't understand that she didn't lust after the naked bodies of strangers in posters, and she wanted to see life, not just Blu-tacked pictures of women's breasts all the way to Mandalay.

On ships discrimination in the eighteenth century meant women had to seem as if they were boys in order to be allowed to sail. Disguised women who were discovered, after working perfectly effectively, implicitly upended stereotypes about what women could actually do. In doing so they exposed that the underlying problem was actually that their exclusion was all about ideas of what women were *supposed* to do, not about the realities of what they genuinely could, and did, do. Similar gendered expectations in the nineteenth century restricted women to domestic work and made it hard for women such as emigrant matrons to win respect or wield authority. In the early twentieth century the struggle was, still, for a woman to get other than domestic work, or even a job at sea at all if she was under 30 and conventionally attractive. Stewardess Violet Jessop dealt with this by deliberately making herself look dowdy and old, literally discarding her hat's pink artificial roses at the interview. She too disguised herself. In the late twentieth century women's challenge was to be accepted as someone capable of doing jobs normally done by men. Some of the veteran pursers such as Frances Milroy managed this by stickability as well as being impeccably good at their work.

Christel Wiman, chief executive of the Ports of Stockholm, declared in 2005: 'one could almost believe that the sector has a quota-based recruitment policy, i.e. 100 per cent men … Why is that? Well, the [recorded] history of transport, especially sea transport, is equal to the history of brave and adventurous men, often naval officers, travelling around the world.'[4]

Modern women who *have* managed to ignore this history, refute the bias, and find sponsorship to support them through college and into placements then discover the main challenges when in the job are still: initial access; discriminatory behaviour that forces them into grit-your-teeth-and-get-on-with-it mode; progressing fairly according to seniority and merit; and finding a way to have children and a career (a far greater problem for deep-sea seawomen who can't go home to their children at night). Men still call women 'fish at sea' and 'cabin furniture'. Modern seawomen battle on with lips largely sealed. At the sharp end, Filipina seawomen, who bear racism as well as sexism, have tellingly devised these strategies to defend themselves from sexual harassment: 'don't drink anything which is not sealed [for fear of spiked beverages] … keep yourself unattractive … don't shave your underarms … don't brush [your teeth] in the morning … keep hair very short … look for a protector'.[5]

I've been shocked at how much sexualised bullying features in today's seawomen's lives. It reveals the power relations that still trouble our societies. Only once did I encounter self-pity, and that was not even when women recounted near-rape. But I heard many exhausted and outraged seawomen's stories of how they secluded themselves in their cabin to avoid hassle, instead of enjoying the voyage; of women who had to wake a colleague to accompany them to the loo, because drunk and stoned men in the night-time corridors were such a threat; and of women who found the ultimate patriarch, the captain, was their unprincipled predator, rather than someone who'd protect them from forcible sexual attention.

Enduring problems in a place you can never escape from can cause 24/7 agony. Most oppressed seafarers don't protest. But at least bullied men will have another male on board to speak to, whereas women can still be the only female on some vessels. Keeping silent, never showing you're fazed, means the stress builds up. Expectation of reprisals is one of the main reasons why so many of my story-givers wanted to be anonymous, or even withdrew the accounts they'd initially given me. The maritime industry is losing good women for bad reasons, unnecessarily.

Has women's difficult and uneven path towards equality at sea been so inevitable? Certainly occupational progress by employees who are seen as minorities, such as black people or women, is seldom linear or straightforwardly incremental. This is especially true now that the 1970s days of flowers and champagne for 'the first woman' this or that are almost over. Women's novelty value has worn off, which means that women are incontrovertibly in the maritime workforce to stay. The good news is that many men admit that the evidence of what real women do disproves the negative stereotypes. Researching Greece, which has the largest fleet in the world, Ioannis Theotokas and Chrysa Tsalichi in 2013 found that about 35 per cent of the country's seamen respondents agreed with the statement about women shipmates: 'I made a mistake at the beginning. She is admirable.' And a similar percentage said, yes, co-operating with women helped them revise their opinions on women's skills and abilities. Many, however, still tended to think a ship was not a suitable working environment for a woman.[6]

Facing men's continuing and puzzling hostility towards women on floating Hislands has been easier for women doing 'women's work', such as hotel department jobs, than for high flyers in deck and engine work, because they weren't challenging the status quo as much – other than by wanting a fair share of the tips. And so-called working vacationers (who've temporarily accepted low-status roles in return for 'free' trips round the world and transocean partying), have had it easier too, because they could shrug and just tell themselves that any hardships were temporary, and the price you pay for fun. But for those interested in a seafaring *career*, particularly on the technical side, it's been harder.

Breaking Through: What Helped

It seems to me that there were six key changes that enabled women to increasingly take to the waves, which are set out here in order of the potential magnitude of their impact.

1. The increasing comfort afforded on ships from the 1840s, after steam developed, meant women passengers increasingly sailed. (This was coupled with the idea that it was morally right for women workers to look after women, and the nineteenth-century growth of hotel-mindedness and consumer culture. It brought the advent of stewardesses.)
2. The rise of mass tourism first in the 1920s and then cheap cruising from the 1960s onwards. It brought not only more women passengers but economic pressure to offer luxury services such as beauty care, many of which were delivered by women workers.
3. Mass migration and the accompanying moral fears, after the 1850s, which eventually led to matrons, and then the first women officers: conductresses.
4. Equalities legislation in the 1970s coupled with the rise of the Women's Liberation Movement, which changed cultural attitudes as well as employers' restrictions on women.
5. Shortages of seafarers, especially from the late 1960s. Women had to be mobilised if ships were to be sailed by British seafarers. This applied to the Royal Navy too, and meant that in 1993 all new women joining the RN became liable for sea service.
6. The building of ships with ensuite staff cabins or/and separate bathroom facilities for women, in the 1970s, which meant women workers could no longer be rejected on grounds that there was nowhere seemly to put them.

It's a privilege to look over two and a half centuries and see the patterns in an occupation, which are not necessarily clear to women today doing that job. From this perspective, if I were assembling the ingredients to make a metaphorical cake called 'Success in breaking through into sea life, over the years', I'd find they were C, A, D, B: Conditions, Ability, Determination and Backing.

CONDITIONS

Crucially, young women – and adventurous older ones too – have been able to go to sea because conditions have been favourable. By 'conditions' I mean the era in maritime/naval development, and women's social and legal position in society. Shortages of personnel have given women a way in. The advent of typewriters – and the subsequent idea that the 'dainty-fingered' species were the most appropriate people to operate them – meant women entered shipboard purser's departments.

Laws and regulations have been a key (often inadvertent) factor in enabling women to progress. The 1963 Robbins Report and subsequent legislation stipulating that higher-education students should receive grants led to a huge increase in working-class women studying for degrees, including those doing business degrees that got them into management jobs on the newly hotelised ships of the 1970s. Flukes had an impact.

For example, Buries Markes director H.H. Mann, who introduced women-only catering teams on his tramp ships in a bold 1950s experiment, was apparently interested in publicity; the move may have been rather a stunt. Current anxieties about paedophilia mean there are extra opportunities for women photographers on ships because statistics show that children are usually safer in women's hands. And oddly, everyone's growing expectations of privacy and adequate accommodation (a requirement long-urged by unions) worked particularly in women's favour, after the 1970s, since more and more ships are now being designed with ensuite crew cabins. This means that the old and frequent objection, 'there isn't a separate bathroom and toilet area for women, therefore we can't employ them', is less and less used.[7] Hot-bedding (people on different shifts taking it in turns to sleep in the same bed) was once advanced as a reason why women shouldn't work on submarines. But the development of nuclear technology now means vessels are so spacious no one needs share a bunk.

ABILITY

Gaps still exist between women's real capabilities and the tasks men imagine they can be entrusted to do. As I wrote this book it kept dawning on me that very often it was known that women *could* do lots of useful things, as proved in emergencies. The problem was the idea that females *shouldn't* be doing such work, especially at sea. And Maria Scott, Wista International president in 2007, said: 'Too many women are, however, in spite of their competence, far too modest.'[8] One woman's modesty can act as a brake that hinders all the women around her. Ferry stewardess Alice Pickles wanted me to make clear to readers that even today: 'It's not just good enough being as good as the men. You've got to be better, because otherwise you won't be recognised.' And you've got to *show* your abilities too.

Distinguished maritime journalist Michael Grey in 2008 affirmed 'that there are almost no "mediocre" women in the maritime industry, and all the ones I have ever interviewed or encountered over the years are people who clearly excel. Perhaps they have to be rather special, to succeed as such a minority.'[9]

Many times I've asked the story-givers in this book if and how women seafarers differ from their male colleagues or whether that's too generalising a question. After all, in psychological and sociological research about gender difference the juries are still out – and arguing heatedly.[10] But seawomen tend to see the following traits in each other. These may be products of hard-wiring as well as learned through socialisation, and they're not true of all women.

Partly because women have to prove themselves to those who believe they can't do much and shouldn't be there, women try very hard indeed. They tend to read the manuals to make sure they know how to succeed at a job, rather than just diving in. On courses women do well, because they need to prove themselves. This then brings up standards in the industry, not least because men don't want to be beaten by women. However it also brings hostility from men angry at being outshone.

Engineers find that women often foresee problems and try to take early evasive action. And fortunately, the average woman's testosterone level is 15–70 nanograms per decilitre (the average man's is 270–1,070 ng per dl).[11] Low testosterone means people make decisions rationally and cautiously, and they are less aggressive and competitive.

Relatedly, some men drink heavily as a proof of masculinity. Women aren't usually interested in seeming masculine, which means they're more likely to turn up for duty and without a hangover. People in authority on ship notice women seem to be keen to do the next job and the next, rather than imagining that evading duties is a clever way of getting one over on bosses. Because they usually lack macho defensiveness women don't feel they lose face if they accept instructions or ask for advice (although some women deck and engine pioneers did bone up privately, if they were contending with femiphobic situations where they had to seem on top of information). Doing your duty well and alertly is vital when failure can have fatal consequences for the thousands on board.

Seawomen also tend to be emotionally literate, good at co-operating, communicating and helping colleagues (including those who are the butt of xenophobia). If they're bosses, they usually listen. Hard-wired emotional literacy can mean women often have a greater supply of the emotional courage to tackle interpersonal problems when they first occur, rather than letting them fester. Such collaborative communication matters in an intense cauldron where people mutually depend on each other for survival.

By contrast, failings that matter on a ship seemingly can include women being too tentative about imposing order on men (at times there *has* to be a hierarchy) and too emotionally concerned about colleagues' responses to them. I haven't yet met any woman who thinks the chestnuts that women have poor spatial awareness and that they readily cry when flummoxed is true of her. Most say they *do* multi-task, but that male shipmates do too.

Women's competence and diligence in preparing to do jobs, learning them and then doing them very well indeed has led to wider acceptance and respect. It's paved a way for the women following them too.

DETERMINATION

I've been awed at the way girls decided as early as age 7 that 'the sea's the life for me' and then gone for it, despite ignorance and hurdles that would daunt most people. For instance, at age 16, 1970s deck cadet Nina Baker took steps to get herself ready for sea work, switching to a school that would give her more experience of males. As a schoolgirl Lisa Jenkins insisted on taking science lessons that would help her become an engineer.

BACKING

Parents, far-sighted mentors and policy-makers in the maritime industry have been crucial in helping girls and women get on. Support includes ship-owning fathers who trusted their daughters so much that they made them masters, wise shoresiders in Human Resources who selected the right ships for new female cadets, shipmates who can see beyond gendered stereotypes, or mothers who look after their seagoing daughter's children for months. Women at sea have been helped in their careers by others who respected their choice, whatever their own views about women at sea. Equal opportunities policies, backed by organisations such as the Maritime Training Board, really do help competencies emerge and strengthen. Worker organisations such as maritime unions, the International Maritime Organisation (IMO) and the International Transport Workers Federation (ITF) have been crucial in backing women's rights, and in educating all those who don't yet see that women have a legitimate place on ships.

And women are backing each other too. They network, and tell each other about the steps they took, including the jokes they made as a way to deal lightly with situations, and share inspiring stories of the way they stood their ground. In 2006 Fleetwood Maritime College cadets set up a Female Forum to share experiences and guide each other. For example, some who'd not already had sea experience had been shocked at the swearing and banter. Claudine Piper from James Fisher tankships was able to offer them the useful information that: 'It's not because men are being nasty. They just don't think.'[12]

Women recognise one another's special needs, which is why the RN has its Naval Servicewomen's Network. Co-founded by Ellie Ablett, by 2014 it had grown to over a hundred members in just two years, and is crucially aware of women's need for support in balancing seagoing career and family.[13]

Other factors, too, now improve the outlook for women at sea. They include affirmative action, such as 50 per cent quotas for women in some maritime situations. These are no longer unusual, and have worked. Indeed, the World Maritime University (WMU) in Malmö, Sweden attracted so many women by sponsoring places for them that it's been nicknamed 'Women's Maritime University'. Women's number there rose from five in 1996 to twenty-eight in 2000 after the WMU committed itself to a target of 30 per cent women by 2010. By 2007, this percentage had already been achieved. UK schools are now mostly co-educational,[14] which means men have grown up with women. Therefore at sea men's behaviour is more informed and relaxed about difference. Better sex education on ships, and the availability of condoms and morning-after pills, means that women who have heterosexual sex may be less at risk of losing their jobs by becoming pregnant. (However, the many late abortions seafaring women seek the moment a ship docks for long enough must act as a signal that the on-board support still needs to be stepped up.)

Four decades of assertiveness training and the enduring impact of the Women's Liberation Movement also must be helping women challenge men who fail to respect them as equals. Certainly the Royal Navy is very good at training senior women to take authority and men to respect it. And above all, the number of women who've gone before, done well and now moved into management roles on land are crucial models and mentors for women, especially those doing non-traditional jobs.

Many people on twenty-first century multicultural ships are from countries where alcohol intake is highly controlled or prohibited by religious rules. This means that there is a less boozy culture (indeed US Navy ships are totally dry and UK Navy ships only allow two cans of beer or lager per day). Women are, therefore, less at risk from inebriated shipmates and their own drunken mistakes.

Hospitality work continues to attract women. This trend will mean British women officers increasingly do such work, including on the new futuristic mega cruise vessels which are now being built to carry 5,000 guests. Cruising is still the fastest expanding sector of the travel, tourism and leisure industry, with a 2,100 per cent growth since 1970. Globally it involves 13.4 million passengers a year.[15] Further advances in new technology will mean technical work becomes lighter and lighter, and therefore can be done by women, who continue to be smaller and slighter than men.[16] Weaker handgrip is still a problem, but the increase in women generally doing strength training at gyms could ameliorate that somewhat.

Shortages of officers worldwide mean suitable women can step through open doorways, and that companies who want to retain these officers will have to act on the many suggestions about how to retain women. Childcare support is slowly but increasingly being arranged for both women and men as a way to halt the brain drain. If the flagging-out system is stopped (as so many seafarers dream it will) then not only will all seafarers get better rights, but also women will be especially helped if their employing countries have good anti-discrimination policies.

And if it does get tough on a voyage, at least the availability of mobile phones and the internet can help women who need to off-load and seek help. Much of the world's ocean is out of signal range, but greater connectivity is being worked on.

WHAT DOES THE FUTURE LOOK LIKE?

There's still a way to go before the golden age of gender-free shipping that Linda du Pauw predicted back in the 1980s. And, after all, no period ever is simply golden, but also grey, and multi-coloured. That which glitters can be deceiving. However, the era 2010–30 could be a golden-*ish* time for several reasons, not least that women in professional and technical jobs have now 'proved women's value', because so many have done their jobs so well.

Most observers doubt that women will ever be 50 per cent of the seafaring population. A maximum of 30 per cent seems more feasible. Admiralty pilot Rachel Dunn, who managed to become a master and have three children, thinks: 'Even in fifty, sixty, seventy years' time you're still going to have that male/female divide. I don't think anything can *change* it, only *improve* it. We'll all change slowly.'[17]

Factors that will accelerate progress include the industry's need for skilled, competent people. The many very able women high flyers who've emerged on ships in the past decades, such as social director Margaret Newcombe in the 1970s and Captain Sarah Breton in the 2000s, are important examples who show that being born a woman is far from being a bar to competence.

'What will help women at sea is *more* women at sea' goes a common adage. The useless ice has been broken. Most companies will employ women seafarers. In the twenty-first century men are less inclined to see women as upstart, privilege-seeking interlopers coming in to 'steal' their jobs, which are men's by divine right. Some of the first women captains who began training in the 1970s are in positions of authority on ships and ashore, which means they can bring about a more respectful culture. This generation of women is well positioned to make organisations more responsive to the needs of women seafarers and to put in place the many recommendations of the IMO and other organisations (see panel), some of which are already being worked on.

Ideas for Helping More Women Go to Sea (Some of Which are Controversial)

◈ At least two women to be on a ship, so they can support each other.[18]

◈ A target 50 per cent quota for women.

◈ Shipping companies should recruit and support more women officers.

◈ Better publicity for maritime industry careers, showing women role models.

◈ All countries should uphold laws against sexual harassment and sexual discrimination. Victims should be encouraged to report sexual harassment and harassers should be banned from maritime work.

◈ Automatic maternity benefits and better child support, to enable women to continue their jobs. No automatic assumption that women are the half of the labour force with a 'sell-by date', a biological clock that will always render them temps.

◈ More gender-sensitivity training for all seafarers, including at college. Captains should not be the only ones given dossiers on how to deal with women.

◈ Colleges and employers should work harder to recruit women. They shouldn't assume women will 'see through' any recruitment material picturing only men and offering only male case-studies. (Already there's a huge improvement in this.) And they can lay a good foundation by discussing discrimination and nipping in the bud any unwitting practices, at the start of maritime careers.

Ships are places where pulling your weight can be a life-or-death matter. Thousands of women have now proved that they do indeed stand shoulder to shoulder with shipmates. Sometimes it's becoming the case that gender is not considered an issue. Indeed, a few young people thought I was rather old-fashioned in asking about it.

And there's still a need for fair but firmly enforced shipping company policies to ensure that men from less-progressive cultures, particularly deck officers from Eastern Europe and stevedores in Arab countries who won't take orders from a woman, will more readily accept women's authority. Repeated professional proximity with clearly respect-worthy women will continue to break down men's gendered assumptions.

Putting more family-friendly policies in place could have a positive impact on the conflict some women have between a deep-sea career and their desire to have children and be at home with them. Future changes may include companies allowing shorter spells at sea, and more vessels emulating Scandinavian ships with on-board crèches for staffs' children. This could usefully breed a generation of children like those who sailed with nineteenth-century masters and their wives. The acceptability of house-husbands is already making a difference; several active women masters benefit from supportive partners at home rearing the children. One of the factors enabling Indian women marine engineers to advance is the cultural expectation that other people are paid to look after the children; a mother's absence is not a problem.[19] Acceptance of the African adage that it takes a village to bring up a child can be really helpful here.

Women will have a greater place on Royal Navy ships as new vessels are built, and now that they are no longer prohibited from sailing on submarines. It's been suggested that the answer to men's problems with women on ships may be women-only ships. (Famously China in the 1960s and 1970s had a cargo ship officered entirely by women, the *Fengtao*.[20]) Generally it's not expected that women-only ships will become a reality. Anyway, most seafarers think it would be a loss, because diversity makes life so rich and enjoyable.

A survey in 2000 showed that young women cadets liked the social side of going to sea (the men were keener on extrinsic benefits, such as pay and leave).[21] So it may be that women will continue to be more attracted to jobs on the more populated vessels, meaning cruise ships. (Low staffing levels on cargo vessels and tankers will mean they can never offer sociable enough environments.) Overall, it's clear that women will sail in increasing numbers. But UK women may find it harder to obtain non-officer jobs, because employers prefer ratings to be overseas workers who will accept lower pay. But for women using the job as a means to see the world, and for those for whom ship handling is a passionate vocation, seafaring is an attractive life that – most of the time – feels more than worth the hassle.

AND THE JOY OF DOING IT, TOGETHER …

Every seafaring woman's story is different. But if there's one phrase that keeps coming up it's: 'I wanted to go to sea and I've loved seeing the world that way.' Working even within Hislands' and sweatships' constraints doesn't spoil their explorations of the world and their own potential. Many have spent what they see as the best part of their lives at sea. They became confident, well-informed, tolerant and deeply able to deal with all sorts of vicissitudes. Seafaring often means they take on new identities.

Most who've left the sea to have children don't regret the loss, not least because the seafaring can pall. It can feel unreal and it's hard to always be away from land and unable to sustain solid links with all those people who matter to them. But the seafaring women I've met definitely celebrate having gone to sea, before motherhood, because it expanded their understanding of human beings in the wider world. Travel does broaden the mind, even if you have to do it in a hard-slog cocoon when you're tired out and distressed by *mal de mer* and injustice. Meeting people from other countries, on ship as well as off, is crucial to a sense of connectedness, wonder and truly common wealth. In particular, the world of tall training ships, where so many women are in leading jobs and therefore in a position to create an enjoyable culture, offers modern women the chance to remake the past. This time around they *can* be included, cross-dressed or not.

'I love it' were the words with which so many story-givers finished their briefings. And they say, 'Yes, even with all its faults, especially these days, I'd recommend it to any young woman, as long as she's prepared to work hard, can thicken her skin and tolerate being in a goldfish bowl. It's a great life. And the camaraderie is to die for.'

The IMO slogan for its campaign to integrate women into seafaring is 'Go to sea together'.[22] That's absolutely what seawomen want: the co-operation and comradeship of women and men voyaging amicably across the world's oceans, together, safely, ethically and with mutual respect.

Voyages are always voyages *in*, too. This special sort of mobility brings all sorts of beneficial changes in identity, wisdom and understanding to the women who determinedly go up that gangplank and live on the waves, voyaging into new worlds.

Appendix 1

A Note on the Thinking Behind This Book

SOURCES

This book surveys a huge period and both navies. Therefore it would take several lifetimes to fully research all the primary sources. I have been studying women and gender at sea for thirty-five years, so that gives me a useful and unusually broad basis. But in some cases, particularly with the early history of women in the Royal Navy, I have used secondary, not primary sources where good ones exist, such as Suzanne Stark's excellent work, *Female Tars*. The bulk of my primary research has been concentrated on post-1918 women, in particular interviewing those never before interviewed: women who did not see themselves as 'historical' until they met me.

I have also used conversations from internet chatrooms, which some traditional academics feel is too skewed a source. Oral testimony is similarly mistrusted. Usually the main objection is that is unreliable and subjective. But I don't believe that such personal accounts are any more troubling than any written and official document. This approach supports the contemporary view that there is no such thing as objectivity or the truth, only subjective versions. Exercising our scepticism makes reading history an adult and interactive process rather than merely the passive reception of 'expert knowledge'.

STYLE

I have written this book for non-academic readers, but using scholarly expertise. For general readers I have deliberately avoided using two key theoretical words, 'patriarchy' and 'hegemony', but have found no substitute in everyday language to 'gendered' hence it appears sometimes.

In referring to little-known subjects, for example the women-officered Chinese ship of the 1970s, I have given the fullest possible reference to the source, to assist later researchers. However, in the interests of reducing notes I have not given references for material that anyone can easily find on the internet by googling, for example 'Ten-Pound Poms'.

Language is always a tricky matter. Take the central word 'seawoman'. Like 'seaman', it implies someone lower down the ladder. The usual general term, which includes officers, is 'woman seafarer'. In the 1980s English speakers started saying 'seafarer' instead of 'seamen' and 'women seamen'. Usage changed slowly. Only in 2000 did the Mission to Seamen charity altered its name to use 'seafarers' instead.

A boat is a small vessel, which could in theory be taken on a ship. But a ship cannot be taken on a boat. Purists wince if you refer to a ship as a boat. Merchant Navy people tend to be more relaxed about the words being used interchangeably. Also the RN used to say 'in' a ship, not 'on', but usually today seafarers in both navies say 'on'.

Some gender theorists argue that the titles Mrs and Miss should not be used because women should not be distinguished by whether they happen to have tied the knot. Normally I agree, but in some cases I have used a woman's title to make the point that marital connections have affected women's relationship with the sea. It would have been anachronistic to use the modern term Ms.

In writing at length about someone I have chosen to refer to them sometimes by their first name and sometimes by their more formal title, for example 'Edith' and 'Miss Sowerbutts', for variety and to indicate the varying distances human being have from each other. It's an uneasy decision, not least because when they were alive I might well have addressed them only in a formal way, because it was respectful to do so then.

It's puzzling, but when seafarers say 'crew' they don't actually mean everyone on board, only lower decks crew. Rather than using the cumbersome term 'officers and crew' I have avoided it by using terms like 'ship's complement' or 'ship's company', 'personnel' or 'staff'.

Turning from people to their ships, several things need to be made clear about terminology. The three departments of a passenger ship's staff are deck, engine and what is now called service, but was once called catering, or victualling. Sometimes people call the crucial divide 'operation and technical' versus 'service'. Or they say 'marine' and 'hotel'.

It's no longer customary to write SS and HMS before the name of a ship. I have occasionally used a prefix to make a distinct situation very clear. Ships are referred to as 'it', not 'she', in line with Lloyd's 2002 policy decision (see Appendix 5). In quoting past texts I have left the capitalisation as it was then, which creates some stylistic inconsistencies.

SCOPE

The book deals with both the Royal and Merchant navies. A traditional view emphasises the difference between the two. Some naval historians argue that naval history is a separate category to maritime history. They see it as maritime history's brother, rather than a subsection. In writing of both navies here I recognise their inter-relationship today: armed forces are now seen as part of the military–industrial complex; merchant ships and their women crews can actually be taken up for war purposes.

Similarly, I have referred to other countries too. My broad take is simply that we live in globalised times. It is appropriate, as well as interesting, to compare British women's experiences with those of seawomen in other countries. Overseas progress has been sometimes faster (as in Scandinavia) and sometimes slower (as in Greece), as well as very different for women ashore in the maritime industry as opposed to at sea. Elsewhere, fairer opportunities sometimes came earlier but only briefly (as in the Soviet Union or China), or came later but were accelerated (as in India today).

CHRONOLOGY OF SELECTED LANDMARKS IN WOMEN'S SEAFARING HISTORY

(Many women have been acclaimed as 'the first …', sometimes mistakenly. Sometimes this is to do with tiny nuances, such as the women being ocean-going or uncertified. This list should be read as provisional. The author would be happy to receive further information, especially about significant non-UK dates, so that a worldwide chronology can eventually be created.)

1600–1699

1690   Apparently the first seawomen disguised as men are discovered: an unnamed woman was on the *Edgar* and Anne Chamberlyne (1667–91) was on an unnamed ship

1696   The first women serve on RN ships as laundresses and nurses

1700–1799

1720   The first women pirates, Anne Bonney and Mary Read, were sentenced to be hanged

1800–1899

1821   First stewardesses recorded in the census

1834   The first women convict matrons sail

1840   Betsy Miller, seemingly Britain's first woman captain, first takes command of the brig *Cloetus*

1852   The Passenger Act makes provision for matrons, paving the way for the first women officers

| 1855 | Mary Ann Brown Patten, a captain's wife, becomes the woman to most famously take the helm, in a crisis on the US ship *Neptune's Carr* from Macao to San Francisco |
| 1884 | The first US woman gains her steam master's ticket, Mrs Mary M. Miller of New Orleans |

1900–1969

1908	The first woman purser's assistant sails, Catherine Leith on the *Carmania*
1913	The first woman doctor, Elizabeth MacBean Ross, sails on the cargo ship *Glenlogan* to Japan
1918	Italy's first woman captain, Elise Belluomini Viareggia, qualifies
c. 1919	The first women emigrant conductresses sail from Britain to Canada
1922	Victoria Drummond is allowed to sail, on the *Anchises*, the world's first woman marine engineer
1923	Hilda James becomes Cunard's first social hostess, on the *Franconia*
1935	Anna Shchetinina is acclaimed as the first ocean-going woman captain, in the Soviet Merchant Navy
1939	Molly Kool, of New Brunswick, claimed by some to be the first woman ship's captain in North America
1943	Wrens begin doing ciphering and coding, sailing on the troopships
1947	Pearl Hogg becomes Australia's first woman master, on the PS *Kookaburra*
1947	Buries Markes employ Britain's first all-women catering crew
1948	Elizabeth Sayers becomes one of the first lady assistant pursers, in Cunard
1959	Angela Firman becomes the first British woman radio officer to sail (but on Scandinavian ships)
1960	Rotterdam Nautical Academy takes on its first woman deck cadet
1967	Sheila Edmundson becomes the first woman deck cadet (taking the graduate route)

1970–1990

1972	US women officially allowed to sail on warships
1972	Nina Baker becomes the first woman cadet, in BP (on the direct-entry route)
c. 1972	Rachel Savage becomes the first British woman ship's photographer
1973	Liz Datson is acclaimed Australia's first women master
1974	Rosemary Daulton became the first women deckhand on Irish Shipping's the *Irish Oak*
1974	The organisation that would become Women's International Shipping and Trading Association (WISTA) began

1974   Women allowed to study at US's Merchant Marine Academy, Kings Point (after Samuel Stratton pushed a bill through Congress to do so.

1976   An all-women officer team, probably the world's first, head the Chinese cargo ship *Fengtao*

1979   Rosalind Yeandle, who later becomes New Zealand's first master, becomes New Zealand's first female deck cadet working with the Union Steamship Company

1980   Cinema projectionist Lucy Wallace wins the first UK sex discrimination test case against a shipping line

1980   Women's Maritime Association founded in the US

1981   The Royal Netherlands Navy becomes the first to allow women to serve on board their vessels, on the Hr Ms *Zuiderkruis*

1990   Wrens first work at sea in substantial numbers, initially on HMS *Brilliant*

1990   Lieutenant-Commander Darlene Iskra becomes the first women in the US Navy to be appointed to command a ship, the rescue towage and salvage ship *Opportune*

1991   The Royal Fleet Auxiliary appoints its first seagoing women officer, Dr Victoria McMaster

1991   Stephanie Hornby and Christine Davies become the first two women on the council of NUMAST, the Merchant Navy officers' union

1993   The WRNS becomes part of the Royal Navy, and all women eventually become liable for sea duties

1993   Helen Marshman becomes the first merchant seafarer to ever win Young Woman Engineer of the Year prize

1994   The Royal Fleet Auxiliary appoints its first women officer cadets: Rosellia Guite, Sarah Robinson and Claire Sullivan

1995   The New Zealand Women's Maritime Association is founded

1996   Ghanaian Beatrice Vormawah becomes first woman captain in Africa (Ghana) and probably the world's first black woman captain

1997   In the US the International Longshoremen's and Warehousemen's Union (ILWU) is renamed the International Longshore and Warehouse Union following action by members Lila Smith and Lee Hewitt

1997   Women and the Sea network begins at National Maritime Museum, co-ordinator Jo Stanley

1998   First two women captains in the British Royal Navy, Lieutenant Suzanne Moore and Lieutenant Melanie Robinson, command 65ft fast training boats *Dasher* and *Express*

1998   Controversially the London International Transport Workers Federation Executive reserved five places for women, the first time this kind of positive discrimination occurred in the UK maritime field

1998   The German Women and the Sea network begins: Verband Frauen zur See e.V.

1999   Exhibition on *Women at Sea* opens at Southampton Maritime Museum, curated by Sheila Jemima

1999   The Mission to Seamen changes its name to the Mission to Seafarers. The vote was ninety-eight for and thirty-eight against

1999   Barbara Campbell becomes the first women master in the Sail Training Association and the first British modern woman captain of a square-rigger

1999   Deborah Harrison receives Queen's Award for her bravery in dealing with pirates

1999   In the US, the first African-American female captain, Rear Admiral Michelle Janine Howard, takes command of the Navy's first Smart-Ship (meaning one that evaluates commercial technology such as machinery control for future fleet use), USS *Rushmore*.

1999   Myrna Galang Daite becomes the Philippines' first woman to become a ship's officer: third mate on the *Ramon Aboitiz*

1999   Women at Sea exhibition opens, *Frauen zur See: Weibliche Arbeitskrafte an Bord deutscher Handelsschiffe seit 1945*, Flensburger Schiffahrtsmuseum, Germany, curator Christine Keitch

2000–2015

2000   Transporting Gender conference, National Railway Museum, York

2000   Dane Marina Aramburu becomes the first Danish woman captain of a naval gas carrier

2003   Wang Yafu, of the Guangzhou Ocean Shipping Company, becomes the first female chief engineer in China

2003   Malin Andersson becomes Wallenius Lines' first female captain (Sweden)

2003   Colleen Beattie become the first female submariner in Canada after law changed in 2002

2003   *Free a Man for Sea – from Domestic to Destroyer. WRNS, Rationing and Role Reversal*, WRNS exhibition at the Royal Navy Submarine Museum in Gosport, curator Debbie Corner

2003   Jennifer Jewell becomes the first UK woman to graduate (with distinction) with the dual qualification of BSc (Nautical Science) and her first professional certificate from Glasgow

2004   Shell appoints first woman LNG (liquefied natural gas) master, Carol Jackson, as master of the *Gallina*

2004   Captain Wendy Maughan, Captain Barbara Campbell and Princess Anne become the first three women to be honoured as 'brethren' of Trinity House

2005   Argentina's first captain, Natalia Prosdocimi, fights through her union to secure women's maternity and lactating rights

2005   The Catholic Apostleship of the Sea takes on its first two women port chaplains (Sally Bennett and Louise Cuming)

2006   Laurie Royston becomes the first female captain of the Isle of Man Steam Packet fleet

2006   *Women at Sea* exhibition launched on the Sea Your History web-based exhibition, Royal Naval Museum, Portsmouth, curator Victoria Ingles

2007   Gender, Emotion, Work and Travel: Women, Transport, Workers and Passengers, Past and Present conference, Greenwich Maritime Institute

2007   Swedish Karin Stahre Janson becomes first woman captain of a cruise ship, Royal Caribbean's *Monarch of the Seas*

2007   China's first female warship captain, Lieutenant-Commander Hsieh Ai-chieh, takes control of her 500-ton Chinchiang-class patrol vessel

2007   Caroline Lallement becomes first French woman master, of SeaFrance's Calais-to-Dover freight ferry

2010   Sarah Breton becomes the first woman master in P&O's 173-year history, on the cruise ship *Artemis*

2010   Inger Klein Olsen takes command of the *Queen Victoria* in 2010, Cunard's first woman captain

2010   Safmarine cadet Akhona Gevesa's disappearance brings new worldwide public awareness of the extent of shipboard bullying and sexual harassment, not only of women

2010   Catherine Williams becomes the only female chief officer at cruise company Holland America Line

2008   Lis Lauritzen takes command of RCI's *Vision of the Seas*

2011   Three Durban women become Africa's first black, female marine pilots with open licences: Precious Dube, Bongiwe Mbambo and Pinky Zungu

2011   RN women allowed to serve on submarines

2012   Sarah West is first woman to take command of a major British warship

2013   Carmen Chan becomes the first female master on ocean-going vessels in Hong Kong, for China Navigation, a subsidiary of Swires

2014   Captain Katharine Sweeney successfully brings a sex-discrimination case over her failure to get a pilot's post in Puget Sound. She wins US$3.6 million, but not a job

APPENDIX 3

WOMEN SEAFARERS WHO DRESSED AS MEN[1]

PART 1: WOMEN WHO JOINED THE ROYAL NAVY OR MARINES (BY DATE OF REVELATION OF THEIR GENDER)

1690	unnamed woman on the *Edgar*
1690	Anne Chamberlyne
1692	unnamed woman on *St Andrew*
1720s	Mrs Coles
1740	Anne Mills
1750	Hannah Snell/James Gray
1757	unnamed woman on the *Resolution*
1760	Samuel Bundy
1761	William Prothero (Marine)
1761	Hannah Whitney (Marine)
1762	Jane/John Meace/Mace
1760s	Charley Waddell
1771	Mary Lacy
1781	George/Margaret Thompson
1802	Mrs Cola
1807	Elizabeth Bowler
1807	Tom Bowling
1807	Rebecca Ann Johnston
1807	Lizzie/John Bowden
1815	William Brown

PART 2: WOMEN WHO JOINED THE MERCHANT NAVY (BY DATE OF REVELATION THAT THEY WERE FEMALE)

1757	Arthur Douglas
1780s	Anna Maria Real/William Henry Renny
1802	two sisters from Bradford
1807	Elizabeth Bowler
1808	Rebecca Ann Johnson
1811	Marianne Rebecca Johnson
1812	Almira Paul
1814	William McDonald
1835	Anne Jane Thornton
1836	George Wilson
1837	Elsa Jane Guerin
1839	Mary Anne Arnold
1840	Mary Anne/Thomas Walker
1841	Ellen/Charles Watts
1842	Lavender Cavendish/Albert Douglas
1843	Margaret Johnson
1846	William Johns
c. 1847	Jane Gallagher
1847	unnamed woman in Derby
1860	Thomas Stewart
1865	Charlotte Petrie/William Bruce
1868	Thomas Brown
1873	Billy (n/a)
1873	William Armstrong
1886	Kate Rundle
1887	Elizabeth Taylor
1898	Alice Lincoln/Amelia Garfield McKinley/Thomas McKinley
1899	unnamed woman from Newport

APPENDIX 4

BETWEEN NAVIES

Many countries have two navies, the commercial one and the defensive one. The introduction explained their different meanings. But there were what might be seen as organisations in between, which gave civilian girls and women the chance to be at sea, albeit voluntarily rather than as paid workers in some cases. This appendix explains what they were.

GIRLS' NAUTICAL TRAINING CORPS

The GNTC is now part of the mixed-gender Marine Society & Sea Cadets. It no longer formally exists but seems to be a strong separate entity in people's minds. Membership of the MSSC offers girls and women the chance to be on ships and be involved in the Royal Navy without actually working full-time. Founded in 1942 as the Girls' Naval Training Corps, it was a training organisation for girls, for the rest of the Second World War the GNTC went into abeyance. This was possibly because of fears that militarising civilian girls, or raising their hopes of seagoing role, would cause controversy with the general public. 'Nautical' replaced 'Naval' in its title in the late 1950s. It revived and was particularly strong in the 1950s and 1960s. Today, though, many units of girls exist within MSSC. They are led by adult officers who were usually from the Navy and Wrens; it can feel like their way of continuing service life. MSSC girls usually don't go on to join the MN or RN. The very few who do so join the RN, not the MN. They are schooled in RN ways, so the progression can feel natural.[1]

SEA RANGERS

By contrast, the Sea Rangers also continues today, as a girls-only organisation which emphasises fun, recreation and adventure. It began twenty-two years earlier than the GNTC, in 1920, as part of the Girl Guide movement. Its many units (with their own small boats) were led by ex-Wrens, especially in the 1920s and 1930s. Its members seldom go on to work in either navy.

MARITIME VOLUNTEER SERVICE

Begun in 1994, this service now has the strap line 'Training in maritime skills'. It has thirty units throughout the UK. In 2015 the MVS's webpage was dominated by a photograph of a happy young woman sailing. Clearly it's an equal opportunities organisation. MVS took over and expanded many former Royal Naval Auxiliary Service roles (see below). [2]

MERCHANT NAVY IN TIMES OF CONFLICT

Civilian seafarers in times of war contributed hugely, often unrecognised and undertrained for this role. Merchant Navy commercial shipping companies had to be ready to allow the government to convert some of their ships for war use.[3] This happened as recently as the 1982 Falklands Conflict when fifty-two ships in Britain's one hundred-strong fleet were Merchant Navy STUFT vessels (Ships Taken Up from Trade).[4] In such cases, the people who normally worked on the ship were asked if they were prepared to sail on this new basis. In the First World War MN women were stopped from sailing, whether or not they were willing to take the risk. Usually they were left on land, for their own protection.

In the Falklands Conflict at least forty women sailed, including laundresses, nurses, public room stewards and pursers. Some were trained to use the guns if they wished, on their now sort-of warship. Similarly, in both world wars a few women, such as shop assistant Mrs Runciman, nurses, and Dr Nancy Ambler, were on merchant ships that could be said to be warships in that they were carrying troops to fight and were armed. Under international protocols hospital ships (which were usually converted liners) were supposed to be safe and neutral, though in fact some were attacked. They had QARNNS and Army nurses on board, such as Katy Beaufoy.

MERCHANT NAVY RESERVE

From 1989 to 2000 this Reserve existed and recruited merchant seafarers of all ranks and ratings who had been at sea in the previous ten years. The aim was to 'ensure the availability of a modest number of British Merchant Seamen to help crew UK vessels and maintain supplies to Western Europe in the event of an attack by the Warsaw Pact.'[5] There is apparently no information about whether women were part of it. I think it highly unlikely, as at that time it was seen as inappropriate to send women into combat.

QUEEN ALEXANDRA'S ROYAL NAVAL NURSING SERVICE RESERVE

QARNNS, usually pronounced 'Quorns', is the naval nursing service, and was so named in 1902. It's a small full-time force of around 300 and has a reserve, QARNNS (R), which was formed in 1910 and continues today, as part of the Royal Naval Reserve. Civilian nurses, as reservists, have been able to nurse at sea (and on land with the Navy) as QARNNS (R) for over a century. They had some of earliest seagoing opportunities of civilian women connected with the RN. The Royal Marine Reserves and the RNR together make up the Maritime Reserve Force, which is part of the British Armed Forces Volunteer Reserves. In 2014 the head of the Maritime Reserve was a man, Commodore Andrew Jameson.

As the chapter on health-care workers at sea showed, QARNNS (R) nurses were at sea in both world wars; hundreds augmented the small regular QARNNS force. In 2015 there were thirty-four QARNNS reservists, of whom over 60 per cent were women. Their training includes exercises at sea. Since 2003 almost 50 per cent have been mobilised. Their commander (who would once have been called matron-in-chief) is currently Pauline Small.[6]

ROYAL FLEET AUXILIARY

Women sail in the RFA, which is a kind of cross-over or bridge between the RN and the MN. Civil servants, these women and men go deep sea on the thirteen Ministry of Defence-owned ships that sail as part of the Royal Navy's support network. They're not Navy, though they may look it. Their work includes replenishing far-away warships with fuel, food and ammunition. The RFA began in 1905 and women sailed from 1991. They worked mainly in stewarding and catering roles.

Dr Victoria McMaster, the RFA's very first seagoing woman in 1991, wrote a report which the RFA used in making future decisions on women's employment. Three years later Claire Sullivan, Rosellia Guite and Sarah Robinson became the RFA's first women cadets.[7] They went to Warsash, which can be seen as the Dartmouth (meaning the Britannia Royal Naval College, where all officers go for initial training) of the Merchant Navy. Today, like RFA men, RFA women do their officer training at Dartmouth. In 2014 women were just 6.7 per cent of the RFA's 1,860-strong force.[8]

ROYAL NAVAL RESERVE

Most armed forces have a reserve, which suitable civilians join so that they can offer support in a crisis such as war. The Army Reserve, formerly called the Territorial Army, is the best-known UK example. By far the greatest number of women reserves were civilian nursing sisters whose hospitals registered them to be part of the Army and Navy Reserves. The Royal Naval Reserve (its name has differed slightly over the years) began supporting the Royal Navy in 1859. Until recently it was informally referred to as the Wavy Navy, because officers' stripes were wavy not straight. Women's earliest role in it doesn't seem to be traceable. It's likely to have been miniscule, and land-based, given the idea that women should not be in combat. The RNR was merged with the Royal Navy Volunteer Reserve (RNVR) in 1958. It later incorporated the former Women's Royal Navy Volunteer Reserve (WRNVR), about which very little is recorded, and QARNNS (R).

In the 1970s women joined the RNR because they wanted to stay in a Navy-related situation, often as ex-Wrens or members of the Sea Rangers and Girls' Nautical Training Corps. It was a way to go to sea (on exercises sometimes) although it's not a seagoing position. They rose up its ranks. In 1997 ex-Wren Second Officer Muriel Hocking (b. 1945) became its first woman commodore, the most senior person.[9] Her successor in 1999 was not a woman, because the most appropriate person for promotion happened to be a man. The RNR still exists and its website clearly shows women are expected to play a significant role.

ROYAL NAVY AUXILIARY SERVICE

From 1963 to 1994 a Royal Navy Auxiliary Service (RNXS) existed. Like the RNR it was a way to sail 'in the Navy' by the back door. Women volunteers sailed long before 1990 when Wrens were allowed to go to sea. The RNXS was formed in 1963 as a way to deal with the nuclear threat. It brought together the Royal Naval Minewatching Service and the Admiralty Ferry Crew Association, in which women are reputed to have been involved in delivering ships, just as women delivered planes in the Second World War.[10] In 1966 a historian of the RNXS commented:

> The RNXS has a pleasant family flavour and in many units there are husbands and wives, and in some cases daughters as well, training together for the job is best suited to their former experience and physical capabilities. There cannot be many services in which the family can enjoy a week's training cruise together, either in the Western Isles, perhaps in French waters if a unit is based on the south coast.[11]

Denise St Aubyn Hubbard (b. 1924) became famous as its first women skipper in 1978. Defence cuts led to the disbanding of the RNXS in 1994.[12]

APPENDIX 5

SHIPS AS 'SHE'

Is a ship a 'she' or an 'it'? The subject is brought up oddly often when people discuss women and the sea. And it may be relevant to women seafarers because it reveals the odd division that exists between idealising Woman as a respect-worthy unworldly representative of all that is high and noble, versus imagining her to be a frighteningly unruly threat to decent innocent men. In the Madonna–whore split, it's argued, how can a real woman be accepted as the complex and ordinary person she is? If such extreme ideas are in circulation, how can a woman sailor 'on a lady' be accepted as just another fallible, flesh-and-blood, valuable shipmate?

Anthropological explanations for the ancient and grand origins of the practice of feminising this vehicle are that early seafarers believed the ship represented their mother. So to call a ship 'she' was to express reverence and wonder for the feat that is a ship – and someone with reproductive abilities, for a mysterious, almost magical force that is responsible for your life. More psychoanalytically, it's been argued that being on board is like being in the womb: the ship as amniotic sac. Very interestingly, some say 'in' not 'on' a ship. Nina Baker, BP's first deck cadet, remarked:

> I had always thought you called a vessel 'she' because you have to take good care of the ship if you want it/she to take care of you … When people are cooped up for years at a time and not really allowed to show each other affection, perhaps it is natural that the human desire for tenderness is transferred to this inanimate object on which their lives depend. I found that two weeks from home, when you lose the worst of your homesickness, get to know your colleagues and to feel like a group … the ship becomes all … and it is not surprising that loyalty becomes warmth, even for a rustbucket.[1]

And men who were heterosexual (or careful to appear so) would clearly choose to anthropomorphise their beloved as 'she', not 'he'. But saying 'she' is not a simple matter, nor something common to every country's language. In Latin, a language which makes nouns neutral, feminine or masculine, both *barco* and *navio* (ships) are masculine. In Russian, gender varies with the ship's type: the words for ship, trawler and cruiser are masculine; but the words for a boat and a launch are feminine.

I myself sometimes find I think of ships as 'she' when I am on them, especially when with seafarers who refer respectfully to their ship as feminine. But ships are 'it' when I am writing about one I don't personally know. Modern seafarers use both 'it' and 'she', but increasingly the rational but less poetic 'it' is used.

More colloquially – indeed, even on gift-shop tea-towels – ships have been called 'she' for stereotypical reasons which appear to have more to do with boats and seaside postcard risqué jokes than with deep primal feelings of awe. Here's a list of the lighter claims:

Hoary Justifications for Calling Ships 'She'

- ◈ They're fickle
- ◈ They are big in the beam, have a waist and stays
- ◈ They show their topsides and hide their bottoms
- ◈ It takes a lot of paint to keep them good looking
- ◈ They need a good mate to handle them correctly, otherwise they're uncontrollable[2]

Shipping journal *Lloyds List* in 1998 aroused ire when the editor enquired whether readers thought a ship is a 'she' or an 'it'.[3] The subject went quiet until 2002 when the journal formally broke 268 years of tradition. Editor Julian Bray wrote: 'I decided that it was time to catch up with the rest of the world, and most other news organisations refer to ships as neuter.' Seeing ships as simply 'maritime real estate', he recognised that: 'However, I don't think there is anything wrong with calling ships "she" in conversation. It's a respectable maritime tradition,' and columnists were 'free to refer to ships as female'. Bray stood by for a 'full and vibrant array of letters' from readers.[4] He got them.[5] Ships are now, in most cases, called 'it'.

GLOSSARY

AB	able seaman, a deck rating
ass. mats	assistant matrons
AWOL	absent without leave
BISN	British India Steam Navigation Company
boatie	someone who sails a small boat, such as a recreational small yacht. It implies passion
body-basher	masseuse/masseur, term used post-1970s
bo'sun	the senior petty officer in charge of all the deck ratings
bridge (the)	literally the place on deck from which a ship is navigated. Anthropologists see it as a primal centre of symbolic power ruled by the patriarch
certificate of competence	the title of maritime qualifications, hence the term 'certificated engineer'
chilly hos	children's hostesses
concessionaire	someone working for a company that has bought the right (concession) to run a business on a ship, e.g. a branch of a high street chain
ETA	electro-technical assistant
ETO	electro-technical officer
F&B	food and beverage
flagging out/flags of convenience	shipowners' practice of registering a ship in another country (under another national flag) to avoid UK restrictions, e.g. on minimum wages
floatographer	ship's photographer
galley	kitchen area
GMDSS	Global Maritime Distress and Safety System – satellite-based system for enabling safety communications at sea, replacing wireless after 1992

GNTC	Girls' Nautical Training Corps, now part of the Sea Cadets Corps
GPO	General Post Office (what became British Telecom)
hairy	shipboard term for a hairdresser
HND	Higher National Diploma
ILO	International Labour Organisation
IMarEST	Institute of Marine Engineering, Science & Technology
IMO	International Maritime Organisation
IWM	Imperial War Museum
ITF	International Transport Workers' Federation
LAP	lady assistant purser (in some companies called FAP, WAP, or AP(F))
LGBTI	lesbian, gay, bisexual, transgender and intersex
LL	*Lloyd's List*
MCA	Maritime and Coastguard Agency
mess	the eating and socialising area for a particular shipboard group, say engineers
MMA	Merseyside Maritime Archives
MN	Merchant Navy
MRC	Modern Records Centre, University of Warwick
NAAFI	The Navy, Army and Air Force Institutes, who provide shops to the UK Forces, the equivalent to the US's PX stores
Nautilus International	Trade union for MN officers (previously NUMAST)
NCOL	not counted on location (referring to affairs)
NMM	National Maritime Museum, Greenwich, London
NMRN	National Museum of the Royal Navy, Portsmouth
NUMAST	National Union of Marine, Aviation and Shipping Transport Officers, the former name for Nautilus International
NUS	National Union of Seamen
Panamax	ships of a size allowed to travel through the Panama Canal
P&O	Peninsular and Oriental Steam Navigation Company
patriarchy	a social system in which males, particularly as father figures, hold power over women and children. It often looked benevolent
petty officer	an officer who is not commissioned but works their way up from rating
PMT	pre-menstrual tension

QAIMNS	Queen Alexandra's Imperial Military Nursing Service – Army nurses (later called Queen Alexandra's Royal Army Nursing Corps)
QARNNS	Queen Alexandra's Royal Naval Nursing Service – Navy nurses
RAMC	Royal Army Medical Corps
rating	someone working on ship who does not have officer or petty officer status
RFA	Royal Fleet Auxiliary
RMG	Royal Museums Greenwich, also National Maritime Museum
RN	Royal Navy
RNXS	Royal Navy Auxiliary Service
RO	radio officer
R&R	rest and recreation
shoppie	a post-1970s shipboard term for shop assistant
STCW	Standards of Training, Certification and Watchkeeping
steam queen/steam fly	A ship's laundry women
STEM	science, technology, engineering and mathematics – the cluster of academic disciplines that campaigners feel are not made sufficiently attractive to women
TNA	The National Archives, formerly the Public Record Office, Kew.
TO	telephone operator
VAD	Voluntary Aid Detachment
watch	the equivalent of a shift. On ship watchkeepers were seen as a very different category to people working nine-to-five hours, not least because their sleeping areas had to be kept quiet to cope with people sleeping unsocial hours.
WES	Women's Engineering Society
WRNS	Women's Royal Naval Service, a part of the Navy, whose ratings were called Wrens

NOTES

Introduction

1   Linda Grant De Pauw, *Seafaring Women*, Houghton Mifflin, Boston, 1982, p. 212.

2   Reports appeared in the South African *Times*, 17, 19 and 24 July 2010. See www.timeslive.co.za, accessed 19 March 2014. Jo Stanley, 'Sexual Harrassment at Sea – & Akhona's Tragedy', Gender, Sex, Race, Class – and the Sea, www.genderedseas.blogspot.com, 23 July 2010.

3   Foreword, in Jean Ebbert and Mary-Beth Hall, *Crossed Currents: Navy Women in a Century of Change*, Brassey's , Washington DC, 2007, p. x.

4   Elizabeth Louise Williams, rail.co.uk, 30 March 2012, www.rail.co.uk/blog/rail-women/, accessed 13 July 2014. I am grateful to Helena Wojtczak for pointing this out to me.

5   Wong Joon San, 'Joanne All Set to Take the Helm', *South China Morning Post*, 3 March 1993, www.scmp.com/article/20478/joanne-all-set-take-helm, accessed 2 April 2014.

6   *Emigrant Accommodation on Board Atlantic Steam Ships. Report with regard to the accommodation and treatment of emigrants on board Atlantic steam ships, and minute thereupon*, 1881 [C.2995] LXXXII, 93.

7   Joan Druett, *Petticoat Whalers: Whaling Wives at Sea 1820–1920*, Collins, Auckland, New Zealand, 1991; *She was a Sister Sailor: The whaling journals of Mary Brewster, 1845–1851*, Mystic, Connecticut, 1992; *Hen Frigates: Wives of Merchant Captains Under Sail*, Simon & Schuster, New York, 1998; *She Captains: Heroines and Hellions of the Sea*, Simon & Schuster, New York, 1999. Suzanne J. Stark, *Female Tars: Women Aboard Ship in the Age of Sail*, Naval Institute Press, Annapolis, MD, 1996. Linda Grant De Pauw, *Seafaring Women*, Houghton Mifflin, Boston, 1982. Minghua Zhao, 'Globalisation and Women's Employment on Cruise ships', *Maritime Review*, 2001.

8   For example, Margaret S. Creighton and Lisa Norling (eds), *Iron Men, Wooden Women: Gender and Seafaring in the Atlantic world, 1700–1920*, Johns Hopkins

Press, Baltimore and London, 1996; Valerie Burton, '"Whoring, Drinking Sailors": Reflections on Masculinity from the Labour History of Nineteenth-Century British Shipping', in Margaret Walsh (ed.), *Working Out Gender: Perspectives from Labour History*, Ashgate, Aldershot, 1999, pp. 84–91.

1 – Britain's Forgotten Women Seafarers, pp. 19–44

1   Susi Newborn, *A Bonfire in My Mouth*, Harper Collins, London, 2003 and emails to the author, spring 2014.

2   Charles Johnson, *A General History of the Pyrates*, Ch. Rivington, J. Lacy, and J. Stone, London, 1724, and on line at https://digital.lib.ecu.edu/17001; David Cordingly, 'Bonny, Anne (1698–1782)', *Oxford Dictionary of National Biography*, http://dx.doi.org/10.1093/ref:odnb/39085, accessed 11 April 2014; Robert Baldwin, *The Tryals of Captain John Rackham and Other Pirates*, 1721, The National Archives (hereafter TNA), CO 137/14f.9.

3   They are summarised in Jo Stanley (ed.), *Bold in Her Breeches: Women Pirates Across the Ages*, Pandora, London, 1995.

4   In maritime lore people made a crucial distinction between sailing *before* the mast, and *after* the mast. Working in front of the mast originally meant you were doing 'manly' seafaring work on the vessel, something to be proud of. Working to the rear of the ship meant labouring rather safely in the low-status food and sleeping area: 'women's work', even if it was done by men.

5   Statistics on modern seafarers are very approximate, because of the methods of collecting and organising data. The UK data are based on material from the Department for Transport (DfT) and the Maritime and Coastguard Agency (MCA). It uses published tables, as well as gendered breakdowns kindly extracted at my request, summer 2014. With thanks to Alice Marshall of the DfT and Vanessa O'Sullivan of the MCA for their active help with this data. The international data are in several ILO and Seafarers' International Research Centre surveys in Phillip Belcher, Helen Sampson, Michelle Thomas et al., *Women Seafarers: Global Employment Policies and Practices*, International Labor Office, Geneva, 2003, especially pp. 9–11.

6   William Richardson, *A Mariner of England: An account of the career of William Richardson as told by himself*, John Murray, London, 1908, p. 169.

7   Jedediah Stephens Tucker (ed.), *Memoirs of Adml the Right Honourable, the Earl of St Vincent*, vol. 1, Richard Bentley, London, p. 193.

8   Joan Druett's many works are listed in footnotes to the introduction.

9   De Pauw, *Seafaring Women*, p. 169.

10   *The Journal of Eliza Underwood*, Dixson Library, State Library of New South Wales, DL MSQ 366. Much appreciation to Joan Druett for finding the

original and making it accessible through depositing her typed transcription there too. Joan's summary of Eliza appears in *Petticoat Whalers: Whaling Wives at Sea 1820–1920*, Collins, Auckland, New Zealand, 1991, pp. 90–3, 133, 199.

11 Elizabeth Linklater, *A Child Under Sail*, Brown, Son & Ferguson, Glasgow, 1938, p. 120.

12 The old refuge in 195 Mare Street ran from 1849 to 1913. In her history of the refuge Claudia Jessop implicitly shows us the haven Thomas/Mary sought: 'The Elizabeth Fry Refuge', The Hackney Society, www.hackneysociety.org/page_id__259.aspx, accessed 20 August 2014.

13 Genealogy and Family History, www.londonancestor.com/street/str-south.htm.

14 'A Gender Variance Who's Who', http://zagria.blogspot.co.uk/2012/11/thomas-walker–1842-ship-steward-porter.html#.U_MmvaNcOuQ; Feòrag Fearsithe, 'Thomas/Mary Anne Walker, the "Female Barman"', 4 November 2012, http://feorag.livejournal.com/528324.html, both accessed 18 August 2014.

15 Derek Hudson, *Munby: Man of Two Worlds: The Life and Diaries of Arthur J. Munby 1828–1910*, Abacus, London, 1974, p. 237.

16 Arlie Russell Hochschild, *The Managed Heart: The Commercialization of Human Feeling*, University of California Press, Berkeley, 1983.

17 Denise Donnelly interviews with author, 6 August 1986 and 14 June 1996, and some phone calls, as well as correspondence with Denise Reed, her daughter, 2014.

18 Inger Klein Thorhauge correspondence with author, August 2014.

19 Masefield, 'Cargoes' written prior to 1948, http://allpoetry.com/cargoes, accessed 14 March 2013.

20 Sara Miller (later Coxon), email to author, 21 October 2014.

21 Freda Price (later Taylor), typescript life story kindly loaned to the author by her husband Frank Taylor.

22 Ronald Hope, *The Merchant Navy*, Stanford Maritime, London, 1980, p. 35.

23 Muriel Arnold, *Tiaras and T-shirts: A Working Life at Sea*, Librario, Moray, 2007, p. 25.

24 Sha Wylie, account written for author, January 2014.

25 The term 'sweatship' is used by maritime writer Leon Fink, and is also the title of a damning report published by the British charity War on Want.

26 Freda Price, typescript life story.

27 Samson C. Stevens and Michael G. Parsons, 'Effects of Motion at Sea on Crew Performance: A Survey', *Marine Technology*, vol. 39, no. 1, January 2002, pp. 29–47. Only one study has made this finding. Anecdotal evidence I've collected both confirms and refutes it.

28   Information on relevant physical differences at sea from osteopath Marina Urquhart-Pullen, by phone and email to author, 20 April 2013.

29   Druett, *Hen Frigates*, p. 96.

30   Druett, *Hen Frigates*, pp. 91–2.

31   The payback information comes from an email to author from Gary Hindmarch, 20 November 2013. The National Union of Seamen situation in the 1980s is revealed by a letter from Jack Kinahan, special services officer, 5 May 1982, 'Female staff' folder, NUS archive, Modern Record Centre, MSS175a, Box 106, University of Warwick (hereafter NUS at MRC) and his correspondence to colleagues and a pregnant member Ms B.W. (initials only are used in this book, not in the original material, to protect her privacy), September 1985, in NUS at MRC, MSS 175a/39/22. General information on modern merchant seawomen's maternity situation is based mainly on telephoned information from MaryAnne Adams and Jessica Tyson, January 2015; the UK Maritime and Coastguard Agency, *Guidance Note MGB 460 (M+F), New and Expectant Mothers*, 2010, p. 8; and ITF, *Women Seafarers, Maternity*, www.itfseafarers.org/ ITI-women-seafarers.cfm, accessed 19 January 2015.

32   Interview with author, 31 October 2014, emails and phone calls, and extract from Robina's unpublished essay 'Ambitions', which she kindly shared with the author.

33   Michelle Thomas, 'Research Shatters the Myths That Set Back Women Seafarers', *Nautilus Telegraph*, November 2013, p. 18.

34   In a recent UK government survey 2.5 per cent of females and 0.4 per cent of males reported experiencing some form of sexual offence in the previous twelve months. One in five women had experienced some form of sexual violence since the age of 16. Ministry of Justice, Office for National Statistics and Home Office, 'An Overview of Sexual Offending in England and Wales', www.gov.uk/government/statistics/an-overview-of-sexual-offending-in-england-and-wales, accessed 3 March 2015.

35   'Bullying Rife Among British and Dutch Officers, Says Maritime Union', *Lloyds List*, 4 July 2011; Nautilus International, 'Protect and Respect', 2013, www.nautilusint.org/.../Protect-and-Respect-pack-anti-bullying-guide.pdf, accessed 12 March 2014.

36   Esther Boylan, 'Aye, Aye – Ma'am', ILO internal document, Geneva, November 1980.

37   Momoko Kitada, 'Women Seafarers and their Identities', PhD thesis, Cardiff University, 2010, www.sirc.cf.ac.uk/Uploads/Thesis/Kitada.pdf, accessed 13 March 2015.

38   For example, a 1960s ship's laundress had her novel typed up and turned into a book by the *Daily Mail* recently. It is not yet available for distribution.

2 – Different Times, Different Possibilities, pp. 45–54

1 Flagging out, meaning registering ships overseas in order to avoid the UK's (expensive) protective legislation, began in the 1950s and escalated. Most women working today will have been foreign-flagged for most of their career. Over half of the entire world's merchant ships were registered with open registries or at Panama, Liberia, and Marshall Islands among others, according to 2009 figures. Even on the few remaining UK-flagged ships it's become increasingly less necessary to employ British staff. This began with first stipulating that ratings didn't have to be British. Then only the top four had to be British. Then the top two had to be British. The introduction of the tonnage tax to the UK in 2000 (an attempt to reduce companies' tax liability) further meant ships could be staffed by people of any nationality. An example of this trend can be seen in the fact that in 2005 there were 1,417 women ratings in hotel and catering work on ships. By 2010 this had nearly tripled to 3,658.

2 This refers to ships of 100 GRT or over, either UK directly owned, parent owned or managed by a British company. MCA, 'UK Ship Register', Gov. UK, 2014, www.gov.uk/uk-ship-register-for-merchant-ship-and-bareboat-charter–100gt, accessed 5 May 2015.

3 MCA Table FLE 501, 'World Fleet Registered Vessels', Gov.UK, 2014, www. gov.uk/government/statistical-data-sets/fle05-world-fleet-registered-vessels, accessed 5 May 2015.

4 Anon, 'Did Somebody Say Ship Life?', Working on Cruise Ships, Facebook, 14 February 2013, www.facebook.com/permalink.php?story_fbid=101512 29425691207&id=194016591206, accessed 11 March 2014.

5 Raw data compiled for author by Robert Merrylees, UK Chamber of Shipping, August 2014. The statistics are based on just twenty-eight companies which compile detailed statistics and must therefore be seen as a snapshot, not a comprehensive or typical summary. Overall figures come from Table SFR0110, 'All UK seafarers active at sea, 2002 to 2013', from the Maritime and Coastguard Agency, workings based on UK Chamber of Shipping manpower surveys. To get a more accurate picture of who is sailing at what level it's best to use figures from the licensing agency, the MCA, showing those people possessing certificates of competence. This can be used alongside the data from their trade union, Nautilus International, but the three sources don't add up. They just give indications. Emails to author, July 2014, from Andrew Linington at Nautilus International, Alice Marshall of the Department for Transport and Vanessa O'Sullivan of the MCA.

6 Phillip Belcher et al., *Women Seafarers: Global Employment Policies and Practices*, ILO, Geneva, 2003, p. 7.

7   Ellie Ablett correspondence with author, May to September 2014; Emma Barnett, 'Meet the Commander Giving the Royal Navy a Female Touch', *Telegraph*, 8 March 2013. www.telegraph.co.uk/women/womens-life/9915261/International-Womens-Day-2013-Meet-the-commander-giving-the-Royal-Navy-a-female-touch.html, accessed 12 March 2014.

8   This weight refers to Builders' Old Measurement, a method used to estimate tonnage based on calculation of a ship's width and beam. It was replaced in 1849 by the Moorsom System which calculates a ship's size on the basis of the tonnage it can carry. Frances's story is recorded in *The Remarkable World of Frances Barkley, 1769–1845*, ed. Beth Hill, Gray's, British Columbia, 1978.

9   Peter Kemp, *A Social History of the Lower Deck*, JM Dent & Sons, London, 1970, p. 133. There were wives and 'wives' who were not necessarily legally married.

10   Suzanne J. Stark, *Female Tars: Women Aboard Ship in the Age of Sail*, Naval Institute Press, Annapolis, MD, 1996, pp. 88–110.

11   Stark, *Female Tars*, p. 101. Stark points out the very double standard: men who dressed as men were seen as despicable and undermining all that was admirable about maleness. By contrast women dressing as men were tolerated and even seen as 'merely amusing', just as a child dressing up as an adult is amusing (p. 113). Indeed, some men could feel flattered that of course a woman would want to look like a member of the 'superior sex'. Equally, of course, she could never truly aspire to be a member of that elite, as the many plays and ballads about cross-dressers reiterate.

12   Brian R. Mitchell, *Abstract of British Historical Statistics*, Cambridge University Press Archive, Cambridge, 1971, p. 218.

13   Margaret S. Creighton, '"Women" and Men in American Whaling, 1830–1870', *International Journal of Maritime History*, vol. 4, no. 1, June 1992, p. 195.

14   Creighton, '"Women" and Men', p. 198.

15   Naval wives Mary Ann Riley and Ann Hopping (aboard the *Goliath* in 1798) and Jane Townshend (aboard the *Defiance* in 1805) are the best known of the wives on board naval ships, because in 1847 they applied for the Naval General Service Medal awarded to survivors of major battles.

16   Ian Friel, *Maritime History of Britain and Ireland*, British Museum Press, London, 2003, p. 230.

17   Lucy Delap, '"Thus Does Man Prove His Fitness to Be the Master of Things": Shipwrecks, Chivalry and Masculinities in Nineteenth- and Twentieth-Century Britain', *Cultural and Social History*, vol. 3, no. 1, 2006, pp. 45–74. Actually it's useful to give priority to anyone who doesn't have sea skills (all passengers and most hotel-side workers today come into this category). However, a modern study has since found that women's survival rates were poorer if the Birkenhead Drill was followed, because selection holds up

evacuation. Mikael Elinder and Oscar Erixson, 'Every Man for Himself: Gender, norms and survival in maritime disasters', Department of Economics Working Paper 2012, no. 8, University of Uppsala, www.nek.uu.se/Pdf/wp20128.pdf, accessed 26 March 2013. And some men were too intent on saving themselves to be gallant.

18   It could be treble that number because the census didn't record all the people who were at sea. Statistics for other deciles appear to indicate that approximately three times as many women were actually working as stewardesses than appeared in the census. But all such numbers should be treated with caution.

19   Hannah Cowley, *Who's The Dupe?*, Charles Wiley, New York, 1824, archive.org/details/whosdupefarceint00cowl, accessed 13 May 2014.

20   Stark, *Female Tars*, p. 79.

21   Statistics for the MN given by Lloyds Register Information Centre, email, 11 April 2013; Hope, *The Merchant Navy*, p. 20.

22   It's very difficult to calculate how many seafarers there were, especially as the Registrar of Shipping and Seaman didn't note gender in some periods. Census summaries are useful as a *simple* indicator of gender patterns. Therefore, we have to infer data from the seafarers who were at home on census night, and who are recorded in much more detail. It is likely that there were three times more women seafarers than those enumerated as at home. I base this suggestion on the 1951 census, the only one to give figures for women ashore *and* afloat. It shows that 31 per cent of the total female maritime workforce was at sea on census night (Industry Tables, no. 7, *National Census of England and Wales*, HMSO, London, 1951, p. 380). On that calculation (and simply by multiplying by three, the women enumerated ashore), the total number of stewardesses in 1911, based on 596 at home, is likely to have been around 1,788. It's a crude measure but indicative.

23   See many images on the excellent Russian-language website about Anna: ljwanderer.livejournal.com/150094.html, accessed 11 July 2014.

24   'US Merchant Marine at War', www.usmm.org/women.html, accessed 13 September 2014.

25   Statistics for the MN given by Lloyds Register Information Centre in email 11 April 2013. This includes colonial ships.

26   The MN statistics are from 'Keep Our Merchant Navy', a 1993 budget submission from trade union NUMAST, Nautilus Archive, p. 1.

27   Arthur Marsh and Victoria Ryan, *The Seamen: History of the National Union of Seamen*, Malthouse Press, Oxford, 1989, p. 206.

28   Hope, *Merchant Navy*, p. 35.

29   Friel, *Maritime History* p. 280.

30   Only 4 per cent of UK train drivers on ordinary trains are women. Deirdre Claffey, 'Meet the Women Doing "Men's Work"', 26 April 2013,

www.theguardian.com/lifeandstyle/2013/apr/26/meet-women-doing-mens-work. By contrast, there is no statistical data on women driving vintage trains (a volunteer job), only anecdotal evidence that they are accepted more readily.

31 RN Statistics from Richard Hill, 'Royal Navy: The New Requirement and the New Structure', *Naval Review*, vol. 79, no. 3, July 1991, p. 189. The MN statistics are from 'Keep Our Merchant Navy', p. 1.

32 Email to author from Netherlands Institute of Military History, 3 June 2015.

33 Maritime Labour Convention, 2006, *ILO*, www.ilo.org/dyn/normlex/en/f?p=NORMLEXPUB:91:0::NO::P91_SECTION:TEXT, accessed 14 July 2014.

3 – From 'Boy' to Captain: Working on Deck, pp. 56–81

1 Michael Fabey, 'Pirates, Ports and Defense', *Daily Press*, Hampton Roads, Virginia, 11 November 2001, frankfordelstop.com/articles/presspirates0001.pdf, accessed 14 August 2014.

2 'Pirate Shoot-out "Was Not Like in the Films"', NUMAST *Telegraph*, (hereafter *NT*), February 1998.

3 'Shell Officer Gets Bravery Award', *NT*, September 1999.

4 'Drummond Award for Dual "First"', *NT*, November 1997.

5 About 4,000 seafarers worldwide are affected by criminal piracy, according to Kaija Hurlburt of the project Oceans beyond Piracy. The trade in which Anne Bonney and Mary Read earlier sailed is not romantic swashbuckling. Seafarers suffer death, workplace stress, long-term post-traumatic stress disorder and family trauma. Attacked seafarers sometimes can't get a job again because employers fear they will break down on a future voyage. Kaija Hurlburt, 'Human Cost of Piracy', Al Jazeera, YouTube, www.youtube.com/watch?v=JM-BrPRPNOQ, accessed 3 August 2014.

6 One source of data is the Department for Transport, which explains that it uses Maritime and Coastguard Agency (MCA) statistics and bases some of its data re officers on the UK Chamber of Shipping (CoS) returns. In 2012, the CoS data surveyed approximately 5,000 known UK-nationality officers and a further 3,300 officers of unknown nationality. Based on the MCA data, the DfT estimated that in 2012 the number of certificated UK nationality officers active at sea in 2012 was 10,840. 'Thus, for UK national officers, one could make a rough estimate that the CoS data represents just under half of all UK officers.' (Email to author from Alice Marshall, DfT, 4 September 2014.) Of the 870 women officers (according to DfT figures) there are at least 284 women deck officers (according to Nautilus International, the officers'

union, which is a good measure of who is working currently). According to the union, but not DfT, out of a total of 564 women seafarers with various certificates of competence, women deck officers are 2.7 per cent of the 21,149 total seafaring officers with such certificates. (Nautilus International statistics in emails to author, 2014. By contrast, an MCA breakdown shows that in early 2014 a total of 367 women held certificates of competence in deck tasks, of whom 122 were masters, 53 were chief mates and officers of the watch were 92. (Email from Vanessa O'Sullivan of MCA to author, 7 August 2014). The DfT shows 2,708 seawomen in total, of whom 870 are certificated women officers of all kinds (not just deck and engine) and 1,838 are ratings. Those overall figures come from Table SFR0110, 'All UK Seafarers Active at Sea, 2002 to 2013', and SFR0201, 'Age Profile of Deck Officers Holding Certificates of Competency', 2013. These workings are based on UK Chamber of Shipping manpower surveys. Thanks to Alice Marshall of the Department for Transport Statistics and Vanessa O'Sullivan of the MCA for help with this data.

7   The data on masters are from DfT Table SFR0210, 'Age Profile of Deck Officers Holding Certificates of Competency', 2013, which does not give a gender breakdown. Roughly 4.5 cent of the 2,708 UK women seafarers have a certificate of competency, compared with 71 per cent of the 18,132 male seafarers. Holding a certificate doesn't mean you're actually working in that role, just as having an HGV driving licence doesn't mean you're driving big trucks every day, or even at all. On ships you normally work for several years at a lower level before a senior job becomes vacant. Probably proportionately fewer certificated women have command of their own vessels than do men. Similarly in air work. It's estimated that only 450 (0.34 per cent) of the world's 130,000 pilots are women captains.

8   An OOW is any officer who can take charge of a watch. (Effectively, a watch means a shift. A watch is one of the two or three teams which take turns to do shifts. Watches used to be four hours on, eight hours off, but now ships are so unregulated and understaffed there's greater variety.) The statistics are from an email from Vanessa O'Sullivan of the MCA to author, 24 July and 7 August 2014.

9   'You Have to Live the Job', *NT*, November 2001.

10   'Savage Boatswain', *LL*, 19 December 2000; *Seafarers' Log*, Seafarers' International Union, Camp Springs, MD, December 2000 and November 2014, www.seafarers.org/seafarerslog/2014/November2014/Documents/November2014Log.asp, accessed 14 March 2015.

11   These points are made by many experts including Michelle Thomas, 'Get Yourself a Proper Job Girlie!' Recruitment, Retention and Women Seafarers', *Maritime Policy & Management*, vol. 31, no. 4, 2004, pp. 309–18; Susan Dolan,

'The Case of the Female Deckhand', 27 November 2006, the-triton.com/article/the-case-of-the-female-deckhand.html, accessed 4 August 2014.

12   Of the 63,182,000 people in Britain, 32,153,000 are women and 31,029,00 are men, according to the 2011 census.

13   Byron Clayton, 'Captain Lis Lauritzen', *Ship Monthly*, 2013, www.shipsmonthly.com/features/view-from-the-bridge/1346-captain-lis-lauritzen, accessed 4 August 2014.

14   In 2008 there was public outcry in the UK because the forty-one admirals, rear admirals and vice-admirals outnumbered warships; it seemed like overkill.

15   'First Woman to Command a Major Navy Warship Takes up Post', Ministry of Defence press release, 22 May 2012; Mark Nicol, 'Disgraced Female Commander of Navy Warship Quits Service …', *Mail On Sunday*, 6 December 2014, www.dailymail.co.uk/news/article-2863252/First-female-commander-Navy-warship-quits-service-removed-post-alleged-affair-junior-officer.html; all accessed 3 February 2015.

16   Dian Murray, 'One Woman's Rise to Power: Cheng I's Wife and Pirates', in Richard W. Guisso and Stanley Johannesen (eds), *Women in China: Current Directions in Historical Scholarship*, Philo Press, Youngstown, New York, 1981, p. 154.

17   J. W. Bennet and J. C. Dewhurst (eds), 'Cheshire Quarter Sessions 1559 to 1760', *Record Society of Lancashire and Cheshire*, vol. 94, 1940, p. 221. Thanks to Terry Kavanagh for this reference. The original newspaper source for Sarah's story is untraceable.

18   *National Gazette*, quoted in the *Chester Chronicle*, 10 September 1841. Thanks to Terry Kavanagh for alerting me to this story.

19   Astronomer and navigation expert Janet Ionn, later Taylor, (1804–70) taught, wrote widely used books on navigation, and invented as well as manufactured navigational devices, including an octant. At least three others set up small private schools: Mrs Mitchell of Polruan; Sarah Jane Rees in Llangrannog; and Ellen Edwards.

20   Rebecca Ann Johnson/George Johnson was sailing on the *Christopher Mitchell*, a US whaler, in 1848 in the Pacific. She doesn't fit within the remit of this UK-focused book so her story will not be told at length here. Jacqueline Kolle Haring, 'Captain, the Lad's a Girl!', Nantucket Historical Association, www.nha.org/history/hn/HNharing-captain.htm, accessed 3 February 2014.

21   *Glasgow Herald*, 29 March 1876.

22   Undated *Sea Breezes* cutting 1939.

23   'Betsy Miller, 1792–1864: First Female Sea Captain', North Ayrshire Heritage Trails, www.ers.north-ayrshire.gov.uk/heritage/heritagetrails_betsymiller.cfm, accessed 18 June 2014; *Glasgow Herald*, 20 February 1852.

24 '"Whither You Go I Shall Go": Merchant and Whaling Wives, Women and the Sea', Mariners' Museum, www.marinersmuseum.org/sites/micro/women/goingtosea/whither.htm, accessed 14 October 2014.

25 John Mahon, *Kate Tyrell, 'Lady Mariner': The Story of the Extraordinary Woman who Sailed the Denbighshire Lass*, Basement Press, Dublin, 1995.

26 'Sailor Women', *Palace Journal*, 14 August 1889, p. 4, www.library.qmul.ac.uk/sites/www.library.qmul.ac.uk/files/archives/peoples_palace/QMC_PP_14_6_Issue_92.pdf, accessed 13 February 2015.

27 'Girl Ships as Sailor; Extraordinary Story: The Heroine a Native of Newport', *Western Mail*, Cardiff, 31 October 1898.

28 Joan Lowell (1902–67), a silent-film actor, was the daughter of a captain but had never grown up at sea nor harpooned a whale as she claimed. Her parents' neighbour blew her story, after it sold well. Seven years later she did indeed marry a captain. Corey Ford parodied Joan's book in his *Salt Water Taffy*: 'The Cradle of the Deep', 1929, Museum of Hoaxes, hoaxes.org/archive/permalink/the_cradle_of_the_deep, accessed 20 October 2014.

29 'Girl is Skipper on her Own Boat', *Spokane Daily Chronicle*, 20 December 1933, news.google.com/newspapers?nid=1338&dat=19331220&id=99JXAAAAIBAJ&sjid=7fQDAAAAIBAJ&pg=7313,4460136, accessed 16 September 2014. NB. Her surname is also spelt Wamboldt.

30 Christine Welldon, *Molly Kool: First Female Captain of the Atlantic*, Nimbus Publishing, Halifax, NS, 2011.

31 Pamela, who married her windjammer captain Sven Eriksson, was a predecessor to women on sail training ships today. Her books are *Out of the World*, Geoffrey Bles, London, 1935 and *The Duchess: The Life and Death of the Herzogin Cecilie*, Secker & Warburg, London, 1958. Another Cape Horner from 1940s sailing ships is Jocelyn Palmer, summarised at www.caphorniers.cl/Cuentos/Jocelyn_Palmer_english.htm, accessed 14 March 2014.

32 Sidney Webb, 'Freedom under Soviet rule', *Current History*, 1933, pp. 399–407.

33 Undated scrap of cutting, *Journal of Commerce*, c. August 1936.

34 Handbook, *Girl's Nautical Training Corps*, n.d. but c. 1950, kindly loaned by Denise Gravestock.

35 Patricia O'Driscoll, 'A Woman in the Hold', *PLA Monthly*, April 1968, vol. 43, no. 510, pp. 134–8.

36 *Fengatao women crew*, www.shtong.gov.cn/node2/node2245/node4507/node55734/node55736/userobject1ai41495.html, accessed 22 June 2015.

37 Correspondence on Ships' Nostalgia, August 2008–November 2009, www.shipsnostalgia.com, accessed 24 November 2013.

38 Email to author, 28 November 2013.

39 Varied sources including correspondence on the Ship's Nostalgia website, op. cit.; 'Lass Would Skip the Hash … Settle for the Marks'; Associated Press story in *Ithica Daily Press*, 20 July 1968; 'Champagne for Sheila – But No Command', *NT*, December 1980.

40 Letter from Mobil Marine Services, 12 May 1970, Nina Baker's personal archive.

41 Interview with author, 26 April 2013.

42 'Women on the Watch', *BP Wavelength*, London, June 1974, p. 6.

43 Interview with author, 7 May 2013.

44 British Parliamentary Papers: Report of the committee of inquiry into shipping industry ('the Rochdale Report'), Cmnd. 4337, HMSO, London, 1970.

45 Esther Boylan, 'Aye, Aye – Ma'am', ILO internal document, Geneva, November 1980, ITF Archive .

46 Graham Wallace, 'BP Female Navigating Cadets', Ship's Nostalgia, 6 January 2011, www.shipsnostalgia.com/showthread.php?t=37109&page=2, accessed 3 April 2015.

47 Interview, 7 May 2013.

48 Hansard, Lords Sitting, Merchant Navy, HL Deb 28 April 1993, vol. 545, cc. 388, hansard.millbanksystems.com/lords/1993/apr/28/merchant-navy, accessed 14 November 2015.

49 Denise St Aubyn Hubbard, *In at the Deep End*, Janus, London, 1993; Jo Stanley, 'Women Taking the Helm', *Maritime Heritage*, vol. 2, no. 4, November/December 1998, p. 37.

50 Stanley, 'Taking', pp. 34–8.

51 Phone briefing with author, 20 November 2013. The RFA was better than other MN companies where top women seafarers were still unusual. Susan's treatment when pregnant in 2008 resulted in her resigning from her ferry company and moving into shoreside management.

52 Leslie Leyland Fields, *The Entangling Net: Alaska's Commercial Fishing Women Tell their Lives*, University of Illinois Press, Urbana and Chicago, 1997.

53 'On Top from Down Under', *NT*, June 1999, p. vii.

54 Sandra Speares, 'First Female Master Finds Life at Helm is a Cruise', *LL*, 4 June 2007.

55 Sandra Fraser, 'A Job Less Ordinary', *Seafarer*, spring 2007, pp. 18–19.

56 Email to author, 14 May 2014. Name disguised as writer has subsequently not responded.

57 Interview by author, 26 September 2013.

58 *The Aerial*, June 1920.

59 Birgitta Gustaffson, her draft English translation of chapter ten of her book, 'Women Wireless Operators'. The book is *Radion och radiotelegrafisten: från gnistepok till satellite*, Borås, Sweden, 1991.

60   Willie Williamson, archivist for the Radio Officers' Association, kindly shared his research on this. Emails to author, autumn 2013.

61   With thanks to M.J. Fish for sharing these statistics with me, summer 2014.

62   Jessie Kenney draft typescripts, memoir, principally 'Notes for chapter 1, What made you go to sea?' There are several versions of this. KP/JK/4/2/11, as well as the draft article, 'Is the Tipping System Played Out?', University of East Anglia, Kenney Papers, KP/JK/ 4/3.

63   Statistics with thanks to M.J. Fish for compiling and sharing them.

64   Joy Bennington, many briefings with author, 2013–14.

65   Olive J. Roeckner 'Women in Wireless', www.spectralumni.ca/women_in_wireless.htm, accessed 12 May 2013. Roeckner is the main historian of women sparks and has also written the autobiographical *Deep Sea 'Sparks': A Canadian Girl in the Norwegian Merchant Navy*, Cordillera, Vancouver, 1993.

66   Joan Deppa, '"No Guy In Every Port": British Merchant Fleet has First Woman Officer', *Pittsburgh Press*, 19 August 1970.

67   Esther Boylan, 'Aye, Aye – Ma'am', ILO internal document, Geneva, November 1980, ITF Archive.

68   *NT*, March 1972. I'm grateful for Graham Wallace's help in tracking down BP women.

69   Rose King's multiple briefings to author, 2013–15.

70   Bobby Khan phone briefing to author, 12 August 2013.

71   Gustaffson, *Radion*, p. 6. She's citing *Nautisk Tidskrift*, 1971, p. 274.

72   This was one of the many harassment stories I was told on the proviso that they were off the record. And one woman RO's distressing stories have actually been taken down from the Ship's Nostalgia website, 2014.

73   Gustaffson, *Radion*, p. 7

4 – From Sail-Shifter to Chief Engineer: Propelling the Ship, pp. 82–100

1   Multiple briefings to author, 2013–15.

2   Statistics from Clyde Marine Training, 2011, with thanks to Katy Womersley. Although women were 1 per cent of trainees, they were 3 per cent of engineering applicants. Experts in the industry think this gap is because some sponsoring companies are resistant to taking on women.

3   IMareEST, www.imarest.org/policy-news/newsroom-press/item/931-imarest-supports-national-women-in-engineering-day, accessed 13 May 2015.

4   Anne Madsen, formerly James, interview with author, 27 April 1913. All subsequent quotes refer to this interview and emails afterwards.

5   All quotes are based on Lisa Jenkins's emails to author, 2013–15.

6   Statistics on women currently holding certificates, from the licensing agency, the Maritime and Coastguard Agency, email to author, 24 July 2014. With thanks to Vanessa O'Sullivan.

7   H. Campbell McMurray, 'Technology and Social Change at Sea: The Status and Position on Board of the Ship's Engineer, circa 1830–60,' in Rosemary Omner and Gerald Panting (eds), *Working Men Who Got Wet*, Memorial University of Newfoundland, Newfoundland, 1980, p. 40.

8   'Death of Lady Parsons', *The Mercury* (Hobart, Tasmania), December 1933, trove.nla.gov.au/ndp/del/article/24888812, accessed 14 March 2015.

9   'Death of Lady Parsons'.

10   Anecdote kindly passed on by Henrietta Heald, correspondence with the author, autumn 2013–spring 2015. I am grateful to Henrietta for her help, as she prepares her forthcoming book, *Rachel Parsons, Queen of the Machine*, 1916, tbc.

11   Sources include Heald, op. cit.; Edmund Raphael, *Rachel Parsons (1885–1956), Woman Engineer*, www.rachelparsons.co.uk/?page=life, and phone briefing by Edmund to author; Institute of Naval Architects, *Transaction, 1919*, p. xxviii, with thanks to RINA; and Peter Smith-Keary, correspondence with author, 2013–15.

12   I am indebted to Peter Smith-Keary for his help in researching his mother, correspondence 2013–15; and Jackie Sullivan, archivist, Roedean School, email, 27 September 2013.

13   Ann Day, 'The Forgotten "Mateys": Women workers in Portsmouth Dockyard, England, 1939–45,' *Women's History Review*, vol. 7, no. 3, 1998; and with Ken Lunn (eds), *Inside the Wall: Recollections of Portsmouth Dockyard*, University of Portsmouth, Portsmouth, 1998.

14   Hugh Murphy, '"From the Crinoline to the Boilersuit": Women Workers in British Shipbuilding During the Second World War', *Contemporary British History*, vol. 13, no. 4, winter 1999, pp. 82–104.

15   Ministry of Labour, *Women in Shipbuilding*, HMSO, London, 1943, p. 10.

16   Rozelle Raynes, *Maid Matelot: Adventures of a Wren Stoker in World War Two*, Castweasel Publishing, Thoresby Park, Nottinghamshire, 2004, p. 117.

17   Marjorie H. Fletcher, *WRNS: A History of the Women's Royal Naval Service*, Naval Institute Press, Annapolis, MD, 1989, p. 39.

18   Women and Manual Trades, www.wamt.org, accessed 6 April 2014.

19   *Merchant Navy and Airline Officers' Association Telegraph*, March 1977.

20   Information based on interview with author, 27 April 2013 and subsequent emails.

21   Femiphobia is the irrational fear of, aversion to, hatefulness or aggression towards, or discrimination against females. A femiphobic person is someone who hates or disapproves of females, female sexualities, behaviour and

mannerisms. This form of bigotry is often based on both personal history and social norms.

22   In fact women had been marginally involved in Freemasonry since the eighteenth century. But there was a major distinction between *co-freemasonry* (from which women were largely excluded until recently) and the specifically *female* women's Freemasonry organisations, which were marginal. In that second category was one of the most influential 'Lady Masons', Florence Burleigh Leach. She was Britain's 'Chief Soldier' in the First World War, the Major General of the Women's Auxiliary Army Corps. Order of Women Freemasons, www.owf.org.uk/news/Lady-Freemasons-War-Efforts, accessed 11 March 2015.

23   Correspondence with author, 18 October 2013; interview by Sheila Jemima, n.d. but *c.* 1993, Southampton City Heritage, M0119.

24   Lisa's correspondence with author, op. cit.

25   'U. S. Navy Engineer Charlene Albright on Missile Test Ship, Calif', *Los Angeles Times*, 2 November 1978.

26   *Made in Govan: An Oral History of Shipbuilding on the Upper Clyde, 1930–1950*, Glasgow. 1991, p. 30.

27   *Navy News*, January 1981.

28   Sophie-Shaughnessy, Zoom, www.zoominfo.com/p/Sophie-Shaughnessy/1200208367.

29   *Navy News*, June 2008, www.publishing.yudu.com/Adgnv/NavyNewsJune08/resources/21.htm, accessed 1 March 2015.

30   IMarEST, op. cit.; Alexander Lawrie and Oliver Farrimond, 'Descendent of Heroic Scots Sea Captain Honoured With Medals', deadline, 23 July 2009, www.deadlinenews.co.uk/2009/07/23/descendant-of-heroic-scots-sea-captain-honoured-with-medals–1449; Melissa Marino, 'She's at Ease With Seas and Grease', *The Age*, Melbourne, 2 February 2003, www.theage.com.au/articles/2003/02/01/1043804567003.html, both accessed 4 April 2015; email from Claudene to author, 20 February 2015.

31   Sara Smith, 'This is a Man's World …', Cunard, wearecunard.com/2011/07/this-is-a-mans-world, 20 July 2011, accessed 3 March 2015.

32   Briefing from Jane Nilsen to author, 2 January 2015 and subsequent emails, January 2015.

33   www.seavision.org.uk/career/oil-gas/marine-engineer, accessed 14 March 2015.

34   'Careers at Sea Begin to Catch the Public's Attention', *LL*, 6 August 2007.

5 – From Steward's Wife to Chief Housekeeper: Doing the Domestic Tasks, pp. 102–119

1   Interview with Fiona Rush by author and subsequent correspondence, particularly email, 6 December 2012.

2   Pamela Marrero, 'A Day in the Life of a Stewardess', Cruise ship jobs, www.cruiselinesjobs.com/a-day-in-the-life-of-a-stewardess, accessed 10 December 2014.

3   Seafarer Statistics, Department of Transport, www.gov.uk/government/publications/seafarer-statistics-2013, accessed 4 May 2014, with additional breakdown data from Alice Marshall, Department of Transport, email to author, 7 May 2014, re Table SFR0110: 'All UK Seafarers Active at Sea, 2002 to 2013', with many thanks to Alice. International statistics are from Belcher et al., *Women Seafarers*.

4   'Catering Assistants', Royal Navy, www.royalnavy.mod.uk/careers/role-finder/roles/rfacateringassistantsteward, accessed 12 December 2014.

5   Interview with author, 3 April 2014.

6   Geraldine Lee-Treweek, 'Women, Resistance and Care: An Ethnographic Study of Nursing Auxiliary Work', *Employment and Society*, vol. 11, no. 1, March 1997, pp. 47–63; Thorstein Veblen, *The Theory of the Leisure Class: An Economic Study of Institutions*, Penguin, New York, 1994, first published 1899, p. 47. Veblen rails against the waste this system produces. A modern example would be the daily changing of towels.

7   Caroline Davidson, *A Woman's Work is Never Done: A History of Housework in the British Isles, 1650–1950*, Chatto and Windus, London, 1982, pp. 128–32.

8   Marcus Rediker, *The Slave Ship: A Human History*, John Murray, London, pp. 269–70.

9   Mary Lacy, *The Female Shipwright*, introduction by Margarette Lincoln, Caird Library Reprints, National Maritime Museum, London, 2008, pp. 68, 69, 83.

10   Memo to all Captains, 14 July 1796, *Memoirs of Admiral the Right Hon Earl of St Vincent*, vol. 1, ed. Jedediah Stephens Tucker and Richard Bentley, London, 1844, p. 193.

11   Stark, *Female Tars*, p. 51, citing John Harvey Boteler, *Recollections of My Sea Life from 1808 to 1830*, ed. David Bonner-Smith, Navy Records Society, London, 1942, pp. 94–5. I am grateful to Suzanne Stark for drawing this to public attention.

12   Hill, *The Remarkable*, pp. 86, 122.

13   Joan Druett, *Hen Frigates: Wives of Merchant Captains Under Sail*, Simon & Schuster, New York, 1998, p. 50.

14   Elizabeth Morrison, *Jane Penelope's Journal: Being the Unique Record of the Voyages of a Sea Captain's Wife in the Indian Ocean and Persian Gulf in the Opening Years of the Nineteenth Century*, West Meadow Books, Cambridge, 1995, p. 26.

15   Charles Dickens, *American Notes for General Circulation*, Penguin, London, 2000, pp. 12–13, first published by Chapman & Hall, London, 1842.

16   'A Female Sailor', *Aberdeen Journal*, 22 January 1873.

17   'Third report by Captain Wilson upon Miss CG O'Brien's indictment against the operation of the passengers Acts', *Emigrant Accommodation on Board Atlantic Steam Ships. Report with Regard to the Accommodation and Treatment of Emigrants on Board Atlantic Steam Ships, and Minute Thereupon*, [C.2995] LXXXII.93. HMSO, London, 1881, original page 74, reprinted as page 79.

18   Thos Gibson Bowles letter to *The Times*, 17 November 1897, p. 11, citing Board of Trade statistics. In 1886 there were 655 stewardesses recorded, nineteen of whom were foreign. This figure omits those sailing deep sea at census time.

19   Valerie Burton, 'The Work and Home Life of Seafarers', PhD thesis, University of London, 1989, p. 51.

20   More than any other girls' novelist Bessie Marchant (1862–1941) wrote 105 novels starring girls with derring-do, or what we would call a sense of agency. They could and did get through any outback adventure, but they were still feminine enough to be capable of putting the kettle on for tea. Marchant's fictional world presaged the climate in which the Girl Guide movement could emerge. She was seen as the equivalent of Thomas Henty, the leading boys' adventure writer. Her *Jill's Rhodesian Philosophy* inspired conductress Edith Sowerbutts.

21   Veva Karsland, *Women and Their Work*, Sampson Low & Company, London, 1891, pp. 144–6.

22   Jake Simpkin, 'SS Stella Disaster', www.jakesimpkin.org/ArticlesResearch/tabid/84/articleType/ArticleView/articleId/4/SS-Stella-Disaster.aspx, accessed 2 February 2015; *The Times*, 10 April 1899, p. 7. For more see her obituary in the *Oxford Dictionary of National Biography*.

23   These are my calculations based on my study of 171 interwar BISN stewardesses listed in NMM, BIS 30/34, 35, 36. They may not match the experience of other companies in other periods, but this is the only raw data in Britain that is available, to my knowledge.

24   Violet Jessop, *Titanic Survivor: The Memoirs of Violet Jessop, Stewardess*, ed. John Maxtone-Graham, Sutton Publishing, Gloucestershire, 1997.

25   These figures are based on M.J. Fish's work on WRNS records, with thanks to him for sharing the data.

26   My calculation from crew agreement for *Duchess of York*, Liverpool to Montreal trip October 1934–January 1935, Maritime Archive, Memorial University, Newfoundland.

27   Paul Fussell, *Abroad: British Literary Travelling Between the Wars*, Oxford University Press, New York and Oxford, 1980.

28   Edith Sowerbutts, 'Memoirs of a British Seaman' typescript, *c.* 1976, IWM, private papers, p. 165 (old p. 191).

29   Maida M. Nixson, *Ring Twice for the Stewardess*, John Long & Co, London, 1954.

30   This is in comparison to 130 Second World War sailings, only thirty-one of which had women aboard, NMM, BIS 30/35 and 36.

31   Margaretta Godefroy seems to have been an adventurous woman, gaining an air pilot's licence and marrying into a noble French family of air aces.

32   'Ex-Wrens Will Not Displace Men on Ships', *Daily Mirror*, 23 August 1946. Piecing together oblique newspaper reports it seems that union and employer came to some sort of compromise, but that the women lost out.

33   Obituary, *Telegraph*, 29 July 2013, www.telegraph.co.uk/news/obituaries/10209917/Juanita-Carberry.html, accessed 13 August 2013; Juanita's memoir, *Child of Happy Valley*, Arrow, London, 2000 (which stops short of covering her time on ships); anecdotes told to author by Juanita's shipmates.

34   Interview with author, 27 September 2013.

35   See Sari Mäenpää, 'A Woman at Sea: Women on the Sailing Ships of Gustaf Erikson 1913–1937', *Nautica Fennica*, 1995, pp. 23–33.

36   Lily Brown-Try, 'Woman at Sea', in Ronald Hope (ed.), *The Seaman's World*, Harrap, London, 1982, pp. 100–2.

37   P&O attempted to cut the wage bill by making 500 of the 2,300 staff redundant, cutting weekly wages by £25 a week (which was about a sixth of some people's wage), setting up rotas which meant seventy-two-hour continuous shifts for some, and requiring seafarers to work an extra month a year. The strike (February 1988 to June 1989) ended in defeat. It effectively broke the union as courts sequestered its funds, and was seen as the last Alamo in a period of Conservative union-breaking in the UK.

38   Briefing with author, 3 April 2014.

6 – From Loblolly Boy to Surgeon: Caring for Health, pp. 120–138

1   There's no published general history book on British women doctors, but there are many websites, articles and a very useful online thesis: Mary Ann Elston, 'Women Doctors in the British Health Services: A sociological study of their careers and opportunities', PhD thesis, University of Leeds, 1986, www.core.kmi.open.ac.uk/download/pdf/43950.pdf, accessed 22 May 2014.

2   Sally Bell website sallybell.weebly.com/cv.html, and briefing to the author, 25 January 2015.

3   Some also have promiscuous sex in hyper-sexualised ships. A consequence of this is that, despite the availability of morning-after pills, pregnant women cruise ship workers seek terminations immediately they dock in the UK. Southampton hospitals perform a disproportionate number of terminations per year, some late.

4   Maritime and Coastguard Agency, *The Ship Captain's Medical Guide*, www. dft.gov.uk/mca/mcga-seafarer_information/mcga-dqs_st_shs_seafarer_ information-medical/mcga-dqs_st_shs_ships_capt_medical_guide.htm, accessed 26 March 2014.

5   The ship's medical facilities in October 2014 can be seen in a video by Julian Simmonds, www.telegraph.co.uk/news/worldnews/ebola/11161534/ RFA-Argus-loaded-with-supplies-for-Ebola-mission-to-Sierra-Leone.html, accessed 5 February 2015.

6   Jane Yelland's rich correspondence with author, 2013–15.

7   Richard Hill, *A Week at Port Royal*, Cornwall Chronicle Office, Montego Bay, 1855, p. 3.

8   In a modern novel ex-nurse Linda Collison imagined what it might have taken in the 1760s. Her cross-dressed heroine Patricia Kelley was the young widow of a naval surgeon who'd taught her skills. She was then helped by accepting mentors (who saw her as young rather than female) and by having the kind of build that enabled her to pass. *Surgeon's Mate*, Fireship Press, Tucson, AZ, 2010.

9   Obituary, *The Gentleman's Magazine*, July–December 1860, p. 210.

10   Account was written by unnamed aunt of Richard Higham, who seems to be related to Bellamy. 'Henry Giles', Nelson and his world, www.nelsonand hisworld.co.uk/forum/viewtopic.php?f=1&t=266, accessed 23 March 2014.

11   Christina afterwards petitioned the Admiralty for a pension, especially as she had become a widow. Christopher Lloyd, *The British Seaman 1200–1860: A Social Survey*, Collins, London, 1968, p. 224.

12   Stark, *Female Tars*, p. 68.

13   Stark, *Female Tars*, p. 69.

14   Stark, *Female Tars*, p. 70.

15   There were eight additional assistants, so about sixteen staff to deal with patients, for whom there was a capacity for 300. John H. Plumridge, *Hospital Ships and Ambulance Trains*, Seeley, Service & Co., London, 1975, p. 14.

16   Kathleen Harland, 'History of Queen Alexandra's Royal Naval Nursing Service', *Journal of the Royal Naval Medical Service*, London, 1990, p. 4.

17   Stephen McGreal, *The War on Hospital Ships*, Pen & Sword, Barnsley, 2009, p. 1.

18   Rachel Holmes, *The Scandalous Life and Astonishing Secret of Queen Victoria's Most Eminent Military Doctor*, Penguin, London, 2003. Today Dr Barry might

be regarded as an intersex person rather than someone who simply disguised herself in order to gain job opportunities.

19   John Wilson, Royal Navy Medical Officer's Journals, TNA, ADM 101/25/54 No. 38. With thanks to Colleen Arulappu, a volunteer researcher for the Female Convicts Research Centre, for sharing this fragment. Email to author, 13 April 2014.

20   Jane Williams (ed.), *Betsy Cadwaladyr: A Balaclava Nurse – An autobiography of Elizabeth Davis*, Honno, Cardiff, 1987, p. 54.

21   Williams, *Cadwaladyr*, p. 43; 'Elizabeth Cadwaladyr', The National Archives, www.nationalarchives.gov.uk/womeninuniform/crimea_profile.htm, accessed 12 April 2014.

22   Charles Dickens, 'The Life and Adventures of Martin Chuzzlewit', *The Times*, 1843; Anne Summers, 'The Mysterious Demise of Sarah Gamp: The Domiciliary Nurse and her Detractors, c. 1830–1860', *Victorian Studies*, vol. 32, no. 3, spring 1989, pp. 365–86.

23   R. Druitt, *Medical Hints to Emigrants*, Society for Promoting Christian Knowledge, London, 1850.

24   Lynn McDonald (ed.), *Florence Nightingale: The Crimean War: Collected Works of Florence Nightingale*, Wilfrid Laurier University Press, Waterloo, Ontario, 2010.

25   Ziggi Alexander and Audrey Dewjee, *The Wonderful Adventures of Mrs Seacole in Many Lands*, Falling Wall Press, London, 1984.

26   Harland, *History of QARNNS*, p. 17.

27   Sister 'Mack All', a superintendent on a hospital ship, *British Journal of Nursing* (hereafter *BJN*), 20 June 1908, p. 492.

28   The law required shipowners to engage 'any competent person to act as a medical practitioner' on board any passenger ship proceeding on a colonial voyage. 1855 Passenger Act, p. 776, section 230 of 17 and 18 Vict, sections 224, 226 and 230.

29   Tim Carter has summarised crew medical needs and treatments in *Merchant Seamen's Health, 1860–1960: Medicine, Technology, Shipowners and the State In Britain*, Boydell Press, Woodbridge, 2014. Lesley Hall has written many articles on seafarers and venereology.

30   See, for example, ship's surgeon Hugh Wansy Bayly, letter, 'Medical Arrangements on Passenger Ships', *British Medical Journal* (hereafter *BMJ*), 2 July 1906.

31   *BJN*, 21 November 1903, p. 415.

32   'X.Y.Z.', letter, 'Warning: Nurses on Passenger Boats', *BMJ*, 16 January 1904, p. 165.

33   Industry Tables, *Census of England and Wales, 1901*, HMSO, London, 1904.

34   *The Seaman*, 7 February 1913, quoted from the *Daily Telegraph*, 9 January 1913, p. 3.

35   For help with Dr Ross's story I am grateful to the Ross family, Morag Bremner and Margaret Urquhart at Tain Museum, and to Louise Miller, who shared the research findings she'd made during writing *A Fine Brother: The Life of Captain Flora Sandes*, Alma Books, London, 2012. For more local information see Tain Museum website, www.tainmuseum.org.uk.

36   *Daily Telegraph*, 9 January 1913, p. 3, and reprinted in *The Seaman*, 7 February 1913. In fact, it seems to have been assumed that 'person' meant 'man'. In parliament in 1876 Sir Charles Adderley mistakenly referred to the law as 'requiring every foreign-going ship to carry a duly qualified medical *man*' (my italics). HC Deb, 5 May 1876, Hansard, vol. 229, c105.

37   Dr Hare seemingly was a beneficiary of two key forces: feminism and public medicine. She became a mature medical student at the Elizabeth Garrett Anderson hospital and her father, Edward Hare, had been deputy inspector general of hospitals in the Indian Medical Service. A 1917 photograph of Dr Hare by George P. Lewis, Q19705, can be seen at www.iwm.org.uk/collections/item/object/205254067, accessed 14 January 2015.

38   Harland, *History of QARNNS*, p. 151.

39   The most widely accepted number seems to be seventy-seven. But the figure is much disputed, partly because of definitions and categories, for example, hospital *carriers* were more like floating ambulances than floating hospitals.

40   'A trained nurse' (almost certainly Annie Cameron, judging from previous signed articles by her), 'At Anzac in a hospital ship,' *The Navy*, January 1916, p. 8. *Women, War & Society, 1914–1918*, Gale Cengage, BCR 25 4 /16.

41   Harland, *History of QARNNS*; Stephen McGreal, *The War on Hospital Ships*, Pen & Sword, Barnsley, 2009.

42   A fuller story of nurses on hospital ships appears in the author's forthcoming book, provisionally entitled *Risk! Women on the wartime Seas*, Yale University Press, London, tbc. See also Sue Light's nursing history website, Scarlet Finders, www.scarletfinders.co.uk.

43   Erica Nadin-Snelling, *Matron at War: The Story of Katy Beaufoy (1869–1918)*, Brewin Books, Studley, 2014. 'Tragedy on the Marquette', *Nursing Review* (New Zealand), April 2015, Vol. 15, No. 2, www.nursingreview.co.nz/issue/april-2015-vol-15-2/tragedy-on-the-marquette; statistics from Yvonne McEwan, *It's a Long Way to Tipperary: British and Irish Nurses in the Great War*, Cualann Press, Dunfermline, 2006, p. 143.

44   Kenney, 'Tipping System'.

45   J.L.S. Coulter, *History of the Second World War: The Royal Navy Medical Services*, vol. 1, HMSO, London, 1954, pp. 73–86.

46   This rough calculation is based on the assumption that there were at least four complete changes of nursing staff per ship during the war: nurses were rotated to land hospitals, not least to alleviate the boredom at sea. This means

that sixteen to eighty nurses would have served on each ship, depending on its size and occupancy rates. Sister Ivy Bussle's data, including the reference to twenty nurses, appears in her letter to the matron-in-chief, QAIMNS, *BJN*, February 1942 p. 28.

47 *London Gazette*, 13 February 1942, www.london-gazette.co.uk/issues/35457/supplements/757/page.pdf, accessed 11 July 2012. See also Brian James Crabb, *Beyond the Call of Duty: The loss of British Commonwealth Mercantile and Service Women at Sea During the Second World War*, Shaun Tyas, Donington, 2006, p. 61.

48 Citation for her Lloyd's Medal for Bravery, George A. Brown, *Lloyd's War Medal for Bravery at Sea*, Western Canadian Distributors, Langley, BC, 1992, p. 51.

49 Liverpool Ships, www.liverpoolships.org/cilicia___anchor_line.html, accessed 11 July 2012.

50 Obituary, *Medical Women's Federation Quarterly*, summer 1988, p. 29, Wellcome Archive, AS/MWF.

51 Harland, *History of QARNNS*, pp. 103–110.

52 Harland, *History of QARNNS*, p. 110.

53 Wynne O'Mara and Eleanor Buckles, *Gangway for the Lady Surgeon*, Robert Hale, London, 1958, p. 7. I am grateful to her widower Bob Proudlock for all his help; in emails, 2014–15.

54 Emails and phone calls to author from Joy's daughter Sue Freeman, 16 March 2015; *Straits Times* (Singapore), 21 October 1950, p. 7.

55 Industry tables, *Census of England and Wales*, 1951.

56 Correspondence with author from Captain (N) C.J. Brooks, 14 April 1998. He could not be certain of the first woman's name.

57 Nicci Pugh, *White Ship, Red Crosses: A Nursing Memoir of the Falklands War*, Melrose Books, Ely, Cambridgeshire, 2010. Andrew Vine, *A Very Strange Way to Go to War: The Canberra in the Falklands*, Aurum, London, 2012, pp. 35, 37–8, 126.

58 'QARNNS', Haslar Heritage Group, www.haslarheritagegroup.co.uk, accessed 24 March 2014.

59 Phone briefing with author, 10 February 2015.

7 – From Convict Matron to Cruise Director: Supporting the Passengers, pp. 139–159

1 'Women Take Charge of Pacific Pearl', stuff.co,nz, www.stuff.co.nz/travel/cruising/5198521/Women-take-charge-of-Pacific-Pearl cruise director, accessed 23 November 2014.

2 All quotes are from author's phone interview, 28 October 2013.

3   Elizabeth Fry was the figure on £5 notes since 2002. Her 'displacement' by Winston Churchill in 2013 brought feminist outcries at women's absence.

4   *The Original Letters from India of Mrs. Eliza Fay* (1908), first published 1817, archive.org/stream/originalletters00forsgoog#page/n6/mode/2up Eliza, especially pp. 63, 11, 176, 177, 225, accessed 23 November 2014.

5   Slave statistics are still the subject of much debate. Slavery, the so-called Second Atlantic System, began in 1450 and by 1760 the British were the biggest shippers of slaves; that position continued until 1808. When it formally (rather than actually) waned in the early nineteenth century 12 to 15 million had been uprooted. Women tended to be outnumbered two to one but female/male ratios varied according to region, as well as period, argues Jennifer L. Morgan in *Laboring Women: Reproduction and Gender in New World Slavery*, University of Pennsylvania Press, Philadelphia, 2004, pp. 56–61.

6   Alexander Falconbridge, *An Account of the Slave Trade on the Coast of Africa*, J. Phillips, London, 1788, p. 23.

7   Marcus Rediker, *The Slave Ship: A Human History*, John Murray, London, 2007, especially pp. 16, 279–83, 284, 348. He was citing the testimony of Henry Ellison in 1790, re the *Nightingale* and William Butterworth on the *Hudibras: Three Years Adventures of a Minor in England, Africa, the West Indies, South Carolina and Georgia*, Baines, Leeds, 1822.

8   The most accessible summary of this voyage is that by Sian Rees, *The Floating Brothel: The Extraordinary True Story of an 18th Century Ship and its Cargo of Female Convicts*, Headline, London, 2001.

9   John Nicol, *The Life and Adventures of John Nicol, Mariner*, ed. John Howell, William Blackwood and T. Cadell, London and Edinburgh, 1822.

10   It became the British Ladies' Society for Promoting the Reformation of Female Prisoners.

11   George R. Gleig, *Chelsea Hospital, and its Traditions*, vol. 3, Bentley, London, 1838, p. 261.

12   *Convict Ship Exmouth 1831: Free settler or Felon?* www.jenwilletts.com/convict_ship_exmouth_1831.htm, accessed 14 November 2014.

13   Evidence of Mrs Elizabeth Fry, Mrs Elizabeth Pryer, Mrs Jane Pirie and Miss Catherine Fraser to the Select Committee on Gaols and Houses of Correction, 1835, archive.org/details/presentstatedisc00grea. The job title came from workhouses, where the matron was usually the wife of the master. Above all, in a world where men tended to be uneasy with women as an 'other species', matrons were people to whom the care of lowly women en masse could be devolved. 'Matron' didn't mean the all-powerful heads of hospitals who emerged seventy years later, or Hattie Jacques-style figures. Instead, they were on a par with lady housekeepers of institutions and manageresses of orphanages.

14   The last ship to New South Wales arrived in 1850 and to Tasmania in 1853. However, the very last convict ship to Australia did not cross until 1868.

15   Private journal kept by Alice, typescript courtesy of Dorothy Weeks Buck and stored at the Oyster Bay Historical Society, Long Island, cited in Druett, *Hen Frigates*, pp. 27–9.

16   It's possible that the BLFES took on *supervisory* matrons who had worked on convict vessels but unlikely. BLFES-managed matrons were now supposed to use the voyage to train young future domestic workers in domestic skills. It would be an overstatement to say that a corner of the emigrant ship became almost a women's training college. But it did mean these women in authority accrued more status again; as teacher they were becoming even more like officers, although still not employees of the shipping lines.

17   Jan Gothard, *Blue China: Single Female Migration to Colonial Australia*, Melbourne University Press, Carlton South, Victoria, 2001, p. 99.

18   *Hints to Matrons*, SPCK, London, 1850.

19   *Hints to Matrons.*

20   Great Britain Colonial Land and Emigration Commission, *Eighteenth General Report of the Emigration Commissioners*, HMSO, London, 1858, pp. 20–1. This 39/43 satisfaction rate compared well to the fifty positive reports for the ninety-one surgeons (ninety of whom were already experienced in ship's work).

21   All data taken from Tricia Fairweather and Leonie Hayes, 'Bride Ships in all but Name: Miss Monk and the Servant Girls', *Western Ancestor: Journal of the Western Australian Genealogical Society*, June and September 2013, Perth, WA. With much appreciation to the authors for sharing the products of their forays with me.

22   '40 Years a Matron on Immigrant Ships to N.Z.', *Barrier Miner*, Broken Hill, NSW, 21 May 1927, trove.nla.gov.au/ndp/del/article/46008517, accessed 20 November 2014.

23   Elizabeth's task list and tactful recommendations from her Metagama trip in April 1919. Library and Archives Canada, Immigration Branch, RG 76, Vol. 614, file 908571, pt 17. I am indebted to Annette Fulford for this information.

24   Rebecca Mancuso, 'This is our Work: The Women's Division of the Canadian Department of Immigration and Colonization, 1919–1938', PhD thesis, McGill University, 1999, p. 142; and her 'For Purity or Prosperity: Competing nationalist visions and Canadian immigration policy, 1919–30,' *British Journal Of Canadian Studies*, vol. 23, no. 1, May 2010, pp. 1–23. Some emigrators argued about whether chaperones, which were now being called conductresses, were needed for non-British women, or for women travelling in classes other than third. Other companies fiddled the situation by taking British women to American ports, then continuing on with them to Canada, but saying conductresses weren't need on such ships.

25   Edith Sowerbutts, 'Days of Empire Vol. 2, 1896–1924', *c.* 1972, and 'Memoirs of a British Seaman' typescript, *c.* 1976, private papers, IWM; 'Men, Women … and More Passengers,' *Sea Breezes*, January 1989, pp. 9–13.

26   Rebecca Mancuso, 'This is our Work', p. 203.

27   Sowerbutts, 'Memoirs', 'Days', and 'Men, Women', as well as many conversations with her niece, Jan Buttifont, to whom the author gives grateful thanks.

28   Ian Hugh McAllister, *Lost Olympics, The Hilda James Story*, emp3books, Fleet, 2013. See also www.lostolympics.co.uk, accessed 30 October 2013.

29   Records of Stewarding Department, NMM, BIS 30/36. Some newcomers entered immediately as matrons, which suggests it was not seen as a job that required prior experience, just one that women would 'naturally' know how to do.

30   Thomas Wolf, 'Diary of the Diaper Cruise: Ex-War Correspondent Rides the Stork Ship,' *Omaha World Herald Sunday Magazine*, 10 February 1946, www. uswarbrides.com/newsarticles/46feb10mag.html, accessed 22 November 2014.

31   'Assisted Immigration, 1947–75', New Zealand History, www.nzhistory.net. nz/culture/assisted-immigration/the-voyage-out, accessed 22 November 2014.

32   The British Shipping Federation, South Western Area, 'Vacancies for Female Seagoing Personnel', n.d. but *c.* 1971. Document kindly loaned to author by Sara Coxon.

33   Mary Ollis, *Boarders Away: An Account of British India Educational Cruises*, Longman Group, London, 1973.

34   As the older ships wore out, after 1968 the *Uganda* replaced them. During the Falklands Conflict the *Uganda* was used to take troops out to the Falkland Islands and continued to do so afterwards: it was more lucrative than school cruising.

35   On non-school trips, the ass. mat. role became 'children's stewardess'. The matron, who was an officer, became the children's hostess, nicknamed 'chilly ho'; Ollis, *Boarders*, p. 12.

36   Poem shown to author by Marje Ellison, 2013.

37   Interview with author, 28 June 2013 and subsequent phone conversations in November and December 2014.

38   Email to author, 16 November 2014. Miss Groom stopped working as a matron slightly earlier, in 1979.

39   Author's interview with Margaret Newcombe, 14 January 2014, and subsequent phone calls.

40   Author's phone conversations, 2014.

41   Author's interview with Carole Routledge, formerly Critchley, 2 October 2013, and subsequent email conversations, especially 6 December 2014.

42   'Slavery levels in UK "higher than thought"', BBC News, 29 November 2014, www.bbc.co.uk/news/uk–30255084, accessed 12 October 2014.

8 – From Stenographer to Administration Director: Doing the Ship's Business Afloat, pp. 160–174

1   For a clear, up-to-date summary (which unfortunately doesn't refer much to gender stratification) see Philip Gibson, *Cruise Operations Management: Hospitality Perspectives*, Routledge, London, 2012.

2   Caroline Norman, email and phone correspondence with author, 2014.

3   Nicola Russell, 'Women Take Charge of Pacific Pearl', stuff.co.nz, www.stuff.co.nz/travel/cruising/5198521/Women-take-charge-of-Pacific-Pearl, 27 June 2011, accessed 23 October 2014.

4   'Logistics Officer', Royal Navy, www.royalnavy.mod.uk/careers/role-finder/roles/logisticsofficer, accessed 14 October 2014.

5   A.P. Herbert, 'The Way of a Ship', *Pathé Gazette*, Reel 1, 1953, www.youtube.com/watch?v=pT1L7ijVr5U, accessed 5 November 2014 (the film shows women assistant pursers typing). Additional words cited in Nelson French, *Ormonde to Oriana*, Navigator Books, Ringwood, 1995, p. i.

6   These images were circulated on UK cigarette cards in the 1930s and can most readily be seen on eBay.

7   Women were sidelined in business because under common law married women's property and rights were legally subsumed into her husband's realm in England (not Scotland). The principle of *coverture* saw her as 'covered' by him, they were one financial entity, until a century later when the Married Women's Property Act of 1870 was passed after much campaigning by feminists. See also 'Women in Banking: Partners', RBS Heritage Hub, heritagearchives.rbs.com/subjects/list/women–in–banking–partners.html, accessed 23 October 2014.

8   Girls were to be at an educational disadvantage by the early 1800s. In 1851 their literacy rates were only 55 per cent, compared to boys (almost 70 per cent). Feminist agitation opposing the idea that to educate girls was 'against nature' improved matters for *wealthy* girls, after the 1840s. But *state* education after the 1870s was very gendered, for example focusing on domestic skills not what we would now call STEM subjects. See Richard Brown, 'Educating girls 1800–1870', Looking at History, 9 February 2011, richardjohnbr.blogspot.co.uk/2011/02/educating-girls–1800–1870-revised.html, accessed 11 May 2014. June Purvis, *A History of Women's Education in England*, Open University Press, Milton Keynes, 1991, records that free secondary education for girls (and boys) only really began with the 1902 Education Act. It was

not fully established until 1944. Britain was fifty years behind the US in that respect. So US women might well have better equipped to become pursers, had there not been other cultural obstacles.

9   Gregory Anderson, *Victorian Clerks*, Manchester University Press, Manchester, 1976, p. 52.

10 'Women as Pursers', *The Press*, Canterbury, NZ, 29 September 1908, p. 6, paperspast.natlib.govt.nz/cgi-bin/paperspast?a=d&d=CHP19080929.2.28, accessed 1 October 2014.

11 *New York Times*, 28 July 1908.

12 Anderson, *Victorian*, particularly refers to the *Minutes of Evidence, Taken Before the Select Committee on Post Office Servants*, HMSO, London, 1914.

13 I am indebted to M.A. Fish for sharing this unpublished data with me, November 2014. It is derived from a list of all ratings and their jobs at The National Archives (hereafter TNA), ADM/336.

14 Jane Rossiter, interview by Peter Godfrey for *Sailors'Tales*, BBC, February 1981, copy at the National Museum of the Royal Navy's Archive (hereafter NMRN).

15 *Cunard* magazine, vol. 5, 1920, p. 111, Cunard Archive, University of Liverpool, D42/PR5.2. For more detail see the author's 'Finding a Flowering of Typists at Sea: Evidence from a New Cunard Deposit', *Business Archives*, no. 76, November 1998, pp. 29–40.

16 'We Find it Out', 9 March 1939, unattributed newspaper cutting in author's possession.

17 These figures were drawn from M.A. Fish's analysis of the statistics in NMM, DAU/162/2 and DAU/165.

18 This was the 1970s standard. British Shipping Federation, South Western Area, 'Vacancies for Female Seagoing Personnel', n.d. but *c.* 1971. Document kindly loaned to author by Sara Coxon.

19 Margaret Newcombe interview by Sheila Jemima, n.d. but *c.* 1992, Southampton City Archive, M0100. Author's own interview with Margaret, 9 January 2014.

20 One anonymous LAP remembers some women campaigning in the early 1970s to be put on the same pay scale as male pursers, 'but I don't know what became of this'. Email to author, 21 May 2013.

21 Muriel Arnold, *Tiaras and T-shirts: A Working Life at Sea*, Librario books, Kinloss, 2007, p. 38.

22 Linda Simkins email to author, June 2013.

23 P&O picture caption, Hardy Amies uniforms, February 1967, P&O S.N. Co., www.pandosnco.co.uk/pursers.html, accessed 14 November 2014.

24 Briefings with author, 2012.

25 Correspondence from former BI Purser Derek Ings via Sue Spence, June 2013.

26   Briefing to author, 22 March 2014; 'Frances Milroy', Audio transcripts, www.
      liverpoolmuseums.org.uk/maritime/exhibitions/newyork/transcripts.aspx,
      accessed 4 November 2014.

27   'Sonia Browne' interview with author, 30 July 2013 and subsequent phone
      and email conversations.

28   Celia's, Seadogs Reunited, www.seadogs-reunited.com/Celias%20Memories.
      htm, accessed 26 October 2014. Picture shows Heather Yandle, Celia Cowan,
      Annette George, Pauline Miller, Celia Gore-Lloyd and Sandra White.

29   Rosemary Selman (formerly Romy Green) briefing to author and
      correspondence, October 2014.

30   Typescript story by Judie, kindly forwarded to the author by the Browne
      family, email 16 November 2014.

31   Assessment report, signed illegibly by captain, 7 January 1989. Document
      kindly sent to author by Jeremy Chandler Browne, November 2014.

32   Judy's story is pieced together posthumously from many fragmentary sources
      including a briefing to the author by Rosemary Selman, 27 October 2014;
      material from 'Legacy from a countryside lover', CPRE, www.cpre.org.
      uk/how-you-can-help/join-or-donate/make-a-donation/leave-a-legacy/
      item/2488-legacy-from-a-countryside-lover; and some documents and
      feedback kindly given to the author by Jeremy Chandler Browne and Judy's
      friend Susan Browne, November 2014. Judy is pictured at www.seadogs-
      reunited.com/Groups%20Himalaya.htm#PD74, both websites accessed
      27 October 2014.

33   Richard H. Wagner, An interview with Jacqueline Hodgson, hotel manager,
      Queen Victoria, www.beyondships.com/QV-Hodgson.html, accessed 27 October
      2014; and 'Farewell to a true Cunarder', *Cunarder*, August 2014, p. 16.

9 – From Candy Girl to Retail Expert: Working in Shops and Hairdressing Salons, pp. 175–195

1   Harding Retail, a very long-established company on land, moved into cruise
      ships in the late 1980s, including Fred Olsen, Cunard, Crystal Cruises and
      Seabourn Cruises, and now works with eighteen major cruise lines including
      Carnival UK's P&O and Cunard fleets. Harding Retail, www.hardingretail.
      co.uk, accessed 28 August 2014.

2   Nuance, www.thenuancegroup.com/about_us/history; Starboard, www.
      starboardcruise.com, both accessed 23 August 2014.

3   Work on Cruise Ships, www.workoncruiseships.com/members/Interview_
      with_a_Gift_Shop_Assistant_on_a_Cruise_Ship.cfm, accessed 28 August
      2014.

4   Phone briefing with author, 9 January 2015.

5   NAAFI, www.naafi.co.uk; accessed 23 August 2014; email correspondence from John Goddard, January 2015.

6   Caroline Cox, *Good Hair Days: A History of British Hairstyling*, Quartet, London, 1999, p. 70.

7   Cox, *Good Hair*, p. 29.

8   Among the armed forces in that war male officers would have been hot-shaved and trimmed by their batmen. Men of lower ranks were tended by a willing amateur or peacetime barber in their midst. After the war US servicemen were allowed to keep the Gillette safety razors with which they all had been issued in wartime. This enabled lift-off for a new be-you-own-barber climate.

9   Humphrey Carpenter, *Robert Runcie: The Reluctant Archbishop*, Hodder & Stoughton, London, 1996, p. 26.

10   See Miss C. Stewart White's pay rates on the *Asturias*: 'Crew Agreement for Voyage Commencing 13 September 1927', Maritime History Archive, Memorial University of Newfoundland.

11   Women were expected to be the main consumers (but not owners or managers; Elizabeth Harvey, of what became Harvey Nichols, was a high-end exception).

12   Pamela Cox and Annabel Hobley, *Shopgirls: True Stories of Friendship, Hardship and Triumph from Behind the Counter*, Arrow, London, 2015. See also Daniel Miller et al., *Shopping, Place and Identity*, Routledge, London, 1998; and Sally Ledger, 'Gissing, the Shopgirl and the New Woman', *Women: A Cultural Review*, vol. 6, no. 3, winter 1995, pp. 263–74.

13   RMSP, *The Story of a Great Liner*, Royal Mail Line, London, 1924, p. 41.

14   British Banking History Society, 'Banking Life on the Ocean Wave, www.banking-history.co.uk/cunard.html; RBS, 'Women Making a Banking Career', www.rbsremembers.com/our-people/behind-the-counter/women-making-a-banking-career.html, both accessed 13 February 2015.

15   For example, R.E. Higgins's 1933 poster for the LINER railway, 'The Continent via Harwich', and later the SR poster by Eileen Seyd in 1947, 'For Your Shopping – Cheap Day Tickets Are Issued From This Station.'

16   *White Star Magazine*, April to June 1933, p. 214, caption referring to the *Georgic*.

17   'Uniform Requirement', memo from Marine Department pasted into *Arlanza* crew agreement, 30 November 1935, MHA, MUN.

18   *White Star Magazine*, July 1930, p. 409, Special Collections, University of Liverpool Library, (hereafter UoL) D42/PR6/12.

19   Anecdote from Robina Herrington, who sailed with her. Briefing to author.

20   Information from Peter Collinge, phone briefing, October 2013.

21   Collinge, op cit; boards.ancestry.co.uk/thread.aspx?mv=flat&m=96&p =surnames.court, accessed 20 October 2013.

22   'Hairdressers'Wages: Notes compiled by National Union of Seamen Research Department', 1958, MRC, MSS 171/9.

23   Phone briefing to author from Lesley Cox, now Schoonderbeek, 6 June 2015.

24   Email to author, 8 June 2015.

25   Interview with author, 2 July 2013 and subsequent correspondence.

26   Tony Kaye and Richard Seamon, *G-strings and Curls*, Swirl, London 2007, p. 169.

27   Allders International was a chain of department stores begun in 1862. It founded Ocean Trading, which was sold to SwissAir in 1996. Allders were mainly called Allders International but also became Allders Ligabue, Allders International (USA) Inc, and Nuance Global Traders. Allders information from ex-sea staff and 'Allders', www.answers.com/topic/ allders#ixzz3Br7DTVqy, accessed 28 August 2014. Harding Retail detailed in note 1 above.

28   Cunard memo, 'Female Staff on the *Queen Elizabeth*', 1963, UoL, D42/ PR4/46.

29   Briefing to author, 8 December 1991 and subsequent correspondence in 2014–15.

30   Interview with author, 15 May 2012, with many thanks to him for his continued help.

31   Phone briefing with author, 24 March 1999, interview with author 31 October 2014, emails and phone calls 2014–15, and extract from Robina's unpublished essay 'Ambitions'.

32   Interview with author, 15 September 2013. I particularly appreciate all the ways she helped me understand maritime life for women at that time.

33   Interview with author and private briefing, July 2013.

34   Private information from CC to author, August 2013.

35   Facebook story, www.facebook.com/groups/30613287118 on 13 October 2014. Although this is a public website I feel it unethical to publish details as I have been unable to ask the writer's permission.

36   With thanks to Brian White for telling me about Sue's role.

37   'Elaine Fenard', *Hotel Business Review*, n.d. but *c.* 2012, hotelexecutive.com/ author/128/Elaine-Fenard Fenard, accessed 13 February 2015.

38   Emailed account sent to author by Tina, now Mobius, 20 October 2013.

39   Nasdaq, globenewswire.com/news-release/2011/10/06/457938/ 234206/en/Steiner-Leisure-Limited-Announces-New-Agreements-With-Cunard-Line-and-P-O-Cruises.html, accessed 11 March 2014.

40   Kevin Griffin, 'Shipboard Spas: If it's on a ship, it must be a Steiners', The Cruise People, seatravel.wordpress.com/2011/07/05/shipboard-spas-if-its-on-a-ship-it-must-be-a-steiners, accessed 16 February 2014. Art auctions and beauty salons are, he wrote, the focus of most passenger complaints about steep mark-ups.

41   'Alders/international/Ocean Trading Shops/Salons on board Cruise Ships', Facebook, www.facebook.com/groups/30613287118/?fref=ts, accessed 14 December 2014. 'OTT' was used as a popular approving expression in the 1970s. It meant outrageous, bold, daring and excessive, like glam rock of the Gary Glitter kind.

42   'Naafi Girls Serve at Sea', *Navy News*, January 1996, p. 12; 'Bev Has Become NAAFI's First Lady', *Navy News*, November 2000, p. 10.

10 – Women in Many Roles, pp. 196–223

1   Author's briefing by Annie Kaye's daughter, Mrs Hobbes, 29 December 1987.

2   Druett, *Petticoat Whalers*, p. 73, citing Marbles papers, Kendall Whaling Museum, Sharon, MA.

3   'Merry Black' briefing to author, August 1994.

4   Georgine Clarsen, '"A Fine University for Women Engineers": A Scottish Munitions Factory in World War I', *Women's History Review*, Vol. 12, No. 3, 2003, pp. 333–56.

5   Interview by Sheila Jemima, 17 December 1997, Southampton City Archives, MO125.

6   Christopher Love, 'Swimming and Gender in the Victorian World', *International Journal of the History of Sport*, vol. 24, no. 5, 2007, pp. 586–602; and his *A Social History of Swimming in England, 1800–1918*, Routledge, London, 2007.

7   *White Star Magazine*, July 1930, p. 379, Special Collections, UoL, D42/PR6/12.

8   British Shipping Federation, South Western Area, 'Vacancies for Female Seagoing Personnel', n.d. *c.* 1971. Document loaned to author by Sara Coxon.

9   'Death of the First British Lady Telephone Operator', *Telegraph and Telephone Journal*, December 1925, p. 56. Thanks to Vicky Rea of the BT archive for her help in locating this information. 'Women's work' op. cit.; and 'Women in Telecommunications', Connected Earth, www.connected-earth.com/Journeys/Transformingsociety/Theimpactonworkinglife/Womenintelecomms/index.htm, accessed 13 December 2014.

10   *Census of England and Wales, 1931, General Report*, HMSO, London, 1950, p. 148; *Sample Census of Great Britain, 1966*, Economic Activity Tables, part 1, table 2, HMSO, London, 1968, p. 48.

11   Interview with Jo Lock by Sheila Jemima, 5 May 1993, Southampton City Archives, MO102.

12   Briefing from Jane Nilsen to author, 2 January 2015 and subsequent emails, January 2015.

13   With thanks to Rose King and Willie Williamson for all their technical advice on this subject, emails December 2014 and January 2015.

14   See letter to Cunard Chairman Sir Thomas Royden, 28 July 1927, UoL, Correspondence, D42/2/259/3 part 1.

15   Cited in Druett, *Hen Frigates*, p. 95.

16   *Belfast Newsletter*, 8 June 1885.

17   Briefing to author, 24 March 1988.

18   Interview with Isobel Wilson, later Harmsworth, by Sheila Jemima, 20 April 1993, Southampton City Archives, M0098.

19   Pamela Laister, 'Children Aboard', *Sea Lines*, n.d. but *c*. 1990, pp. 51–3.

20   Author's correspondence with Barbara Wells, formerly Symonds, December 2014.

21   After Orient Line merged with P&O, who had their own personnel arrangements, in 1960 Miss Osborn joined P&O public relations staff 'where she remained a backbone of commonsense and administrative calm' until her retirement in 1980. 'Penny Osborn', *P&O Wavelength*, no. 91, March 1980, p. 4.

22   British Shipping Federation, 'Vacancies for Female Seagoing Personnel'.

23   'Best Cruises for Families', Travel and Leisure, February 2013, www.traveland leisure.com/articles/best-cruises-for-families, accessed 14 December 2014.

24   Jon Ronson, 'Rebecca Coriam: Lost at sea', *Guardian*, 11 November 2011.

25   See John Graves's version of MPS's and indeed shipboard photography history, *Waterline: Images from the golden age of cruising*, National Maritime Museum, London, 2004. See also MPS history at www.seadogs-reunited. com/MPS.htm, accessed 11 March 2015. I am deeply grateful to many MPS staff for their reminiscences.

26   Jane Hunter-Cox, *Ocean Pictures: The Golden Age of Transatlantic Travel 1936 to 1959*, Webb & Bower/ Michael Joseph, London, 1989.

27   Telephone briefing to author, 25 June 2013.

28   Telephone briefing to author, 12 June 2013.

29   Interview with author, 26 April 2013.

30   For an informative video about a (male) ship's photographers' life, see Matej Kopecki, 'Life of the Cruise Ship Photographer', vimeo.com/55770553, accessed 6 March 2015.

31   Emailed accounts sent to author be Sarah Craig, June–July 2013.

32   One of the best illustrated summaries can be found in 'Horseback Riding on Ocean Liners', *Popular Mechanics*, December 1924, pp. 929–38, books.google. co.uk/books?id=JdsDAAAAMBAJ, accessed 28 February 2015.

33   Dewi Sant, 'Music on Cunarders', *Cunard* magazine, August/September 1922, p. 55, UoL, D42/ PR5/5.

34   Margaret Myers, 'Searching for Data About European Ladies; Orchestras 1870 –1950', in Pirkko Moisala and Beverley Diamond (eds), *Music and Gender*, University of Illinois Press, Champaign, IL, 2000, pp. 189–211.

35   Phone briefing with author, 21 May 2015.

36   Jane McDonald, *Follow Your Dreams*, HarperCollins, London, 2000, p. 11.

37   Christopher Terrill, *HMS Brilliant: In a Ship's Company*, BBC, London, 1995, pp. 157–8; Stella Bruzzi, *New Documentary: A Critical Introduction*, Routledge, London, 2006, pp. 81–3.

38   Jim Wood started in the mid-1980s with Royal Cruises. Jim Wood, *The Man Who Danced Around the World: Confessions and Life Lessons from a Cruise Line Dance Host*, CreateSpace Independent Publishing Platform, 2012.

39   Equal Opportunities Commission, *Genuine occupational qualifications (GOQs): the cases of Wylie v. Dee & Co. (Menswear) Ltd; Mutch v. Knightsbridge Sporting Club; Wallace v. P&O Steam Navigation Company*, Manchester Equal Opportunities Commission 1985. *Sex discrimination decisions, no. 10*; Ms L. Wallace v Peninsular and Oriental Steam Navigation Company Limited, 1980, Central Office of Industrial Tribunals, 1029/1180; author's informal briefing by the P&O official present at the tribunal, 2013.

40   *The Era*, 23 May 1847. (A bushel of white flour weighed between 42 and 60lb, 19–29kg).

41   Charles Dickens, *American Notes for General Circulation*, Penguin, London, 2000, p. 27.

42   Alexander Quinlan & N.E. Mann, *Cookery for Seamen*, C Tinling & Co., Liverpool, 1894; 'Mann, Miss Ellen E', Robert Mondavi Institute for Wine and Food Science, householdbooks.ucdavis.edu/authors/1646, accessed 18 October 2014.

43   Yuriko Akiyama, *Feeding the Nation: Nutrition and Health in Britain before World War One*, London and New York, Tauris Academic Studies, London, 2008.

44   Theodore J. Karamanski, *Schooner Passage: Sailing Ships and the Lake Michigan Frontier*, Wayne State University Press, Detroit, 2000, p. 89. Women cooks still work on the Great Lakes today. (See Victoria Brehm, *The Women's Great Lakes Reader*, Ladyslipper Press, Tustin, MI, 2001, and Sheree-Lee Olson's novel about women Great Lakes cooks in the 1980s: *Sailor Girl*, The Porcupine's Quill, Erin, Ontario, 2008.

45   'The Lesson of the Depression", *The Seamen's Journal*, 1 June 1933, archive. org/stream/seamensjour4749unse/seamensjour4749unse_djvu.txt, accessed 21 October 2014.

46   Freda Price, later Taylor, from her typescript life story kindly loaned to the author by her husband Frank Taylor and a letter from Freda 31 March 1998.

Background information is from Frank, who spoke on Freda's behalf when she was too poorly. (Frank Taylor, and a letter to the author, 9 January 2014, two phone briefings and an interview in January 2014.)

47   'Ex-Wrens Will Not Displace Men on Ships', *Daily Mirror*, 23 August 1946. Maud McKibbin, interview and correspondence with author, 2014. Author's interview with Kath Lees, and correspondence 2014–15.

48   London School of Nautical Cookery, letters and replies, 1948–60, NMM, SAH/63/4,SAH/63/5.

49   Sha Wylie, account written for author, 2013; 'Stewardettes a Success', *Ships' Telegraph*, vol. 5, no. 1, April 1963, p. 8.

50   'Ship's Cook Stephanie Heads For a Storm', unknown newspaper cutting, 21 February 1976.

51   'MoD Settles Dispute With Female Chef Banned From Royal Marines', *The Caterer*, 6 July 2000, www.thecaterer.com/articles/27957/mod-settles-dispute-with-female-chef-banned-from-royal-marines, accessed 2 March 2015. Her case, like that of Tanja Kreil in Germany and Marguerite Johnstone in Ireland, was seminal in changing European equal opportunities law.

52   Cutting and Sabine Machado-Rettau emails to author, July–October 2014.

53   'Sally Townsend' interview with author, 28 May 2014.

54   'Croupier', National Careers Service, nationalcareersservice.direct.gov.uk/advice/planning/jobprofiles/Pages/croupier.aspx, accessed 29 February 2015.

55   Data compiled by M.A. Fish from TNA ADM 336, and kindly shared with author.

56   Email to author, 8 March and 29 April 2015.

57   Telephone briefing to author, 5 March 2014.

58   Ewen MacAskill 'Women in Military Combat is Nothing New, Just Not British', *Guardian*, 19 December 2014.

11 – Conclusion: Progress and Prognosis, pp. 224–236

1   Email to author from Gary Hindmarch, 20 November 2013.

2   This is only a partial figure reflecting ITF membership. 'ITF Women Seafarers' meeting, 2005', www.solidarnosc.nms.org.pl/pliki/solidarnosc/File/belka_prawa/ITF_Women_Seafarers%27_Meeting_2005.pdf, accessed 14 April 2015.

3   'Ship's officer Daite does a first for Filipinas', *Trade Winds*, 11 November 1999, www.tradewindsnews.com/weekly/158621/ships-officer-daite-does-a-first-for-filipinas, accessed 23 February 2015.

4   'Leading Ladies: A galaxy of stars, part 2', *LL*, 1 September 2005.

5   Lucia Tangi recorded these seawomen's recommendations. Lucia's academic findings are summarised by Maria Aleta O Nieva, ABS-CBN, Manila, 30 September 2008, www.abs-cbnnews.com/pinoy-migration/09/30/08/filipino-women-enter-lonely-difficult-world-seafaring, accessed 11 March 2015.

6   Ioannis Theotokas and Chrysa Tsalichi, 'Employment of Women at Sea: Perceptions, Attitudes and Experiences of Male Seafarers in the Greek Context', Proceedings of the IAME 2013 Conference, 2013, p. 13, www.academia.edu/8883613/Employment_of_women_at_sea._Perceptions_attitudes_and_experiences_of_male_seafarers_in_the_Greek_context, accessed 3 July 2014.

7   Segregated toilets are a symptom of gendered unease, which can be writ large on ships with few women aboard. The subject in general, not at sea, is aired in Olga Gershenson and Barbara Penner (eds), *Ladies and Gents: Public Toilets and Gender*, Temple University Press, Philadelphia, 2009.

8   'Scott Leads the Way in People Business', *LL*, 31 August 2007.

9   Michael Grey, 'Why Shipping Shouldn't Be a Man's World', *LL*, 14 April 2008.

10   See a summary in Linda L. Carli, 'Gender Issues in Workplace Groups: Effects of Gender and Communication Style on Social Influence', in Marilyn J. Davidson and Mary Barrett (eds), *Gender and Communication at Work*, Ashgate, Aldershot, 2006, pp. 69–83.

11   Based on Mayo clinic data. 'Testosterone Levels', Healthline, www.healthline.com/health/low-testosterone/testosterone-levels-by-age, accessed 11 June 2015.

12   'Support Roles', *Nautilus Telegraph*, January 2006, p. 24.

13   'Servicewomen's Network Reaches Milestone Membership', Royal Navy, 22 May 2014, www.royalnavy.mod.uk/news-and-latest-activity/news/2014/may/22/140522-servicewomen, accessed 14 May 2015.

14   In 1966, there were 2,500 single-sex schools in the UK, which had dwindled to about 400 in 2006 (the Department for Education was unable to provide an up-to-date figure). Clint Witchall, 'Should We Sound the Bell on Single-Sex Schools?', *Independent*, 6 October 2011, www.independent.co.uk/news/education/schools/should-we-sound-the-bell-on-singlesex-schools-2367032.html, accessed 14 May 2015.

15   Thomas Frey, 'The Future of the Cruise Industry', www.futuristspeaker.com/2011/01/the-future-of-the-cruise-industry, accessed 24 June 2015.

16   Women in England in 2010 were typically 5ft 3in (161cm) tall and weighed 11 stone (70kg); the average man was 5ft 9in (175cm) tall (an increase of 11cm since 1870). He weighed 13.16 stone (83kg).

17 Interview by author, 26 September 2013.

18 In India Neera Malhotra, deputy director general of shipping in Mumbai's Directorate General of Shipping pointed out that 'it becomes difficult for an owner or manager to employ a lone woman on board a vessel, for security reasons. Therefore, a company is forced to employ two women on board a vessel to ensure safety. The shipmanager [to whom I spoke] was of the opinion that this causes extra work ... and, therefore, the company finds it easier to employ a male and get the job done.' ('Why Indian Women Seafarers Will Fight for Professional Recognition', *LL*, 1 September 2006.)

19 Anecdotal evidence give to author by colleague.

20 A (bad) translation can be made by clicking 'translate' at 'Fifth, the "Fengtao" round female crew', www.shtong.gov.cn/node2/node2245/node4507/node55734/node55736/userobject1ai41495.html, accessed 23 June 2015.

21 Michael Grey, 'An excursion to Warsash Maritime Centre', *LL*, 30 August 2000. He refers to research done by Charles Musselwhite, Colin Stevenson and Dr Mike Barnett with 167 people at induction training.

22 IMO, 'Women in the Maritime Industry', www.imo.org/MediaCentre/HotTopics/women, accessed 4 January 2015.

Appendix 3 – Women Seafarers who Dressed as Men, pp. 245–246

1 Sources include *Nineteenth Century Newspapers Online*, Suzanne Stark's *Female Tars*, *Mariners Mirror* and *Naval Chronicle*. Thanks to Helena Wojtczak for sharing her finds. NB: this list is only what is known at present. Many more may have remained undiscovered, perhaps twenty or a hundred times this number. It can't be ascertained. Sometimes their nationality is unclear in reports. It's also possible that Billy and William Armstrong are the same person. The list does not include the famous Mary Anne Talbot/John Taylor as Stark has found she never actually went to sea. For further reading on these women see Daniel A. Cohen, *The Female Marine and Related Works: Narratives of Cross-Dressing and Urban Vice in America's Early Republic*, University of Massachusetts Press, Amherst, MA, 1997; Diane Dugaw's *Warrior Women and Popular Balladry, 1650–1850*, Cambridge University Press, Cambridge, 1989; Julie Wheelwright's *Amazons and Military Maids: Women Who Dressed as Men in the Pursuit of Life, Liberty and Happiness*, Pandora, London, 1989; and *The Lady Tars: The Autobiographies of Hannah Snell, Mary Lacy and Mary Anne Talbot*, foreword by Tom Grunder, Fireship Press, Tucson, AZ, 2008.

Appendix 4 – Between Navies, pp. 247–250

1   Information here comes from phone interviews and correspondence with many GNTCers in 2014, particularly Denise Gravestock, to whom I am deeply grateful, and the MSCC.

2   Maritime Volunteer Service, www.mvs.org.uk, accessed 25 March 2015.

3   H. Moyse-Bartlett, *A History of the Merchant Navy*, George G Harrap, London, 1937, p. 272.

4   John Johnson-Allan, *They Couldn't Have Done it Without Us*, Seafarer Books, Woodbridge, 2011, p. 20. Other experts claim there were forty-nine Merchant Navy ships.

5   'Merchant Navy Reserve', www.merchant-navy.net/forum/merchant-navy-general-postings/15853-merchant-navy-reserve.html, accessed 7 June 2015.

6   'Reserves', QARNNS, www.qarnns.co.uk/reserves, accessed 7 June 2015.

7   'Women First,' *NUMAST Telegraph*, March 1994. Victoria's email and phone correspondence with author.

8   *The CIA World Fact Book*, 2014; Houses of Parliament written answer, 24 March 2014, www.publications.parliament.uk/pa/cm201314/cmhansrd/cm140324/text/140324w0002.htm, accessed 28 July 2014.

9   Phone briefing and email correspondence, 3 August 2014.

10 Anecdotal evidence about the AFCA women given to author, 12 August 2014 by a male officer who was in the RNXS in the 1960s. It cannot yet be verified. The women pilots delivering planes were part of the Air Transport Auxiliary, often seconded from the Women's Auxiliary Air Force. See John Frayn Turner, *The WAAF at War*, Pen & Sword Aviation, Barnsley, 2011.

11 C.E.E., 'Royal Naval Auxiliary Service', *Naval Review*, vol. 54, no. 2, April 1966, p. 149.

12 Denise St Aubyn Hubbard, *In at the Deep End*, Janus, London, 1993, and phone conversations with the author, February 2014.

Appendix 5 – Ships as 'She', pp. 251–252

1   Nina Baker, emails to author, 19 and 22 August 2014.

2   Compiled from numerous sources including, 'Why a ship is "she"', *Ditty Box*, December 1944, p. 6.

3   'Equal Opportunities', *LL*, 18 July 1998.

4   Those that were fit to print can be found at 'When the "it" Hit the Fan', *LL*, 22 March 2002, www.lloydslist.com/ll/sector/ship-operations/article155107.ece, accessed 28 July 2014. Among the more poignant responses is a protest at this 'bleaching and depletion of the surviving poetry in our lives'. Another

holds the pronoun 'sacrosanct' in view of 'all the beautiful ladies [i.e. ships] that are still sailing'.

5   Andrew Hibberd and Nicola Woolcock, 'Lloyd's List sinks the tradition of calling ships "she"', *Daily Telegraph*, 21 March 2002, www.telegraph.co.uk/news/uknews/1388373/Lloyds-List-sinks-the-tradition-of-calling-ships-she.html, accessed 28 July 2014. I am grateful to Nicola Good for her help in accessing *Lloyd's List* articles on the subject, such as: 'Letter to the Editor: "A Ship's A She Who Must Be Obeyed"', 15 July 1998; 'Lloyd's List Makes Headline News With Style Change', 21 March 2002; 'No Time for Sex as Navigators Face Collision Course With an Electronic Albatross', 23 April 2002. A similar furore hit the Australian National Maritime Museum when it decided 'she' should become 'it' in the late 1990s.

FURTHER READING

WOMEN SEAFARERS (EXCLUDING WOMEN SAILING SOLELY AS CAPTAINS' WIVES)

International

Belcher, Phillip, Helen Sampson, Michelle Thomas et al., *Women Seafarers: Global employment policies and practices*, International Labor Office, Geneva, 2003.

Coons, Lorraine and Alexander Varias, *Tourist Third Cabin: Steamship travel in the interwar years*, Palgrave MacMillan, New York and Basingstoke, 2003.

Cordingly, David, *Heroines and Harlots: Women at sea in the great age of sail*, Macmillan, London, 2001.

Creighton, Margaret S. and Lisa Norling (eds), *Iron Men, Wooden Women: Gender and seafaring in the Atlantic world, 1700–1920*, Johns Hopkins Press, Baltimore and London, 1996.

De Pauw, Linda Grant, *Seafaring Women*, Houghton Mifflin, Boston, 1982.

Druett, Joan, *She Captains: Heroines and hellions of the sea*, Simon & Schuster, New York, 1999.

Dugaw, Diane, *Warrior Women and Popular Balladry, 1650–1850*, Cambridge University Press, Cambridge, 1989.

Fink, Leon, *Sweatshops at Sea: Merchant seamen in the world's first globalized industry, from 1812 to the Present*, University of North Carolina Press, Chapel Hill, 2011.

Greenhill, Basil and Ann Giffard, *Women under Sail: Letters and journals concerning eight women travelling or working in sailing vessels between 1829 and 1949*, David & Charles, Newton Abbot, 1970.

Kitada, Momoko, Erin Williams and Lisa Loloma Froholdt (eds), *Maritime Women: Global Leadership*, World Maritime University Studies in Maritime Affairs, vol. 3, Springer-Verlag, Berlin Sand Heidelberg GmbH, 2015.

Mather, Celia, *Sweatships: What it's really like to work on board cruise ships*, War on Want, London, 2002.

Tansey, Pamela, 'Women on Board: Ten years of the IMO Women in Development Programme', International Maritime Organisation, 2000, www.imo.org/blast/mainframe.asp?topic_id=406&doc_id=1082.

Zhao, Minghua, 'Globalisation and Women's Employment on Cruise Ships', *Maritime Review*, Pacific Press, 2001, pp. 77–82.

— *Seafarers on Cruise Ships: Emotional labour in a globalised labour market*, Seafarers' International Research Centre, Cardiff University, Cardiff, 2002.

— 'Women Seafarers in World Merchant Fleets: Policy, politics and prospect', in J.O. Puig et al. (eds), *Maritime Transport*, UPC, Barcelona, 2001.

The Americas and Canada

Atkinson, Charlene, Sue Ellen Jacobs and Mary A. Porter, *Winds of Change: Women in Northwest commercial fishing*, University of Washington Press, Seattle, 1989.

Becerra, Julia Liliana [chief officer, Argentina Merchant Navy], 'This Much I Know', ITF Women Seafarers, 2013, www.itfseafarers.org/WOMEN-SEAFARERS.cfm.

Fields, Lesley Leyland, *The Entangling Net: Alaska's commercial fishing women tell their stories*, University of Illinois Press, Urbana and Chicago, 1997.

Gwin, Lucy, *Going Overboard: The onliest little woman in the offshore oilfields*, Viking Press, New York, 1982.

Jensen, Vickie, *Saltwater Women at Work*, Douglas & McIntyre, Vancouver, 1995.

Lutz, Jeanne Marie, *Changing Course: One woman's true-life adventures as a merchant marine*, New Horizon Press, Far Hills, New Jersey, 2003.

Pestell, Debbie, 'Experiences with Mixed Gender Submarine Crews' [in Canada], just-thinkin.net/downloads/Canadian%20Navy-women%20on%20submarines.pdf.

Robson, Nancy Taylor, *Woman in the Wheelhouse*, Tidewater Publishers, Centreville, MD, 1985.

The Antipodes

Adam-Smith, Patsy, *There was a Ship: The story of her years at sea*, Penguin, Ringwood, Australia, 1995.

Agostino, Katerina, '"She's a Good Hand": Navy women's strategies in masculinist workplaces', *Journal of Interdisciplinary Gender Studies*, vol. 3, no 1, 1988, pp. 1–22.

— 'Women's Strategies in the Royal Australian Navy', in Ed Davis and Valerie Pratt (eds), *Making the Link: Affirmative action and industrial relations*, Affirmative Action Agency and Labour-Management Studies Foundation, Macquarie University, Sydney, 2004.

Fodie, Sally, *Waitemata Ferry Tales*, Ferry Boat Publishers, Auckland, 1995.

Pignéguy, Dee, *Saltwater in her Hair: Stories of women in the New Zealand maritime industry*, VIP Publications, Auckland, 2001.

Steel, Frances, 'Women, Men and the Southern Octopus: Shipboard gender relations in the age of steam', *International Journal of Maritime History*, vol. 20, no. 2, 2008, pp. 285–306.

Wettern, K.J., *The Geography of Women's Integration into the Royal Australian Navy: 1984–1995* (master's thesis), Australian Defence Force Academy, Canberra, 1995.

Scandinavia

Hansen, H.L. and J. Jensen, 'Female Seafarers Adopt the High Risk Lifestyle of Male Seafarers' [on Danish merchant ships], *Occupational and Environmental Medicine*, vol. 55, no. 1, January 1998, pp. 49–51, www.ncbi.nlm.nih.gov/pmc/articles/PMC1757498.

Hinkkanen, Merja-Liisa, 'Maritime Women' in David Kirby and Merja-Liisa Hinkkanen (eds), *The Baltic and the North Seas*, Routledge, London and New York, 2000, pp. 231–53.

Karjalainen, Mira, *In the Shadow of Freedom: Life on board the oil tanker*, Finnish Society of Sciences and Letters, Helsinki, 2007.

Mäenpää, Sari, 'A Woman at Sea: Women on the sailing ships of Gustaf Erikson 1913–1937', *Nautica Fennica*, 1995, pp. 23–33.

Roeckner, Olive J., *Deep Sea 'Sparks': A Canadian girl in the Norwegian Merchant Navy*, Cordillera, Vancouver, 1993.

Europe

Colakoglu, Y., 'Recommendations of Rules, Regulations, and Codes for Managing the Female Officers in the Turkish Navy', master's thesis, US Naval Postgraduate School, Monterey, CA, 1998.

Guns, N., 'Women on Board: A longitudinal study of attitudes towards and opinions about serving with women at sea in the Royal Netherlands Navy', PhD thesis, Vrije Universiteit, Amsterdam, 1985.

Theotokas, Ioannis and Chrysa Tsalichi, 'Employment of Women at Sea. Perceptions, Attitudes and Experiences of Male Seafarers in the Greek Context', Proceedings of the IAME 2013 Conference, 2013, www.academia. edu/8883613/Employment_of_women_at_sea._Perceptions_attitudes_and_ experiences_of_male_seafarers_in_the_Greek_context.

Deutsche Welle [German broadcaster], 'Captain of the Ship – A Woman at the Helm' [film about Germany's container ship First Mate Julia Petzold], YouTube, 2013, www.youtube.com/watch?v=9Wp5cT7JQiM.

The Soviet Union

Stanley, Jo, 'Soviet Women Commanding Ships', 4 July 2014, http://genderedseas. blogspot.co.uk.

The African continent

Stanley, Jo, 'Ghana's Pioneering Seawomen', 3 January 2014, http://genderedseas. blogspot.co.uk.

Van Wijk, Charles, 'Never, Never Sick At Sea': Gender Differences in Health Care Utilisation on Board South African Naval Vessels, *Journal of Gender Studies*, vol. 14, no. 3, 2005, pp. 251–60.

— and Gillian Finchilescu, 'Symbols of Organisational Culture: Describing and prescribing gender integration of navy ships', *Journal of Gender Studies*, vol. 17, no. 3, 2008, pp. 237–49.

Asia

Aleta O Nieva, Maria, 'Filipino Women Enter Lonely, Difficult World of Seafaring', ABS-CBN, 30 September 2008, www.abs-cbnnews.com/pinoy-migration/09/30/08/filipino-women-enter-lonely-difficult-world-seafaring.

Anon, 'What Men Can Do, Women Can Also Do' (Profile of Filipina Third Engineer on Tankers), Norway: The Official Site in the Philippines, www.norway.ph/news/Maritime/Female-cadets/#.VKfCNcl_SuQ.

Gitte, Nandkishore, 'Dawn of Women Marine Engineers in India', Life at Sea, http://mylifeatsea.blogspot.co.uk/2008/07/dawn-of-women-marine-engineers-in-india.html.

Guo, Jiunn-Liang, and Gin-Shuh Liang, 'Sailing into Rough Seas: Taiwan's women seafarers' career development struggle', *Women's Studies International Forum*, vol. 35, no. 4, July 2012, pp. 194–202.

Stanley, Jo, 'Chinese Women Sailors in Navy', 8 July 2014, http://genderedseas. blogspot.co.uk.

GENDERED TRANSPORT AND MOBILITY

Baker, Paul and Jo Stanley, *Hello Sailor: The hidden history of gay life at sea*, Pearson Education, London, 2003.

Bridges, Donna, Jane Neal-Smith and Albert J Mills (eds), *Absent Aviators: Gender issues in aviation*, Ashgate, London, 2014.

Fernando, Priyanthi and Gina Porter (eds), *Balancing the Load: Women, gender and transport*, Zed Press, London, 2002.

Hochschild, Arlie Russell, *The Managed Heart: Commercialization of human feeling*, University of California Press, Berkeley, 1983.

Law, Robin, 'Beyond "Women and Transport": Towards new geographies of gender and daily mobility', *Progress in Human Geography*, vol. 23, no. 4, 1999, pp. 567–88.

Letherby, Gayle and Gillian Reynolds (eds), *Gendered Journeys, Mobile Emotions*, Ashgate, London, 2009.

Pagh, Nancy, *At Home Afloat: Women on the waters of the Pacific Northwest*, University of Calgary Press, Calgary and University of Idaho Press, Moscow, Idaho, 2001.

Scharff, Virginia, *Taking the Wheel: Women and the coming of the Motor Age*, University of New Mexico Press, Albuquerque, 1999.

Sinclair, M. Thea (ed.), *Gender, Work and Tourism*, Routledge, London, 1997.

Smith, Sidonie, *Moving Lives: Twentieth century women's travel writing*, University of Minnesota Press, Minneapolis, 2001.

Stanley, Jo, 'And After the Cross-Dressed Cabin Boys and Whaling Wives? Possible futures for women's maritime historiography', *Journal of Transport History*, vol. 23, no. 1, 2002, pp. 9–22.

— 'Putting Gender into Seafaring', in Hilda Kean, Paul Martin and Sally J. Morgan (eds), *Seeing History: Public history in Britain now*, Francis Boutle, London, 2000, pp. 81–104.

Wojtczak, Helena, *Railwaywomen: Exploitation, betrayal and triumph in the workplace*, Hastings Press, Sussex, 2005.

WOMEN AT THE SEA'S INTERFACE

Ayers, Pat, 'The Hidden Economy of Dockland Families: Liverpool in the 1930s', in Pat Hudson and W. Robert Lee (eds), *Women's Work and the Family Economy*, Manchester University Press, Manchester, 1990, pp. 271–90.

Bergholm, Tapio and Kari Teras, 'Female Dockers in Finland, *c.* 1900–1975: Gender and change on the Finnish waterfront,' *International Journal of Maritime History*, vol. 11, no. 2, December 1999, pp. 107–20.

Brøgger, Jan, *Nazare: Women and men in a pre-bureaucratic Portuguese fishing village*, Harcourt Brace Jovanovich College Publishers, Boston, 1992.

Burton, Valerie (ed.), 'Comparative Perspectives Symposium: Fish/Wives: Gender, representation, and agency in coastal communities,' *Signs: Journal of Women in Culture and Society*, vol. 37, no. 3, 2012.

Doe, Helen, *Enterprising Women and Shipping in the Nineteenth Century*, Boydell Press, Rochester, New York and Woodbridge, Suffolk, 2009.

Crane, Elaine Forman, *Ebb Tide in New England: Women, seaports and social change, 1630–1800*, Northeastern University Press, Boston, 1998.

Hagmark-Cooper, Hanna, *To Be a Sailor's Wife*, Cambridge Scholars' Publishing, Newcastle upon Tyne, 2012.

Lincoln, Margarette, *Naval Wives and Mistresses, 1750–1815*, National Maritime Museum, London, 2007.

Norling, Lisa, *Captain Ahab Had a Wife: New England women and the whalefishery, 1720–1870*, University of North Carolina Press, Chapel Hill, 2000.

Sampson, Helen, 'The Lives of Women Married to Seafarers in Goa and Mumbai', *Ethnography*, vol. 6, no. 1, March 2005, pp. 61–85.

Stanley, Jo, 'Liverpool's Women Dockers', *North West Labour History Journal*, no. 25, 2001, pp. 2–14.

Thomas, Michelle, *Lost at Home and Lost at Sea: The predicament of seafaring families*, Seafarers International Research Centre, Cardiff, 2003.

Trotter, Henry, *Sugar Girls & Seamen: A journey into the world of dockside prostitution in South Africa*, Jacana Media, South Africa, 2008.

OTHER

There are several general books I recommend. For a really fascinating social history of the grand liners in the late nineteenth and early twentieth centuries see John Maxtone-Graham's works including *The Only Way to Cross* (Patrick Stephens, Cambridge, 1983) and John Malcolm Brinnin's *The Sway of the Grand Saloon* (Macmillan, London, 1972). For a realistic picture of shipping today see Rose George's well-informed and beautifully written book, based partly on her voyage on a container ship, *Deep Sea and Foreign Going* (Portobello Books, London, 2013). It makes a good sister to Christine B.N. Chinn's *Cruising in the Global Economy: Profits, Pleasure and Work at Sea* (Ashgate, Farnham, 2008), and *Consumer Behavior in Travel and Tourism* by Kaye Sung Chon, Abraham Pizam, and Yoel Mansfeld (Routledge, New York, 2010). Anyone who reads *Ship* by Gregory Votolato will never again be able to see ships as just machines for transport (Reaktion, London, 2010). Marcus Rediker's works on early seafaring take a very interesting cultural-studies perspective on seafaring, as do Greg Dening's, although they do not focus on gender.

INDEX

NB: This index uses the surname a woman had when she was sailing, not necessarily her subsequent or current surname.